BIAN Edition 2019 - A framework for the finan

Other publications by Van Haren Publishing

Van Haren Publishing (VHP) specializes in titles on Best Practices, methods and standards within four domains:
- IT and IT Management
- Architecture (Enterprise and IT)
- Business Management and
- Project Management

Van Haren Publishing is also publishing on behalf of leading organizations and companies: ASLBiSL Foundation, BRMI, CA, Centre Henri Tudor, Gaming Works, IACCM, IAOP, IFDC, Innovation Value Institute, IPMA-NL, ITSqc, NAF, KNVI, PMI-NL, PON, The Open Group, The SOX Institute.

Topics are (per domain):

IT and IT Management	Enterprise Architecture	Project Management
ABC of ICT	ArchiMate®	A4-Projectmanagement
ASL®	GEA®	DSDM/Atern
CATS CM®	Novius Architectuur	ICB / NCB
CMMI®	Methode	ISO 21500
COBIT®	TOGAF®	MINCE®
e-CF		M_o_R®
ISO/IEC 20000	**Business Management**	MSP®
ISO/IEC 27001/27002	BABOK® Guide	P3O®
ISPL	BiSL® and BiSL® Next	PMBOK® Guide
IT4IT®	BRMBOK™	PRINCE2®
IT-CMF™	BTF	
IT Service CMM	EFQM	
ITIL®	eSCM	
MOF	IACCM	
MSF	ISA-95	
SABSA	ISO 9000/9001	
SAF	OPBOK	
SIAM™	SixSigma	
TRIM	SOX	
VeriSM™	SqEME®	

For the latest information on VHP publications, visit our website: www.vanharen.net.

BIAN Edition 2019

A framework for the financial services industry

Contributing authors:
Guy Rackham
Hans Tesselaar
Klaas de Groot

Colophon

Title:	BIAN Edition 2019 – A framework for the financial services industry
Author:	The BIAN Association
Contributing authors:	Guy Rackham, Hans Tesselaar, Klaas de Groot
Text editor:	Steve Newton (Galatea)
Publisher:	Van Haren Publishing, Zaltbommel, www.vanharen.net
ISBN Hard copy:	978 94 018 0315 1
ISBN eBook:	978 94 018 0316 8
ISBN ePub:	978 94 018 0317 5
Edition:	First edition, first impression, September 2018
Lay-out and DTP:	Coco Bookmedia, Amersfoort – NL
Copyright:	© BIAN Association and Van Haren Publishing, 2018

Trademarks:
ArchiMate® is a trademark of The Open Group
TOGAF® is a trademark of The Open Group
IFX is a Trademark of the Interactive Financial eXchange (IFX) Forum
ISO20022 is a Trademark of the International Organization for Standardization
FIBO as ontology is a joint effort of the EDM Council and the Object Management Group

This document is provided "as is", and the BIAN Association and its members make no representations or warranties, expressed or implied, including but not limited to, warranties or merchantability, fitness for a particular purpose, noninfringement, or title; that the contents of this document are suitable for any purpose; or that the implementation of such contents will not infringe any patents, copyrights or other rights.

Neither the BIAN Association nor its members will be liable for any direct, indirect or special, incidental or consequential damages arising out of, or relating to, any use or distribution of this document unles such damages are caused by wilful misconduct or gross negligence. The foregoing disclaimer and limitation on liability do not apply to, invalidate, or limit representations and warranties made by the members to the BIAN Association and other members in certain written policies of the BIAN Association.

Foreword

Why this book?

It's been over 10 years now that some influential players in the financial services industry bundled their forces to stop the ever growing cost for IT integration. The Banking Industry Architecture Network was born.

So now after 10 years of hard work of all members in our community we have packaged all the knowledge and insights in this book.

There's never been a more exciting time to be part of the financial services industry. The pace of the change has never been greater, the competitive landscape continues to expand beyond traditional players and emerging technologies are opening doors that allow us to find new ways to differentiate ourselves and explore the art of the possible. But none of this will be possible using traditional approaches.

At BIAN we believe that the Banking industry wastes over a billion dollars each year due to the complexity of our core technologies and integration approaches that only ignore the problem, if not add to the dilemma. This has become one of the primary reason Banks are not getting anticipated benefits from their digital transformations. We must rid ourselves of the anchor that is slowing us down which is proprietary core banking solutions that are today's legacy technologies only to be tomorrows if we do not change. We need to stop trying to predict the future but as an industry start taking responsibility to define a much more efficient and effective approach. This is where BIAN steps in. We are enabling a unique opportunity to migrate away from existing outdated core systems and move into a fully digital new world supported by Industry Standards. An open standard that establishes a utility for the industry. Virtually eliminating integration costs, leveling the playing field for anyone who develops against the standard and unleashing the power of the Cloud by giving Banks the freedom to have a choice to buy interchangeable micro services regardless who develops them.

This book covers all aspects of Architecture for the financial services industry. It should support all involved to help their organizations to enter a truly digital world.

Besides our original Service Oriented view, the authors also included our latest insight on Enterprise Architecture and give you guidance in the fast evolving API arena.

I'll hope you will find what you need to perform your architecture role at its peak.

Enjoy reading.

Steve Van Wyk
Executive Vice President, Head of Technology and Operations, PNC Financial Services Group and Chairman of the BIAN board

Contents

Part I   1

1 INTRODUCTION 3
    1.1   Who this book is intended for 3
    1.2   How to use this book 3
    1.3   BIAN, the Banking Industry Architecture Network 4
    1.4   The BIAN Service Landscape, an overview 5

2 BIAN'S PRIMARY PURPOSE AND APPROACH 7
    2.1   Introduction 7
    2.2   A different approach to a well-established problem 8
         2.2.1   BIAN's capability view versus a traditional process view 8
    2.3   BIAN in the context of other standard efforts in the industry ... 10
         2.3.1   Standardization in the financial services industry 11
         2.3.2   Support for industry standards 12

Part II   15

3 UNDERSTANDING THE THEORY 17
    3.1   Introduction 17
    3.2   Some key terms/concepts 18
    3.3   Business capability partitions 19
    3.4   Modeling real world behaviors 20
    3.5   The BIAN standard can be interpreted in different situations ... 21
    3.6   How to combine a static and a dynamic view in your model 22

		3.6.1	The difference between capability model views (static) and process model views (dynamic)..............................23
		3.6.2	A capability (static) model is better suited for defining a standard 24
		3.6.3	Defining canonical capability partitions......................25
		3.6.4	Why use capabilities as the building blocks for the BIAN model?..25
		3.6.5	Business capability, business capability building block or business capacity?..26
		3.6.6	Picking the right model view for a technical solution............27
	3.7	BIAN's model view on the business.................................28
		3.7.1	Business behavior is modeled using Service Domains 28
		3.7.2	Service Domain interactions................................29
	3.8	What is the purpose of service orientation and how does BIAN apply it?...29
	3.9	The BIAN Framework...30
		3.9.1	The BIAN Framework – an overview.........................30

4 THE BIAN SERVICE LANDSCAPE 33

	4.1	Introduction..33
	4.2	High-level Service Domain definition 37
	4.3	The BIAN Service Domains.......................................39
		4.3.1	The Service Domain Control Record 39
		4.3.2	Rightsizing the BIAN Service Domain 41
		4.3.3	Translating BIAN Service Domain designs into software specifications 42
		4.3.4	The BIAN Service Domain specification.......................43
		4.3.5	Service Operation details...................................44
		4.3.6	The BIAN Business Scenario................................45
		4.3.7	Wireframe models...49
	4.4	The evolving BIAN Framework....................................52
	4.5	Statement of coverage by the BIAN standard 53

Part III   55

5 HOW TO APPLY THE BIAN STANDARD.....................................57

	5.1	Introduction..57
	5.2	BIAN's alignment to TOGAF 57
	5.3	Mapping BIAN to other industry standards (e.g. IFX, ISO 20022)........58
	5.4	Other mapping considerations 59
	5.5	Translating BIAN 'down the stack' 60

		5.5.1 Translating at the business architecture level 60
		5.5.2 Translating at the information architecture level. 60
		5.5.3 The Control Record can be modeled 63
		5.5.4 Translating at the application level. 64
		5.5.5 Translating at the infrastructure level 65
		5.5.6 Translating summary 67
5.6	Applying BIAN Service Domains in different environments 68
	5.6.1 Using BIAN specifications as a high-level implementation design . . 68
	5.6.2 Service-oriented architectures and the benefits of 'externalization' 69
	5.6.3 Defining BIAN's concept of 'externalization' 70
	5.6.4 Externalization in business application design 73
	5.6.5 Business to technical architecture – mapping Service Domains. . . . 74
	5.6.6 Business architecture versus systems architecture views of a Service Domain 76
	5.6.7 Service Domain clusters. 77
	5.6.8 Mapping implementation level functionality to a Service Domain 79
	5.6.9 Possible Service Domain functional specializations 81
	5.6.10 Extending the functional definition of the Service Domain 81
	5.6.11 Mapping Service Operations to messages 82
5.7	Using the BIAN models to define (open) APIs 88
	5.7.1 Semantic APIs 88
5.8	Service-based access 91
5.9	Applying BIAN in different technical architectures 95
	5.9.1 Level 1 - Conventional (legacy/core) system rationalization 96
	5.9.2 Level 2 - Host renewal/ESB integration and application/system assembly 100
	5.9.2.1 Host alignment 101
	5.9.2.2 Multiple candidate hosts 103
	5.9.3 Level 3 - Loose coupled distributed/cloud systems 105
	5.9.3.1 Service information precision. 107
5.10	Support for emerging industry approaches. 109
	5.10.1 Application Program Interfaces (APIs) 109
	5.10.2 Micro-services 110
5.11	Using BIAN Service Domain partitions to define APIs 111
	5.11.1 Cross-technical platform solutions. 113
	5.11.1.1 Specifying point solution requirements – accelerator packs 113
	5.11.2 Business case development 115
	5.11.3 Select and amend Business Scenario(s) 115
	5.11.3.1 Develop a Wireframe model 117
	5.11.4 Define the implementation requirements 117

		5.11.4.1 Feature checklists 117
		5.11.4.2 Service Operations 118
		5.11.4.3 Business Scenarios and Wireframes 119
	5.11.5	Map and assess existing systems/candidate packages 121
		5.11.5.1 Functional coverage 121
		5.11.5.2 Service enablement 122
	5.11.6	Candidate system 'hygiene factor analysis' 123
		5.11.6.1 More general considerations when implementing point solutions 124
	5.11.7	Customization/development 125
	5.11.8	Migration planning 125
5.12	Support for incremental adoption/migration 126
	5.12.1	Using BIAN as an API 'inventory' 126
	5.12.2	API inventory 129
	5.12.3	Three levels of architectural alignment 131
		5.12.3.1 Direct to core 133
		5.12.3.2 Wrapped host 134
		5.12.3.3 Micro-service architecture 136
		Limitations 137
5.13	Case study 138

Part IV   139

6 ASSEMBLING A REPRESENTATIVE ENTERPRISE BLUEPRINT 141

6.1	Building the enterprise blueprint for a bank 143
	6.1.1 Select Service Domains that match the enterprise activity 144
	6.1.2 Adapt the general BIAN specifications as necessary 145
	6.1.3 Assemble Service Domains in a structure matching the enterprise 145
	6.1.4 Matching the enterprise segmentation approach 147
6.2	Case study 148

7 AN ENTERPRISE BLUEPRINT IS A FRAMEWORK FOR ANALYSIS 151

7.1	The BIAN specifications can be augmented 152
	7.1.1 Feature attribution 153
7.2	Track business and technical performance 156
7.3	Overlay resources to identify shortfalls 156
7.4	Analysis supported by the enterprise blueprint 157
7.5	Linking between business and technical assessments 158

Part V   159

APPENDIX 1: SERVICE DOMAIN DESCRIPTIONS (JANUARY XX8) 161

APPENDIX 2: BIAN AND TOGAF'S ADM PHASES 181

- A2.1 Relating BIAN to the phases of the ADM 181
  - A2.1.1 Preliminary phase 182
  - A2.1.2 Architecture vision 182
  - A2.1.3 Business architecture 182
  - A2.1.4 Information systems architecture 183
  - A2.1.5 Technology architecture 183
  - A2.1.6 Opportunities and solutions 184
  - A2.1.7 Migration planning 184
  - A2.1.8 Implementation governance 184
  - A2.1.9 Architecture change management 184
- A2.2 Requirements management 185
- A2.3 Relating BIAN to TOGAF guidelines and techniques 185
  - A2.3.1 Applying the ADM at different enterprise levels 185
  - A2.3.2 Using TOGAF to define and govern SOAs 185
  - A2.3.3 Architecture principles 186
  - A2.3.4 Architecture patterns 187
  - A2.3.5 Interoperability requirements 187
- A2.4 BIAN and the TOGAF Architecture Content Framework 187
  - A2.4.1 Deliverables, artifacts and building blocks 188
  - A2.4.2 Mapping the BIAN deliverables to the TOGAF Content Metamodel 188

APPENDIX 3: THE BIAN ORGANIZATION 191

- A3.1 General Assembly 191
- A3.2 Board of Directors 192
- A3.3 Secretariat 192
- A3.4 Working Groups 192
- A3.5 BIAN special projects 193
- A3.6 Communication between a member and BIAN 193
- A3.7 Official roles of members 193
- A3.8 BIAN events and Chapter Meetings 194
  - A3.8.1 Scope and content 194
  - A3.8.2 Where should members participate? 194
  - A3.8.3 Location and frequency 195

List of figures

Figure 1: Components of the BIAN Service Landscape	5
Figure 2: Comparing enterprise and city planning	8
Figure 3: Building without a plan – shanty town and application portfolio	9
Figure 4: Migrating to a well architected application map	10
Figure 5: BIAN in the context of other standards	11
Figure 6: The central role of ISO 20022	13
Figure 7: Design principles and techniques	17
Figure 8: Static structures and dynamic use	24
Figure 9: The Service Landscape framework	34
Figure 10: The BIAN Service Landscape	36
Figure 11: Periodic table and different BIAN Service Landscape views	38
Figure 12: Key properties of BIAN Service Domains	40
Figure 13: Clarifying points for determining the correct scope	40
Figure 14: Simple Business Scenario with rules	46
Figure 15: Example Business Scenario in MagicDraw	48
Figure 16: A payment transaction mapped on a Wireframe view	50
Figure 17: An example of the Service Operation connections for a Service Domain	51
Figure 18: A Wireframe showing the main Service Operations for a collection of Service Domains	51
Figure 19: Levels of completion of Service Domains	52
Figure 20: Other mapping considerations	60
Figure 21: The association between the BIAN standard and prevailing model views	66
Figure 22: Mapping Service Domains down the stack	67
Figure 23: Point solutions environment: Legacy re-alignment	71
Figure 24: Mapping business applications to Service Domains	76
Figure 25: Aligning utility and common solution application modules to Service Domains	77
Figure 26: Mapping Service Landscape with shared and common solutions	78
Figure 27: Example cluster for a retail financial services business application	80
Figure 28: Four types of input and output parameters	87
Figure 29: Semantic API design scheme	90

Figure 30: Design topics included in the API scheme — 91
Figure 31: Design topics selected for four typical types of exchange — 92
Figure 32: BIAN action terms — 93
Figure 33: Default action term by functional pattern — 94
Figure 34: Example of a BIAN API exchange — 94
Figure 35: Service Domain broken into a functional core and a service wrapper — 96
Figure 36: Using BIAN Service Domain partitions for comparisons — 97
Figure 37: Externalizing Service Domains in an application — 99
Figure 38: The use of BIAN Service Domains to define Service Domains to define a service directory for the ESB — 101
Figure 39: ESB solutions integrating host and cloud-based service solutions — 104
Figure 40: Advanced 'loose coupled' development — 105
Figure 41: Advanced cloud technology solutions — 106
Figure 42: Mapping BIAN to a cloud-based environment — 108
Figure 43: BIAN Service Domains related to (micro)-services — 111
Figure 44: Cloud-based services for a relationship management Service Domain — 112
Figure 45: Example Business Scenario with rules — 114
Figure 46: A payment transaction mapped on a Wireframe view — 116
Figure 47: The completed payments area Wireframe (example) — 118
Figure 48: Feature list for a Service Domain - Customer Credit Rating — 119
Figure 49: Mapping candidate systems to the feature list of a Service Domain — 120
Figure 50: Overlaying current systems on a Wireframe model — 122
Figure 51: Example hygiene factor analysis — 124
Figure 52: The BIAN Service Landscape – First API Inventory — 128
Figure 53: Wave 1, Service Landscape coverage — 130
Figure 54: Offer Management – scoping statement — 131
Figure 55: Offer Management Wireframe — 132
Figure 56: Summary of the API sophistication levels — 133
Figure 57: Level 1 Layout — 133
Figure 58: Level 2 layout — 135
Figure 59: Level 3 Layout — 136
Figure 60: The scope of BIAN's M4 Bank model — 143
Figure 61: From the conventional Service Landscape to the value chain layout. — 142
Figure 62: Three steps in developing an enterprise blueprint — 144
Figure 63: Two value chain elements representing different lines of business — 146
Figure 64: Two lines of business connected to a regional operation — 147
Figure 65: M4Bank with local units, regional and head office reporting — 147
Figure 66: Mapping product and customer types to segmentation views — 148
Figure 67: Enterprise analysis: a measurement framework — 152
Figure 68: Enterprise analysis: a measurement framework for cost of staff — 152
Figure 69: Attribution quadrant with an attributed value chain element — 155
Figure 70: Example approaches associated with an attribution — 154
Figure 71: Systems and operational cost and performance measures — 156

Figure 72: Overlay of systems on an enterprise blueprint revealing shortfalls — 157
Figure 73: BIAN designs applied to point and enterprise solution — 157
Figure 74: Using the enterprise blueprint for planning & analysis — 158
Figure 75: BIAN designs help bridge between point solutions and enterprise viewpoints — 181
Figure 76: Relating BIAN to the phases of the ADM — 186
Figure 77: Different areas of an enterprise — 188
Figure 78: Deliverables, artifacts and building blocks — 189
Figure 79: Mapping BIAN deliverables onto the TOGAF Content Metamodel — 191

PART I

1 Introduction

1.1 WHO THIS BOOK IS INTENDED FOR

This book is intended for those enterprise, business and solution architects in the financial services industry (FSI) who are interested in applying the BIAN Industry Standard in their organization. The authors of the book expect the readers to have an in-depth knowledge of IT architectural principles and methodologies.

For those architects and organizations already familiar with the TOGAF framework, we have added Appendix 2 which describes how one can apply the BIAN standard with the TOGAF framework.

1.2 HOW TO USE THIS BOOK

This book will provide you with in-depth knowledge to help you understand the full construct of BIAN artifacts, how to apply them and how you can contribute to help the BIAN standard fulfill your (organization's) needs. We will start with a short introduction to the BIAN organization, its goals, the deliverables and the future state.

Due to the constant development and evaluation of the BIAN models, additions to this publication will be publicly available at the BIAN homepage (www.bian.org).

This initial chapter gives you a high-level overview of all the topics that we will discuss in more detail in the designated chapters that follow:
- Chapter 2: BIAN's primary purpose and approach;
- Chapter 3: Understanding the theory;
- Chapter 4: The BIAN Service Landscape;
- Chapter 5: How to apply the BIAN standard;
- Chapter 6: Assembling a representative enterprise blueprint;
- Chapter 7: An enterprise blueprint is a framework for analysis.

1.3 BIAN, THE BANKING INDUSTRY ARCHITECTURE NETWORK

The Banking Industry Architecture Network (BIAN) is a global, not-for profit association of banks, solution providers, consultancy companies, integrators and academic partners with the shared aim of defining a semantic standard for the banking industry[1] covering almost all the well-known architectural layers.

The BIAN was formed in 2008 by a group of banks and solution providers with the shared aim of defining a semantic Service Operation standard for the financial services industry. At a later stage other standards bodies, like ISO and IFX, joined along with some academic partners.

BIAN's expectation is that a standard definition of business functions and service interactions that describe the general construct of any bank will be of significant benefit to the industry. When compared to an increasing number of proprietary designs, a dedicated industry standard, like BIAN, provides the following main benefits:

- It enables the more efficient and effective development and integration of software solutions for and between banks;
- It significantly lowers the overall integration costs;
- It improves the operational efficiency within and between banks and provides the opportunity for greater solution and capability re-use within and among banks;
- It supports the current need for more industry integration and collaboration through the usage of (open) APIs;
- It supports the adoption of more flexible business service sourcing models and enhances the evolution and adoption of shared third party business services;
- It supports FinTechs and RegTechs to gain an easy insight in the complex financial services industry structure.

BIAN refers to the collection of designs that makes up its industry standard known as the BIAN Service Landscape. The BIAN Service Landscape's development is iterative, relying on the active contribution of industry participants to build consensus and encourage adoption. The BIAN Association coordinates the evolution of the BIAN Service Landscape on behalf of its members with regular new version releases and seeks feedback to help continually expand and refine its content.

It is helpful to understand that BIAN Working Groups govern Service Domains. Each Service Definition Working Group covers an associated area of business expertise. The scope covered by individual Working Groups is defined in their charter so that, collectively, Working Groups cover the whole landscape with no overlaps between them.

---

[1] This book refers to banking, but all examples and models are applicable for other sectors in the Financial Services Industry.

The governance of Service Domains within a business area is assigned to a Working Group. The Working Group is then responsible for the initial specification and any subsequent updates to its assigned collection of Service Domains. This implies the content creation is driven by the BIAN members using their experts' knowledge and experience.

■ 1.4   THE BIAN SERVICE LANDSCAPE, AN OVERVIEW

The BIAN Architecture is a layered/componentized one. These layers and components are identified in figure 1.

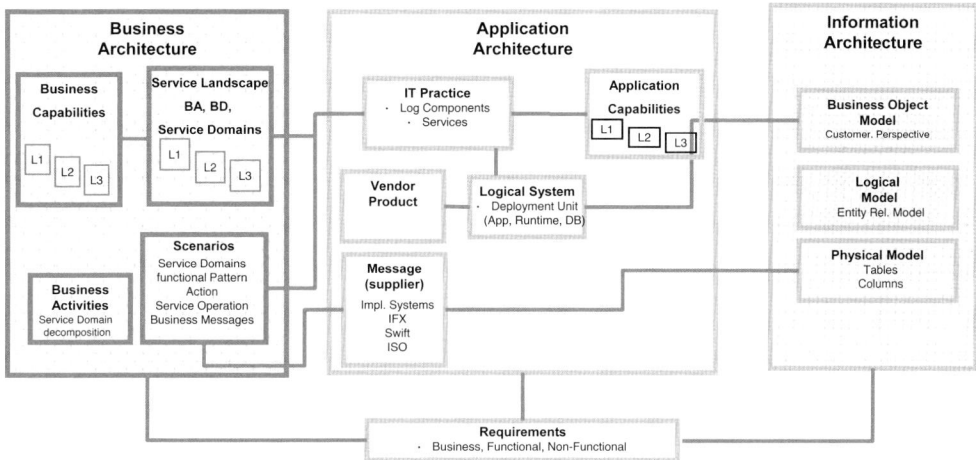

Figure 1: Components of the BIAN Service Landscape

This set of architectural artifacts is defined as the BIAN Service Landscape, it includes:
- The BIAN Meta Model, based on the ISO 20022 Meta Model;
- The BIAN Business Vocabulary;
- The high-level BIAN reference map: the BIAN Service Landscape;
- The BIAN Business Architecture;
- The BIAN Business Capability Model;
- The BIAN Service Domain Definitions;
- The BIAN Service Operations Definitions;
- The BIAN Business Scenario Definitions;
- The BIAN Application Architecture;
- The BIAN Application Capabilities (also called: Vendor Agnostic IT Model);
- The BIAN API/Message Definitions;
- The BIAN Information Architecture;
- The BIAN Business Object Model, fully aligned with ISO 20022;
- The BIAN API Classification Guideline.

The BIAN standard is published in a UML repository, as well as an HTML read-only version which is freely available on the BIAN website (https://www.bian.org/). In addition, a collection of supporting documents is maintained and released with each revised release of the BIAN standard.

The following options are in place to collect and process your feedback:
- BIAN members are encouraged to provide feedback by using the BIAN Wiki, to the Architectural Committee, Architecture Framework & Foundation Working Group or via their representatives.
- Non-members are invited to post their suggestions by using the BIAN website www.bian.org.
- Feedback can also be posted to how-to.guide@bian.org.

2 BIAN's primary purpose and approach

■ 2.1 INTRODUCTION

Since 2008 the financial services industry has faced a series of challenges in respect to their business models, customer relations and information technology. The desired business changes in banks are often slowed down by an inflexible and complex systems landscape. The primary reason for the difficult transformation and modernization of that landscape is the fact that the components are tightly coupled.

The BIAN Association strives to enhance the flexibility and agility of financial services systems by improving the integration with an architecture that is based on services. Those financial services-specific semantic services are the cornerstone upon which to achieve this flexibility. The value of BIAN is the standardization of those functional services based on a well drafted architecture framework with elements carefully chosen from industry best practices. It is the ambition of the BIAN Association to achieve a consensus on the service definition among leading banks and providers in the financial services industry, which in due time should lead to standardized services.

The goal of the BIAN Association is to develop the most important content, concepts and methods in interoperability, supporting the aim of lower integration costs in the financial services industry and to facilitate business innovation and agility by:
- Providing an architecture framework with all of the necessary elements, tools and methodologies for a sustainable operational model through the adoption of and alignment to available market standards.
- Focusing on the definition of semantic services and/or API-definitions to improve the semantic integration of the financial services landscapes.
- Enabling the financial services industry to develop and run successfully a loosely coupled environment.
- Acceptance by the members of the BIAN Association and the industry of the way that the requirements will be implemented by both financial institutions and solution suppliers, resulting in the defined services becoming the de-facto-standard in the financial services industry.

2.2 A DIFFERENT APPROACH TO A WELL-ESTABLISHED PROBLEM

Many financial services industry participants, including the founding members of the BIAN Association, have frequently observed a common and enduring problem: excessive complexity in most application portfolios. This complexity results in inflexible/unresponsive systems, inflated enhancement, increasing maintenance and operational costs, and an inability to leverage rapidly evolving advanced solutions, technologies, approaches and business models.

The BIAN Association was set up to address this issue by developing a common industry standard to define functional partitions and Service Operations that could be used inside any financial organization resulting in the anticipated benefits already noted. However, the objective of the BIAN Association raises a key question: "Why should the BIAN model and approach be successful in addressing application portfolio and interoperability complexity?".

2.2.1 BIAN's capability view versus a traditional process view

At the core of the proposition of the BIAN Association is the adoption of a capability-oriented approach to architecting the systems that support the financial organization. This approach is fundamentally different from the prevailing 'process–centric' designs. To highlight this critical difference, a comparison can be made with architectural disciplines when applied to the highly tangible problem of designing the layout of a city as opposed to the much less tangible design of a commercial enterprise such as a financial institution, see figure 2.

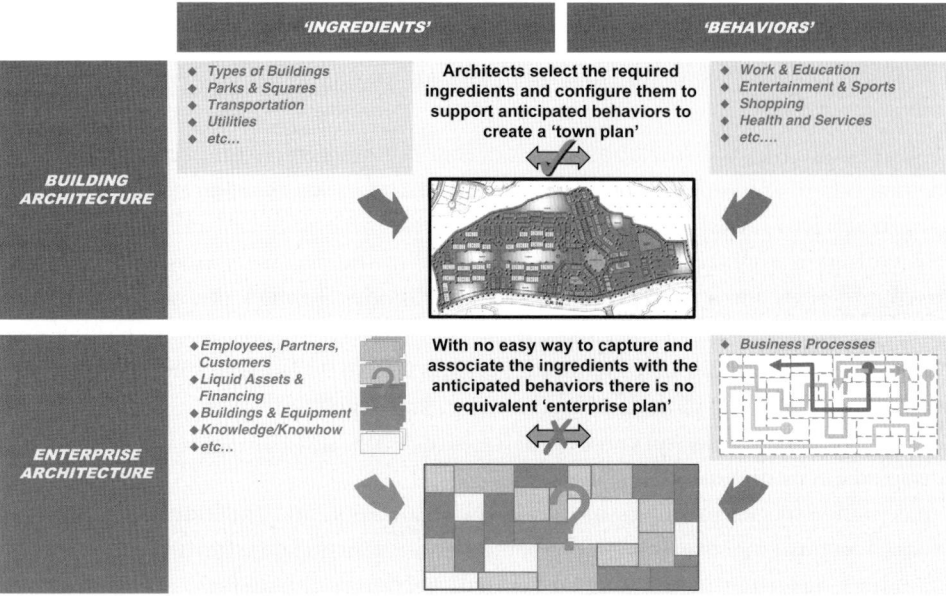

Figure 2: Comparing enterprise and city planning

Any design is a combination of the ingredients that are used and the behaviors that the design is intended to support. The ingredients relate to static or persistent things that are 'deployed' and the behaviors refer to more dynamic patterns of desired responses to anticipated events or triggers. An architect develops an overall design based on an understanding as to how the ingredients need to be configured to support the intended behaviors. In the case of the town planner this is a town plan. The ingredients seen in the town plan are the buildings, parks and communications infrastructure that need to be in place to support the anticipated behaviors of the town's inhabitants. These behaviors could be traced as journeys or 'days in a life' on the town plan.

Comparing building architecture as practiced by the town planner and enterprise architecture that might eventually be used to design the applications for a bank reveals an important shortfall in the arsenal of tools for business architects.

The ingredients that make up the bank are not tangible things like buildings and roads, they are the far less tangible business capabilities that a bank must establish in order to execute business. The behaviors that are modeled as journeys through the town are the business processes that the bank supports. Enterprise/business architects have extensive experience in modeling processes. The key issue for the business architect is defining the generic capability building blocks that they should select and configure to create the equivalent of the town plan for the bank. These capabilities can, in different combinations and sequences, then support those more familiar processes.

The result of building without a governing town plan is a shanty-town – buildings and roads are put up as and when they are needed and, over time, chaos is inevitable. Without a town plan for the business, systems built to meet the immediate needs of the processes as they are today will eventually lead to the same inevitable chaos in terms of overlapping and redundant applications, as shown in figure 3.

A city where new construction is not coordinated with a town plan...

An enterprise where application development is not coordinated with an enterprise plan...

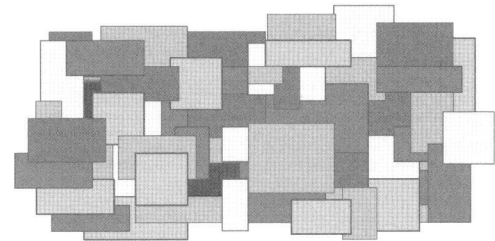

Figure 3: Building without a plan – shanty town and application portfolio

The problem of application complexity goes much further than the obvious problem of redundancy in the overlapping applications. It is greatly exacerbated when the applications need to interact with each other. Every application has its own specific scope and boundary and every point-to-point connection is unique. As the application portfolio grows to several hundred overlapping systems it is no surprise that adding or enhancing any system becomes an exercise in tracing highly complex dependencies.

The functional partitions of the BIAN standard define discrete non-overlapping business capabilities. The BIAN Service Landscape seeks to identify all possible 'elemental' business functions that might make up any bank. A blueprint for a bank, assembled using the BIAN partitions, creates the same organizing blueprint as the town plan – eliminating overlaps and defining standard connections. Figure 4 shows how the BIAN Association anticipates that as the standard is established and adopted, banks will be able to progressively rationalize their application portfolios to eliminate the redundancy and the associated operational complexity.

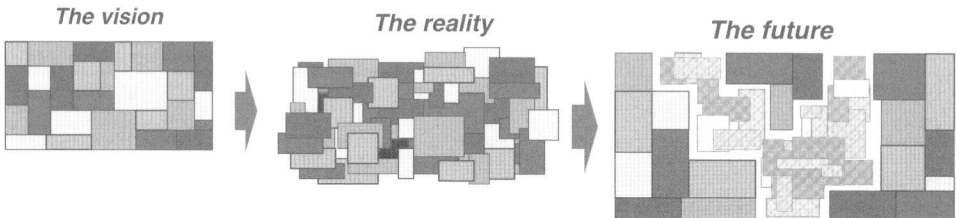

Figure 4: Migrating to a well architected application map

Chapter 4 covers the approach of the BIAN Association to service-oriented architecture (SOA) in detail. It explains how banks can adopt a service-based approach incrementally, targeting those areas where existing complexity is constraining the business most, or where more flexible and responsive systems are most needed to exploit new business opportunities. More recently the BIAN standard and its perspective on a service-oriented architecture has been considered in the context of specifying standard application programming interfaces (APIs) and the adoption of micro-service architectures.

■ 2.3 BIAN IN THE CONTEXT OF OTHER STANDARD EFFORTS IN THE INDUSTRY

There are several domains in which a standardization body can be active. The BIAN Association has developed a clear focus on services for banking software based on semantic business definitions.

Within the landscape of financial services standards bodies, BIAN has a unique position. BIAN specifications are no longer only A2A (application to application). They are now mostly A2A but also cover B2B (Business tot Business) to some extent. The emergence of third-party providers (TPPs), driven by initiatives such as PSD2 (Payment Service Directive 2), means that some of the interactions between Service Domains in

2 BIAN's primary purpose and approach

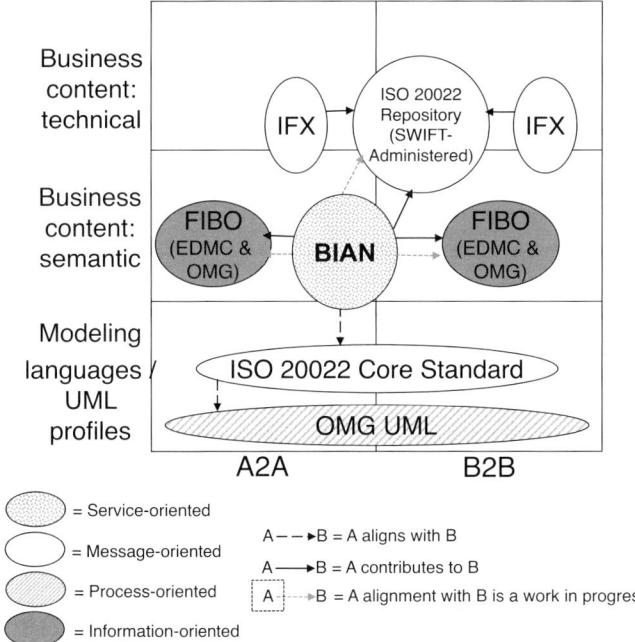

Figure 5: BIAN in the context of other standards

our API Business Scenarios that previously would have been A2A interactions are now B2B interactions because of the involvement of a TPP.

The BIAN Association has a strong working relationship with all of the above mentioned standardization bodies.

2.3.1 Standardization in the financial services industry

The financial services industry is already benefitting from the concrete results achieved to date, which confirms that there is sufficient standardization occurring to demonstrate progress towards our overall goal of interoperability. This is the result of more focus on those areas where BIAN can standardize and add value.

In the period 2018 to 2020, the BIAN Association will place a strong emphasis on the standardization of API specifications. The BIAN Association will follow a multi-approach strategy to further strengthen the position of the BIAN deliverables in the industry standards and financial services communities:

- The priority is to enrich the BIAN Service Landscape with the maximum content, so it will be used as the reference model in the financial services industry with the goal of becoming a de facto standard. This is seen as the horizontal expansion of the BIAN content work.
- In parallel, the BIAN Association is in close cooperation with the ISO 20022 working group, to develop (physical) message definitions (APIs) based on their existing standard. This will include enhanced guidelines and templates to support the

service definition on a more detailed level with regards to both internal and external interoperability. This is referred to as the vertical expansion of BIAN content work.
- In the past the BIAN Association and The Open Group published some papers on how to use the BIAN deliverables in the TOGAF framework. This provides an extra impulse for the adaptation of the BIAN deliverables (see Appendix 2).
- Currently the BIAN Association is investigating if and how the BIAN models can be represented in different modeling languages like ArchiMate. The BIAN Association will look to achieve this by making an UML and an XML version of the models available.

In order to progress all of the above there is a need to focus increasingly on semantics of services and domain definitions. This is perceived as an important element to solve the integration issues of financial services software and to ensure standardization, particularly in terms of cross-vendor requirements. Therefore, building up naming conventions and a financial services business vocabulary are amongst the required concepts. Both will evolve into a so called Financial Services Business Domain Model and BIAN's Service Landscape.

The central role of ISO 20022 is an increasingly important factor. In particular:
- The newest phase of the ISO 20022 project involves the major standardization bodies in the financial services sector working on mapping their standards to the ISO 20022 Business Model.
- The BIAN Association is making major contributions to the ISO 20022 Business Model, and, in so doing, is shaping the ISO 20022 Business Model to fit with the BIAN architecture.
- When the mappings of the major standards to the ISO 20022 Business Model are in place, they will be mapping to a model that is well aligned with the BIAN architecture. This will make it easier for the BIAN Association members (and other BIAN users) when they work on projects that use BIAN in combination with other financial services standards. See figure 6.

2.3.2 Support for industry standards

BIAN as an industry standard defines a unique business architecture model of financial services activity that outlines the discrete, canonical functional components and service exchanges as described in the following chapters of this book. There are two other industry standards with which the BIAN Association is maintaining close alignment that are of specific interest to API development:

- *ISO 20022*. The BIAN meta model has been based on the ISO messaging standards from the outset. The BIAN Association continues to work closely with the relevant ISO working groups to ensure that the standards remain aligned and that any content developed by the BIAN Association builds on ISO content and similarly that any new

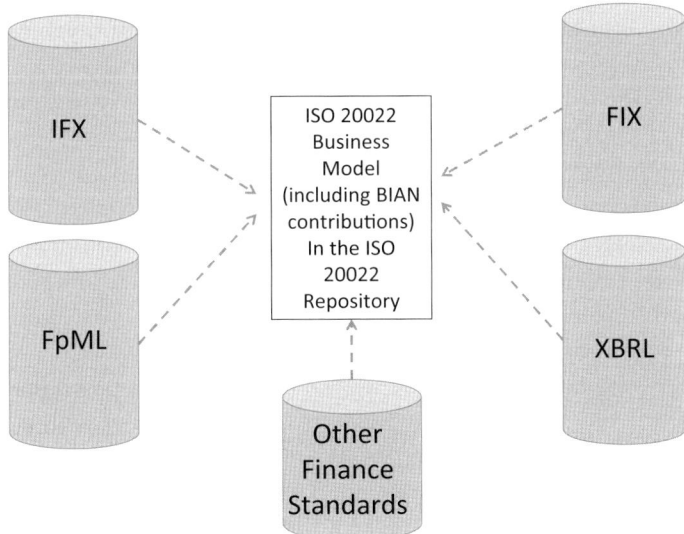

Figure 6: The central role of ISO 20022

content the BIAN Association develops is provided for consideration by the ISO operation when appropriate.

Some time ago, the BIAN Association considered adopting the ISO 20022 Business Object Model (BOM) as the foundation for its own object model. However, on review it was found that structural differences between the way the ISO model is organized and the desired structure of the BIAN BOM precluded this approach. Briefly the ISO BOM models business objects as they occur/are referenced in the external business to business (B2B) message schema. The BIAN BOM needs to associate objects with the asset types and functional patterns that define the foundational Service Domain partitions.

With specific reference to BIAN's API work, the BIAN core team mapped the semantic information content of Service Operations to the ISO 20022 Business Object Model at the level of the Service Domain Control Record. The content of the emerging BIAN BOM is then completed by the mapped content of the ISO model for the listed properties of the Control Record and, where appropriate, finer grained Service Domain Behavior Qualifiers.

The BIAN Association documents any potential additions to the ISO model to support the Control Record mapping and any more detailed information content for their consideration in future versions of ISO 20022.
- *OMG & EDM Council – FIBO.* A joint effort between the EDM Council and the Object Management Group, the Financial Industry Business Ontology (FIBO) can be thought of from one perspective as an industry thesaurus. It defines financial services concepts and allows for these definitions to be specific to a particular business context,

maintaining synonyms and homonyms in addition to the conceptual definitions. As BIAN builds out its own BOM, reference is made to the content of FIBO and the terms used where possible. The content development of FIBO is at an early stage and so the precise mechanics of this collaboration is likely to evolve.
- *Business Architecture Guild.* The Business Architecture Guild® is a community of business architects who have come together to build and expand their profession. The Guild is an international, diverse community of business architecture practitioners, beneficiaries and interested parties. The Guild is also a collaborative collective where individuals can learn with and from their peers, explore and develop new ideas, and further the practice and discipline of business architecture. Whilst developing BIAN's Business Capability model, the Guild discovered that there was an overlap in participation of the BIAN Working Group members and the Architecture Guild membership. Based on this knowledge both organizations granted each other access to their deliverables so that best practices can be shared.

PART II

3 Understanding the theory

■ 3.1 INTRODUCTION

BIAN has developed an approach to enterprise architecture design, business capabilities and associated Service Operations that can be selected and assembled to model any bank (or financial institution). The BIAN designs are 'canonical', meaning they can be consistently interpreted by any financial organization in many different implementation situations. To define canonical designs, the BIAN approach needs to be fundamentally different from more traditional techniques that adopt process-oriented designs. BIAN uses a specific type of service-oriented architecture (SOA).

This section describes the key design concepts and techniques employed in the BIAN approach as set out in figure 7.

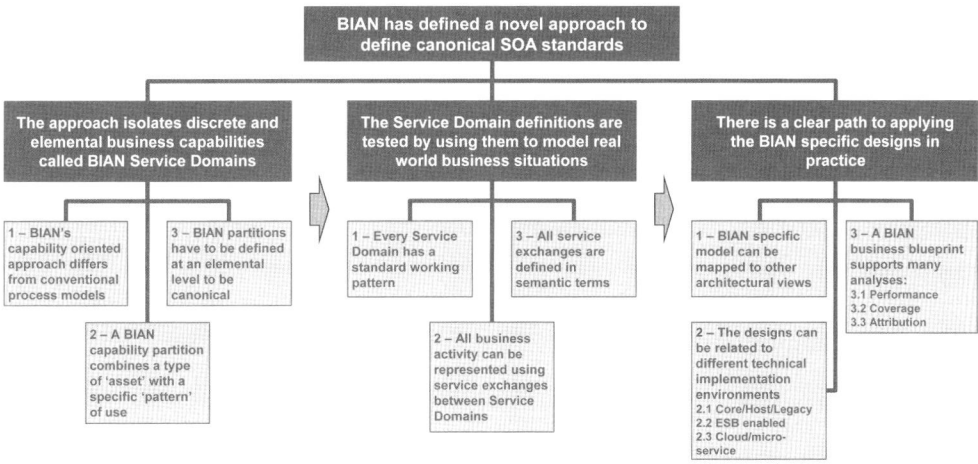

Figure 7: Design principles and techniques

The BIAN design principles and techniques are shown in figure 7 and further explained in the following chapters of this book.

3.2 SOME KEY TERMS/CONCEPTS

Before we look into the BIAN design principles and techniques in more detail, we will explain the key terms and concepts that are used in BIAN to help you better understand the underlying principles.

Application 2 Application - Enterprise Application Integration (EAI) is the use of software and computer systems' architectural principles to integrate a set of enterprise computer applications.

Business Capability - represents a consistent set of actions realizing a specific goal that can be applied to a specific object.

Business Role/Purpose - a Service Domain enables an enterprise to exact value from an object directly through its use (e.g. assign work to an employee) or by influencing the object to ensure/increase its value-generating potential (e.g. pay and train an employee).

Business Scenario - like any process model, the Business Scenario defines a linked sequence of interactions between Service Domains in response to a business event. The Business Scenario also clearly defines the specific Service Domains and Service Operation exchanges responsible for each action involved in the sequence.

Canonical Level - rather than a definition of the term, the implication of this concept needs to be spelled out. The basis for BIAN defining Service Domains and their associated Service Operations needs to establish precisely why these designs are canonical. For example, if two independent designers applied the BIAN techniques to identify Service Domains for the same requirement, they would necessarily derive the same partitions.

Control Record - manages the lifecycle state of the Object within the Service Domain.

Enterprise - describes an organizational unit, organization, or collection of organizations that share a set of common goals and collaborate to provide specific products or services to customers.

First Order Connection - the First Order Interactions for a Service Domain establish its required service connections. These connections provide an aspect of the definition of the Service Domain as a business capability building block.

Functional Pattern - each Service Domain has a dominant Functional Pattern associated to the Service Operations that classifies the role of the Object within the Service Domain.

Implementation Agnostic - the high-level semantic Service Operation designs do not include anything specific to any particular implementation approach. They can, for example, be interpreted in a wrapped legacy host, a three-tiered architecture and a fully service enabled 'cloud' architecture, or any combination of these.

Lifecycle - a Service Domain handles all relevant states of instances of the object it acts on. These states define a 'lifecycle' that reflects the role/purpose of a Service Domain.

Object - is a tangible or intangible thing the bank can own or influence its behavior e.g. a customer relationship, cash or a payment capability.

Semantic Level - in approximate terms this can be defined as the spoken language description. It is important to note that when the model is complete, all the main business concepts will be addressed such that in further, more detailed, interpretation no new concepts are required. It will simply be a matter of establishing better definition and resolution of those concepts.

Service Domain - the BIAN Service Operations define interactions between business capability building blocks that are more fully defined in terms of the organization, procedures and associated information systems that support them. In general attention is more typically aligned to the supporting information systems and systems interfaces, but this focus should not obscure the fact that a Service Domain represents a coherent aspect of the business enterprise combining its people, procedures and systems.

Service Landscape - is a reference model containing one of each identified Service Domains, organized in groups to help with their identification and selection.

Service Operation - lifecycle changes are triggered through Service Operation (action) calls between Service Domains, or they can result from internally scheduled activity (such as periodic analysis).

Technology Agnostic - the BIAN Service Operation specifications are unbiased towards the use of different technology tools to solve different problems.

Wireframe - is a narrow selection of Service Domains (with the available service connections between them) needed to address an area of business activity. For example, all the Service Domains directly and indirectly involved in customer relationship development.

■ 3.3 BUSINESS CAPABILITY PARTITIONS

BIAN's approach is based on breaking all financial services activities down into a collection of discrete business capability building blocks called BIAN Service Domains. The collection of BIAN Service Domains is intended to be comprehensive so that all business activity can be supported by a suitable selection of Service Domains interacting through their associated Service Operations. In order to explain the BIAN Service Domain concept further, consider the following three points:

1. **Compare BIAN's capability view to a process representation** – the more conventional business models typically use a process description of an activity, where a process view represents a business activity as a linked series of (pre-defined) steps or tasks that are worked through to get to a specific goal. However, BIAN models the same business activity by identifying discrete business capability building blocks that need to be involved without prescribing any specific sequence of interaction. An analogy can be made by considering road and town planning for a city. A business process is analogous to charting a route through the city. On the other hand, BIAN business capability building blocks are equivalent to the town plan showing all the different types of buildings and infrastructure that would be 'visited' or 'involved' in this (and indeed any possible) journey.
2. **A BIAN Service Domain combines an asset and a use** – the technique used to isolate a BIAN Service Domain defines its associated business function to be the combination of a type of action or use applied to a type of asset or entity. BIAN has identified a standard list of uses (called functional patterns) and has developed a hierarchical decomposition of the assets or entities (tangible and intangible) that may make up any bank. Each Service Domain combines a single primary functional pattern (for example: 'maintain reference details', 'define and execute a plan') with an asset or entity type (for example 'a piece of equipment', 'a customer relationship').
3. **BIAN Service Domains are elemental in scope** – in order to define canonical capabilities each Service Domain must fulfill a single/elemental business role. If a Service Domain covers multiple functions, then different combinations could apply in different deployment situations and the behaviors would cease to be canonical/standard. The functional patterns and asset decomposition mentioned in the previous section help to identify 'elemental' business roles. Some additional considerations are included that are necessary to ensure the designs are indeed canonical for some specific financial services activities.

■ 3.4 MODELING REAL WORLD BEHAVIORS

The specifications of the BIAN Service Domains are tested and refined by modeling business behaviors to check that the business function that each Service Domain performs is indeed well defined and discrete and to reveal the interactions between Service Domains (the semantic 'Service Operations').

1. **BIAN Service Domains share a common structure** – all Service Domains fulfill a unique business purpose by acting as a 'service center' and providing access to their business functionality through offered Service Operations and drawing on the

services of other Service Domains as they may require. Every Service Domain has an operating pattern characterized by the handling of its 'Control Record'.

The Control Record reflects the combination of the Service Domain's functional pattern that is applied to its associated asset/entity type. Because the functional pattern takes the verb form describing a behavior, BIAN associates a generic artifact with each functional pattern. The generic artifact refers to something more tangible that better represents the Control Record. For example, for the functional pattern to 'Design' the associated artifact is a 'Specification'. A Control Record instance is created each time a Service Domain fulfills its role and persists from inception to completion. The Service Domain with the functional pattern 'Design' that creates and maintains designs for products has the Control Record 'Product Specification'. It will maintain a Control Record instance detailing the specification of each valid product for as long as it is in use at the bank.

2. **Business activity is modeled as Service Domain interactions** – anything that goes on in a bank can be represented by using a suitable selection of Service Domains and capturing the pattern of service interactions between them. The primary model representation captures transactional activity using the BIAN Business Scenario, similar in purpose to a high-level business process. The Business Scenario is a simple schematic representation of the involved Service Domains and the archetypal flow of service interactions involved in handling/responding to a business event. With Release 6.0 BIAN builds on the use of Wireframe models that capture the known/established service connections between Service Domains. A specific business event may trigger several parallel/concurrent threads of activity that can each be captured as Business Scenarios that resolve asynchronously. These Business Scenarios can be charted as flows across a suitable Wireframe model. This more 'networked' view of business activity is explained in more detail in later sections.
3. **Service Operations are defined in semantic terms** – the interactions between the Service Domains represent the core of the BIAN industry standard. They are described in semantic terms, covering the main business concepts involved in the interaction, in sufficient detail to provide an unambiguous definition that can be consistently interpreted during implementation.

■ 3.5 THE BIAN STANDARD CAN BE INTERPRETED IN DIFFERENT SITUATIONS

The BIAN standard provides a partitioned view of business functionality that can be captured in different technical notations and applied/interpreted in different technical implementation environments. The BIAN standard can be used in two broad ways – one as a high-level design specification for targeted solution implementation, the other to define a stable blueprint of the enterprise for business and technical planning and analysis activities.

1. **BIAN is a business model view that can be mapped** – defined at the business architecture level, the BIAN Service Landscape bridges between the high-level business model/strategy and the many underlying implementation-level architectural views. BIAN's Service Landscape Semantic Service Operations can be consistently mapped to established industry messaging standards and proprietary message definitions. The functioning and role of the BIAN Service Domain can also be related to conventional implementation-level architectural views such as process and data models.
2. **Applying BIAN designs in different technical environments** – the BIAN Service Domain and associated Service Operations define business functional partitions and the interfaces between them. This high-level specification of business behavior can be interpreted as a high-level design for a range of technical environments. Three main environments are considered:
   i. As a framework to better structure/align 'monolithic' legacy technologies;
   ii. As a design for service-enabling business applications using technologies such as an enterprise service bus (ESB);
   iii. As a schema for 'container' type service-enabled partitions for highly distributed 'cloud' type technologies and, more recently, one type of micro-service architecture.
3. **Using BIAN to define an enterprise blueprint** – using the BIAN Service Domains as the building blocks of an enterprise blueprint. A key property of the Service Domain is that its business purpose/role does not change over time. The way a Service Domain works or achieves its purpose can change as practices and enabling solutions evolve but its core business purpose is stable. As a result, a business blueprint that has been defined using Service Domains is also highly stable and suited to different types of analysis. Three general categories are defined:
   i. Setting and tracking performance;
   ii. Mapping and evaluating coverage;
   iii. Associating behavioral attributes to better specify requirements.

■ 3.6　HOW TO COMBINE A STATIC AND A DYNAMIC VIEW IN YOUR MODEL

BIAN's goal is to define standard Service Operations covering the working of banks (other types of financial institution may be included in time). BIAN has adopted a specific approach to modeling business behaviors in order to define Service Operations that are 'canonical', or consistently interpretable in any bank. The approach captures business activity by identifying generic operational 'business capability partitions' – the 'BIAN Service Domains'. An operational business capability partition represents the ability perform some type of well-defined business need such as the capacity to maintain a contractual agreement or the capacity to execute a financial transaction.

A capability-based model of business activity is fundamentally different from the more widely used process-oriented model. The capability model captures the static or enduring facilities/capabilities that collectively make up a bank. For example, a typical bank will have customer contact centers, bank branches, ATM networks, trading floors, and intangible items such as relationships, knowledge and know-how. The alternate process model view captures the dynamic or temporal sequence of linked tasks that happen in response to a trigger or an event. For example, a process model can describe the steps a bank follows when it on-boards a new customer, or the steps it follows when it executes a payment transaction. In other words, a process view is implementation-/organization-specific whilst a capability view is implementation-/organization-agnostic. Therefore BIAN cannot provide standardized process definitions, only examples of use as demonstrated in the Business Scenarios.

3.6.1 The difference between capability model views (static) and process model views (dynamic)

The two types of models are not mutually exclusive. They are simply used to represent different perspectives of a business and so highlight different aspects of the same business activity. The static capability model is particularly useful in highlighting the discrete capabilities/resources/skills needed to respond to any likely event but it does not necessarily detail the precise sequence or thresholds involved in invoking these different capabilities to react to any one business event. Conversely the dynamic process views set out the sequence of dependent actions in a tightly linked series needed to address a specific business event but may not detail the specific capabilities responsible for completing each action. In order to properly model business activity, both static and dynamic perspectives are often needed.

Continuing with the city analogy the limited information needed to describe a journey between two points is simply the directions to follow – turn left, straight on, turn right etc. This description does not include the nature or purpose for visiting specific buildings on the journey. This highlights a limitation of many process models since, as already noted, they do not necessarily formally define the responsible parties along the way in any detail.

As an example of combining static and dynamic views to provide a rich model perspective, let's look at the map of Frankfurt. With the layout and make-up of the town (static elements) combined with a specific journey from point A to B (an instance of dynamic use of these elements - in this case a journey from the BIAN offices to the main station) we create a useful insight. BIAN uses the less common static model view point of business for reasons that we will clarify in more detail.

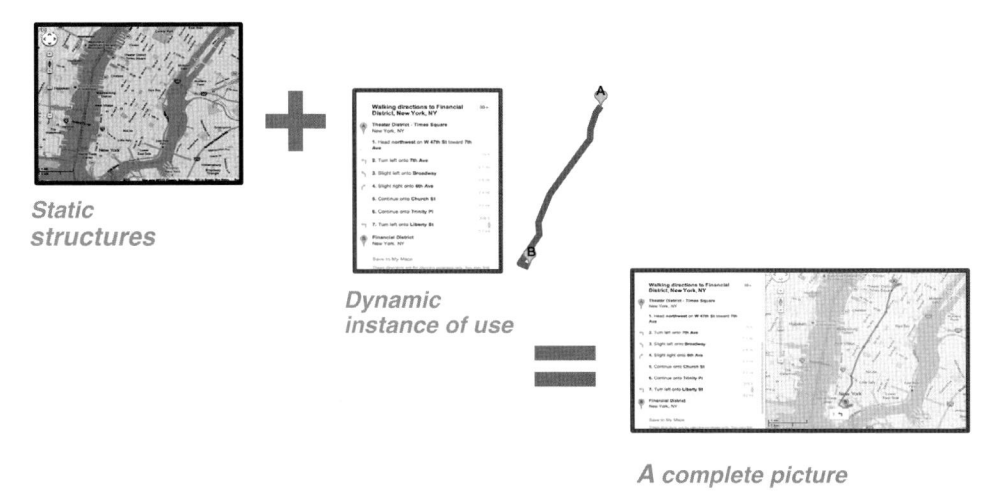

Figure 8: Static structures and dynamic use

The BIAN standard defines discrete business capability building blocks – its Service Domains. These are similar in purpose to the buildings in the city plan, where each Service Domain represents a specific type of building with a discrete purpose (a school building, police station, house, grocery store, park, cinema etc.…). BIAN uses several static model views containing Service Domains for different purposes (these are described in more detail later):

- The BIAN Service Landscape – is a reference model containing one of each identified Service Domains organized in groups to help with their identification and selection.
- A Model Bank View – is an enterprise blueprint assembled from a selection of Service Domains, possibly including duplicates of Service Domains where this is necessary to reflect the make-up of the organization. (For example, if the enterprise operates multiple contact centers in different locations there will be copies of the associated Service Domains.)
- A Wireframe – is a narrower selection of Service Domains (with the available service connections between them) needed to address an area of business activity. For example, all the Service Domains directly and indirectly involved in customer relationship development.

BIAN also uses a representation called the BIAN Business Scenario. This differs from similar views in that it aligns loosely with a dynamic process model. Like a process model, the Business Scenario defines a linked sequence of interactions between Service Domains in response to a business event. The Business Scenario also clearly defines the specific Service Domains and Service Operation exchanges responsible for each action involved in the sequence.

3.6.2 A capability (static) model is better suited for defining a standard

The city analogy also helps explain one key reason why BIAN has used the capability-based model view to define standard Service Operations. The capability model of the city (the town plan) is bounded or finite in terms of its scope. Depending on the selected level of detail, the structural make-up and content of the town plan is quite stable and enduring. It should be possible to draw an unambiguous town plan that everyone can look at and agree on whether it accurately represents the current layout of the city.

To define an unambiguous and comprehensive process model of the city would require capturing every possible 'day-in-the-life' journey that any of its inhabitants might wish to make. Clearly the number of process paths and possible variations needed to exhaustively capture anything that may go on in that city is practically unlimited. It would be virtually impossible to document every possible journey, let alone have everyone agree on the validity of them all.

Process models of a business are extremely useful to capture frequently recurring behaviors that can then be streamlined and/or automated. This view could then be used to determine the optimal configuration for mass transport systems in a town. But because of their flexibility process models are not good for defining canonical standards for anything but the most commodity-based and predictable type of behavior.

3.6.3 Defining canonical capability partitions

To define its standard, BIAN breaks down a bank into its constituent capabilities. BIAN has had to do this decomposition in a specific way that meets a critical objective. In order to create a canonical industry standard, the constituent capabilities that BIAN specifies must represent *common/generic* building blocks that any bank can select from and assemble to create their own particular 'town plan' equivalent of their specific enterprise. The approach BIAN has developed to identify generic capability building blocks is described later.

As noted, the building blocks in the BIAN model are called BIAN Service Domains. The BIAN Service Domains define behaviors at a business architecture level. These high-level definitions need to be related to more detailed systems architecture views for implementation. Some approaches for carrying out this mapping/translation are also outlined later.

3.6.4 Why use capabilities as the building blocks for the BIAN model?

The justification for the BIAN approach described so far explains why a static model view is most appropriate for its purposes (as opposed to a dynamic model view) and further that a functional capability model meets this requirement. But are there any other static model views that could have been used?

A static model captures the enduring elements that make up the subject. The model also represents a finite or bounded dimension of the subject (that can be decomposed into its constituent parts at increasing levels of detail). It is interesting to briefly consider other

static dimensions of a bank to confirm that the functional capability view is indeed the best for BIAN's purposes:
- **Organization/roles** – this is clearly a finite/bounded dimension, but it can be volatile. As a consequence, agreeing a comprehensive set of standard roles and standardizing the service exchanges between them would be difficult and may not relate easily to the supporting applications/systems.
- **Locations** – also clearly a finite/bounded dimension but clearly not a structure that can be easily related to the supporting applications/systems in any general way.
- **Finance/capital allocation** – another bounded dimension but as with locations, it is difficult to relate to supporting applications/systems in a standard/general manner.

From these examples it is hopefully clear that a functional capability model is most likely to provide a standard view that can be sensibly aligned with the supporting applications and systems.

3.6.5 Business capability, business capability building block or business capacity?

So far, we have described a BIAN Service Domain as a business capability partition or business capability building block, which is often abbreviated to business capability. There is, however, an important if subtle distinction between the capability partition represented by a Service Domain and an aspect of a business that is conventionally referred to as a business capability.

A Service Domain represents a discrete and generic business function, or the capacity to perform some action such as: 'maintain reference details about a customer relationship' or 'operate a network'. But a more formal and complete definition of a 'business capability' describes something that the business wishes to be able to do within a defined business context for which some associated value or purpose can be defined.

The business capability combines the capacity to perform with a specific business context. The business function performed by a Service Domain may be leveraged to support different business capabilities with different business contexts and an associated value and/or purpose.

An example will help to clarify this. BIAN has defined a Service Domain that tracks/determines a bank's credit view of a customer (Customer Credit Rating). This Service Domain may be involved in many different business capabilities. Consider the two business capabilities:
- Match products to customers;
- Negotiate product pricing with customers.

Each of the above business capabilities can be modeled using a BIAN Business Scenario. In both cases the scenario will include a reference to Customer Credit Rating, but the value/impact of the bank having an accurate credit perspective of the customer varies between the two capabilities.

If the credit perspective is overly generous it may be that the impact on product matching would be to recommend the wrong product, leading to a missed sale or, even worse, the sale of an inappropriate product. The impact on the pricing business capability would be to offer too generous terms, clearly a different value measurement.

Having the business capability view allows this context-based distinction to be maintained. The BIAN Association is currently developing a business capability model to augment the current Service Landscape that will be available in a later release. In anticipation of this addition, the functioning of a Service Domain is more accurately defined to be a 'business capability building block' (as defined by TOGAF). An alternative term that is used informally within BIAN is 'business capacity'.

3.6.6 Picking the right model view for a technical solution

There are several different ways in which information technology can be leveraged to support business activity. It is important to match the chosen model view with the way the underlying technology solutions are intended to support the business activity.

As mentioned, a process model view is most useful when the goal is to design and build systems that automate/streamline repeating and well-defined activities. In very general terms, a process-oriented view of a bank models it as a factory with highly structured production lines that can be automated. A common goal of the supporting technology is to maximize straight through processing (STP) in order to increase efficiency and consistency. Process models and the process-oriented systems they are used to develop are often most appropriate for the high-volume transaction processing found at the core of most banks.

But there is a wide array of activities that also go on in a bank surrounding this core 'transaction factory'. This includes activities such as product/service ideation, new business development, relationship management, customer servicing and risk management. These activities are not always easily captured using process models as they do not always follow a predictable and repeatable execution path. They are, therefore, best modeled as collections of discrete specialist capabilities that collaborate as and when required in a flexible, loosely connected network.

Different model views have emerged over time to better help design systems that support this kind of business behavior. Of note is object-oriented analysis and design (OOAD) and, more recently, service-oriented architecture (SOA). Recently, some SOA concepts have been adapted/extended to support the definition of standard application program interfaces (APIs). In addition, there are significant similarities between the BIAN view and micro-service architectures.

The BIAN model is a specific type of service-oriented architecture (SOA) applied at the level of business architecture. Its service exchanges can also be aligned to APIs at a semantic level. The interpretation of the BIAN designs into the underlying systems designs is therefore best suited to service-oriented systems design. The BIAN designs can of course be interpreted for process-oriented systems design but many of the advantages of service-oriented design are compromised in doing so. The mapping approaches for both service and process-oriented systems designs are described in Chapter 5.

3.7 BIAN'S MODEL VIEW ON THE BUSINESS

3.7.1 Business behavior is modeled using Service Domains

The general behaviors that might be found in any bank are used to refine the definition of Service Domains and the interactions between them. It is important to note that the developed models of behavior (Business Scenarios) are archetypal and only used to clarify the workings of Service Domains. They are not prescriptive and are not part of the BIAN standard:

- **Standard actions and states are associated with Service Domain exchanges** – all Service Domains have a common operating behavior: they perform a single dominant function to occurrences of a single type of asset or entity – for example one might handle the 'operation' of a 'piece of equipment'. One instance of a Service Domain fulfilling its assigned business role from start to finish is managed using a pattern or structure called a 'Control Record'. In this document several standards/checklist items are used to define the behavior of Service Domains:
  - Service Domain states – based on the working of the Service Domain, general operating states are defined;
  - Service Operation types – a small range of exchange types can be associated with the Service Operations.

- **Archetypal activity is modeled using Business Scenarios** – the main mechanism used to model interactions and clarify the nature of the service exchanges between Service Domains is the Business Scenario. This simple technique identifies the involved Service Domains and the Service Operation exchanges associated with handling a business event or transaction. The modeled flow is archetypal using a representative example to clarify the roles of Service Domains. A Business Scenario is not intended to define a standard process but is simply one viable example of possible behavior. It is also not intended to be exhaustive or complete; it merely needs to include sufficient context to clarify the targeted actions of the Service Domains being considered. The Business Scenarios will often need to reference Service Domains that are handled by other Working Groups and the central BIAN administration helps coordinate these dependencies to ensure the referenced Service Operations are developed by their respective 'governing' Working Groups.

For BIAN Release 6.0 the Model was extended through a Business Capability Model, more detailed service connection descriptions, a Business Object Model and linkage to the ISO 20022 Standard Message descriptions.

3.7.2 Service Domain interactions

Finally, the specification of the Service Operation exchanges between Service Domains is broken down to a level of detail that unambiguously defines the interaction and that is sufficient to match to underlying system message exchanges where appropriate:

- **A framework defines the exchange content** – BIAN uses a simple template that defines generic types of input and output parameters to structure the description of the Service Operation. The business concepts represented by the Service Domain's Control Record and the content of the information exchanged through Service Operations can be modeled using conventional conceptual information modeling approaches. Since BIAN Release 5.0 the description of the Service Operation information content has been expanded and structured specifically to support interpretation of the BIAN Service Operation as a 'semantic API'.
- **A vocabulary and other standard terms are applied** – BIAN has defined a generic set of action terms that characterize the possible range of Service Operations needed to access any business capability to improve consistency in their specifications. The naming of the Service Operations and the content descriptions use terms that are cross-referenced to a BIAN business vocabulary. BIAN has developed a semantic business vocabulary tool that is integrated with the UML-based content repository and presentation tooling to help capture and maintain this vocabulary.
- **The semantic Service Operation can be mapped to messages** – the intent behind the semantic Service Operation is that it can be mapped to the underlying message specifications for machine-to-machine and person-to-machine interactions where they have been defined. The BIAN Service Operations are mapped differently depending on the technical environment and nature of the messages themselves.

■ 3.8 WHAT IS THE PURPOSE OF SERVICE ORIENTATION AND HOW DOES BIAN APPLY IT?

Within banking, there are well established reasons for adopting a service-oriented architecture (SOA). BIAN has developed a specific approach to SOA that is needed to define canonical designs (designs that can be consistently interpreted by any organization). The BIAN designs are assembled in a framework using a range of supporting tools and facilities:

- **What is the purpose of SOA and how has BIAN applied it** – service-oriented architectures model business activity in a way that is intended to leverage service-based operational approaches and technologies. BIAN has extended the general SOA design concept to identify generic capability partitions that can be service-enabled

and, more importantly, that represent the elemental building blocks of any bank as is needed to establish an industry standard.
- **The BIAN Framework** – BIAN's designs are captured in a framework that consists of a high-level reference landscape that encapsulates all the generic business capabilities referred to as BIAN Service Domains. The framework also records the nature of the service exchanges between Service Domains, defined as Service Operations, that are required to support business execution. A modeling technique referred to as the BIAN Business Scenario is a mechanism used to identify and specify the involved Service Domains and associated Service Operations.
- **Content development is supported by tools and facilities** - content is captured using a BIAN web app tool. BIAN's AF&F (Architecture Framework and Foundation) Working Group updates the central UML repository using this content. There is also an integrated vocabulary tool with limited content at the time of BIAN Release 6.0.

■ 3.9 THE BIAN FRAMEWORK

3.9.1 The BIAN Framework – an overview

BIAN's goal is to define standard semantic Service Operations with specific emphasis on the internal operations of any financial institution (as opposed to inter-bank exchanges) to help improve the bank's internal operational performance. Although BIAN Service Operations cover all types of business service exchange, the emphasis is on systems-enabled interactions leading to the more specific implicit goal of improving application-to-application (A2A) interoperability within a bank. The BIAN SOA Design Framework is the informal name given to the collection of BIAN design artifacts used to specify the semantic Service Operations that make up the BIAN standard. It is more commonly referred to within BIAN by the name of its highest-level design component: the BIAN Service Landscape.

The BIAN SOA Design Framework is intended to contain all the business capabilities any bank might employ. (Typically, any one bank will only need a subset of this collection, for example because it supports only certain financial services products.) BIAN has developed a design rationale and supporting techniques to break up financial services capabilities into non-overlapping 'Service Domain' partitions. The collection of Service Domains is arranged in a reference framework called the BIAN Service Landscape.

All possible financial services business activity can be modeled as a pattern of collaboration involving a suitable selection of Service Domains taken from the Service Landscape. BIAN models examples of Service Domain interactions using an informal representation called the BIAN Business Scenario. The BIAN Business Scenario is used to clarify the roles of BIAN Service Domain and their exchanges by providing a contextual illustration of behaviors. The BIAN Business Scenario is not a formal design but merely an archetypal instance of one possible pattern of collaboration.

The exchanges between Service Domains are modeled as 'Service Operations' that are offered and consumed. In practice a Service Domain can be involved in any number of Business Scenarios but because it always fulfills a unique and discrete business purpose, the Service Operations it offers (and consumes) can be defined as a fixed or 'bounded' collection.

With BIAN Release 6.0, BIAN has introduced an additional level of detail to the Service Domain specification. The mechanism used is the definition of 'behavior qualifiers' that break down the behavioral characteristics of the Service Domain's functional pattern. This additional detail is used to expand the description of the business information governed and accessed through its offered Service Operations. It is also used to define a more precise purpose/definition for those individually offered Service Operations when necessary.

The BIAN Service Domain's specification contains the semantic definitions of all its offered Service Operations and provides references to the Service Operations it consumes from other Service Domains, along with an outline of its business purpose or role. The Service Domain Semantic Service Operation specifications define the core of the BIAN industry standard.

BIAN's standard semantic Service Operation specifications are 'implementation agnostic'
Though BIAN's goal is to improve A2A interoperability, to be canonical (i.e. consistently interpretable by any bank in any technical environment) the specifications themselves must be system implementation agnostic. The BIAN Service Operation specifications include nothing specific to, nor reliant on, some feature of any technical architecture or solution approach. BIAN does however provide guidelines as to how its standard can be applied/interpreted in different prevailing systems architectures. See Chapter 5 for more details.

A Service Operation's specification defines the Service Domain exchange in narrative terms as might be described and understood by a business practitioner. In BIAN Release 6.0 a more comprehensive list of the types of business information that might be included in the Service Operation has been produced. The list is specific to a Service Domain's functional behavior. The information list is also structured to recognize different categories of business information to help with the interpretation of the semantic service during system design and implementation.

BIAN intends to capture example information content for Service Domains over time using a vocabulary tool to match the example content to the different information types.

The Service Operation specification is intended to be sufficiently comprehensive such that, where appropriate, it can be interpreted for supporting systems implementation without the need to specify additional business requirements. (Note that significant additional design effort will typically be needed to translate BIAN's high-level semantic Service Operations into the far more detailed code-level message designs.)

The BIAN Service Landscape covers all financial services activity including Service Domains typically having a high dependency on underlying systems support and others that have minimal need for highly integrated information systems. Given BIAN's priority to improve application to application (A2A) interoperability, the designs and associated techniques described relate primarily to Service Domains with a high systems dependency.

Note: increasingly application interoperability will not be limited by 'on premise' restrictions since it will include cloud and third party organizations.

Each component of the BIAN Framework is now described in more detail. Note that these components can be presented in different formats: as documents in standard productivity tools (e.g. Microsoft PowerPoint, Excel and Word); and as structured report extracts from the BIAN UML repository. Different formats are shown in BIAN's WIKI for members and as HTML renditions at BIAN's homepage for ease of presentation and also as explanation in this document.

4   The BIAN Service Landscape

■ 4.1   INTRODUCTION

The BIAN Service Landscape is a reference framework that contains all identified BIAN Service Domains, see figure 9. Its purpose is to provide a mechanism for quickly identifying and selecting Service Domains. The landscape uses a hierarchical decomposition of general financial services industry capabilities at three levels as described below. As noted, it is the goal of BIAN that the BIAN Service Landscape will eventually contain all possible Service Domains. All business activity can then be represented by a suitable collection of one or more Service Domains working together in collaboration. BIAN uses a 'primary' Service Landscape view based on agreed categorizations that have been refined in use over several years by the BIAN membership.

The BIAN Metamodel is a detailed and comprehensive (UML) model that defines all the BIAN design structures – it is fully documented elsewhere in its own guide (The BIAN Metamodel, see bian.org). The Metamodel has three elements that detail the structure of the BIAN Service Landscape.

As seen in figure 9 we identify three levels within the BIAN Service Landscape:
- Business Area – is the highest-level classification. A business area groups together a broad set of business capabilities. In the case of the BIAN Service Landscape they are defined to be aspects of business activity that have similar supporting application and information-specific needs.
- Business Domain – at the next level, Business Domains define a coherent collection of capabilities within the broader business area. In the BIAN Service Landscape the Business Domains are associated with skills and knowledge recognizable in the financial services business.
- Service Domain – is the most detailed level of capability partitioning, each domain defining a unique and discrete business operational capability building block. The Service Domains are the 'elemental building blocks' of the Service Landscape.

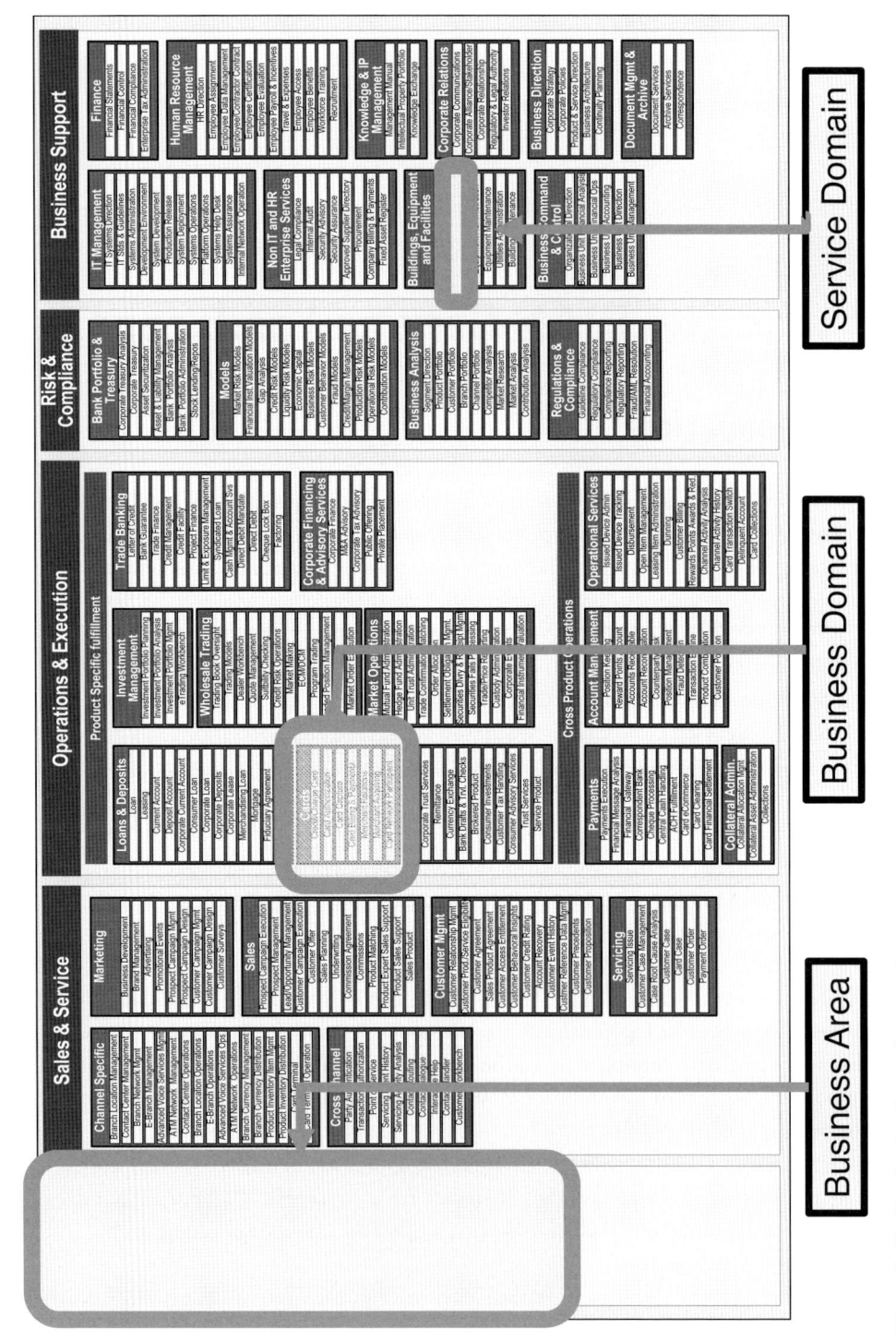

Figure 9: The Service Landscape framework

The Service Domain relates to generic capabilities that do not vary in their scope, but the definitions of the Business Domain and Business Area are classifications that are specific to a Service Landscape layout. The BIAN Service Landscape can be presented in two layouts:

- The historical Service Landscape – this is the matrix layout that BIAN has evolved over recent years. There have been changes in the scoping of some Business Domains to reduce anomalies with product categorization.
- The Model Bank Landscape – this is an informal re-scoping of the Business Areas and Domains and a reformatting of the layout to make it better aligned with the development of a bank 'enterprise blueprint' as explained in Chapter 5 'How to apply the BIAN standard'.

The historical Service Landscape Business Areas have been defined corresponding broadly to types of systems use. They have the following six Business Areas working from left to right:

1. Reference Data – contains Business Domains (and their contained Service Domains) that handle access to both internally and externally sourced information which is widely accessed by different parts of the business.
2. Sales & Service – brings together Business Domains that support the interactions with the bank's customers through all channels, for the purposes of selling and servicing in-force products and services.
3. Operations & Execution – is a large area that combines all transaction processing-oriented aspects of product and service fulfillment, including product-specific activities, 'vanilla' capabilities that can be integrated within many products and shared supporting operational services. Due to its large size, this area is subdivided into two regions. One of these corresponds to groups of product-specific activities and the other to shared product fulfillment support capabilities.
4. Cross Product Operations – contains Business Domains that handle 'generic' financial services such as Payments, Account Management, Operational Services and Collateral Administration.
5. Analytics & Risk – consolidates the Business Domains that support and perform detailed analysis functions. These cover product- and customer-related analyses, business unit performance assessments and all dimensions of risk (e.g. credit, market, instrument, operational and compliance).
6. Business Support – combines the wide range of general management and support activities common to most enterprises, including the executive, finance, staff, systems and facilities functions.

Within these six broad Business Areas, there are approximately 40 more finely grained Business Domains that represent generally recognizable financial services functional groups. Approximately 300 'elemental' Service Domains have then been mapped into this two-tiered reference framework based on their specific business roles, as shown in figure 10.

The BIAN Service Landscape

Reference Data

Party
- Party Data Mngmt.
- Customer Profile

External Agency
- Information Provider Admin
- Syndicate Mngmt.
- Interbank Relationship Mngmt.
- Correspondent Bank Relationship Mngmt.
- Correspondent Bank Data Mngmt.
- Sub Custodian Agreement
- Product Service Agency
- Product Broker Agreement
- Contractor/Supplier Agreement

Market Data
- Information Provider Operation
- Market Information Mngmt.
- Financial Market Analysis
- Financial Market Research
- Quant Model
- Market Data Switch Admin
- Market Data Switch Ops
- Financial Instr. Ref Data Mngmt.
- Counterparty Administration
- Public Reference Data Mngmt.
- Location Data Mngmt.

Product Mngmt.
- Product Design
- Product Combination
- Product Deployment
- Product Training
- Product Quality Assurance
- Discount Pricing
- Product Directory
- Special Pricing Conditions

Sales & Service

Channel Specific
- Branch Location Mngmt.
- Contact Centre Mngmt.
- Branch Network Mngmt.
- E-Branch Mngmt.
- Adv. Voice Services Mngmt.
- ATM Network Mngmt.
- Contact Centre Operations
- Branch Location Operations
- E-Branch Operations
- Adv. Voice Services Operations
- Branch Currency Mngmt.
- Branch Currency Distribution
- Prod. Inventory Item Mngmt.
- Prod. Inventory Distribution
- Card Terminal
- Card Terminal Operation

Cross Channel
- Party Authentication
- Transaction Authorization
- Point of Service
- Servicing Event History
- Servicing Activity Analysis
- Contact Routing
- Contact Dialogue
- Interactive Help
- Contact Handler
- Customer Workbench

Marketing
- Business Development
- Brand Management
- Advertising
- Promotional Events
- Prospect Campaign Mngmt.
- Prospect Campaign Design
- Customer Campaign Mngmt.
- Customer Campaign Design
- Customer Surveys

Sales
- Prospect Campaign Execution
- Prospect Management
- Lead/Opportunity Management
- Customer Campaign Execution
- Customer Offer
- Sales Planning
- Underwriting
- Commission Agreement
- Commissions
- Product Matching
- Product Expert Sales Support
- Product Sales Support
- Sales Product

Customer Mngmt.
- Customer Relationship Mngmt.
- Customer Prod/Service Eligibility
- Customer Agreement
- Sales Product Agreement
- Customer Access Entitlement
- Customer Behavioural Insights
- Customer Credit Rating
- Account Recovery
- Customer Event History
- Customer Precedents
- Customer Reference Data Mngt
- Customer proposition

Servicing
- Servicing Issue
- Customer Case Management
- Case Root Cause Analysis
- Customer Case
- Card Case
- Customer Order
- Payment Order
- Service product

Operations & Execution

Product Specification Fulfillment

Loans & Deposits
- Loan
- Consumer Loan
- Corporate Loan
- Corporate Deposits
- Corporate Lease
- Merchandising Loan
- Mortgage
- Fiduciary Agreement
- Leasing
- Current Account
- Deposit Account
- Corporate Current Account
- Savings Account

Cards
- Credit/Charge Card
- Card Authorization
- Card Capture
- Card Billing & Payments
- Merchant Relations
- Merchant Accounting
- Card Network Participant

Consumer Service
- Corporate Trust Services
- Remittances
- Currency Exchange
- Bank Drafts & Travelers Checks
- Brokered Product
- Consumer Investments
- Customer Tax Handling
- Provide Consumer Financial Advice
- Trust Services

Investment Mngmt.
- Investment Portfolio Planning
- Investment Portfolio Analysis
- Investment Portfolio Mngmt
- eTrading Workbench

Wholesale Trading
- Trading Book Oversight
- Trading Models
- Dealer Workbench
- Quote Management
- Suitability Checking
- Credit Risk Operations
- Market Making
- ECM/DCM
- Program Trading
- Traded Position Management
- Market Order
- Market Order Execution

Market Operations
- Mutual Fund Administration
- Hedge Fund Administration
- Unit Trust Administration
- Trade Confirmation Matching
- Order Allocation
- Settlement Obligation Mngmt
- Securities Dlvry & Receipt Mngmt
- Securities Fails Processing
- Trade/Price Reporting
- Custody Administration
- Corporate Events
- Financial Instrument Valuation

Trade Banking
- Letter of Credit
- Bank Guarantee
- Trade Finance
- Credit Management
- Credit Facility
- Project Finance
- Limit & Exposure Management
- Syndicated Loan
- Cash Mngmt & Account Svs
- Direct Debit Mandate
- Direct Debit
- Cheque Lock Box
- Factoring

Corp. Financing & Advisory Services
- Corporate Finance
- M&A Advisory
- Corporate Tax Advisory
- Public Offering
- Private Placement

Cross Product Operations

Payments
- Payment Execution
- Financial Message Analysis
- Financial Gateway
- Correspondent Bank
- Cheque Processing
- Central Cash Handling
- Card e-Commerce
- Card Clearing
- Card Financial Settlement

Account Management
- Position Keeping
- Reward Points Account
- Accounts Receivable
- Account Reconciliation
- Counterparty Risk
- Position Management
- Fraud Detection
- Transaction Engine
- Customer Position
- Product Combination

Collateral Administration
- Collateral Allocation Mngmt
- Collateral Asset Administration

Operational Services
- Issued Device Admin
- Issued Device Tracking
- Disbursement
- Open Item Management
- Leasing Item Administration
- Customer Billing
- Dunning
- Reward Points Awards & Red.
- Channel Activity Analysis
- Channel Activity History
- Card Transaction Switch
- Delinquent Account
- Card Collections

Risk & Compliance

Bank Portfolio & Treasury
- Corporate Treasury Analysis
- Corporate Treasury
- Asset Securitization
- Asset & Liability Management
- Bank Portfolio Analysis
- Bank Portfolio Administration
- Stock Lending/Repos

Models
- Market Risk Models
- Financial Inst. Valuation Models
- Gap Analysis
- Credit Risk Models
- Liquidity Risk Models
- Economic Capital
- Business Risk Models
- Customer Behaviour Models
- Credit/Margin Management
- Production Risk Models
- Operational Risk Models
- Fraud Models
- Contribution Models

Business Analysis
- Segment Direction
- Product Portfolio
- Customer Portfolio
- Branch Portfolio
- Channel Portfolio
- Competitor Analysis
- Market Research
- Market Analysis
- Contribution Analysis

Regulations & Compliance
- Guideline Compliance
- Regulatory Compliance
- Compliance Reporting
- Regulatory Reporting
- Fraud/AML Resolution
- Financial Accounting

Figure 10: The BIAN Service Landscape Release 6.0

4.2 HIGH-LEVEL SERVICE DOMAIN DEFINITION

Standard high-level definitions are maintained for each Service Domain in the UML repository (some of the technical terms described here are revisited in the following pages in this document):
- **Name** – the descriptive name of the Service Domain.
- **Business Role** – a brief description of the business role.
- **Example of use** – a brief example of some business event/context that involves the Service Domain.
- **Control Record** – a control mechanism that is used to track an instance of the execution of the Service Domain's business role from start to finish.
- **Functional Pattern** – the dominant type of business function performed (BIAN has classified a list of general functional behaviors, one of which will be applicable to a Service Domain). Each functional pattern has an associated *artifact*. The artifact represents the type of document or record that might be used to manage/track the execution of the function.
- **Asset/Entity** – the business asset or entity type that the Service Domain acts upon in the manner as characterized by its associated functional pattern.
- **Comment** – general clarification of the Service Domain's role and any open considerations arising from internal design discussions within the BIAN Association.

The primary use of the Service Landscape is to act as a complete reference framework that organizes the full collection of Service Domains. The current layout has been driven primarily by the need to discover and develop discrete content within the BIAN membership.

Different criteria to those just described above (complete, discrete) can be used to define alternative Business Domains and Business Areas and create alternative layouts (that typically also contain the complete collection of identified BIAN Service Domains). One such alternative arrangement noted above – the *'value chain view'* has been developed to support deployment of the BIAN standard and is shown in figure 11.

As the examples in figure 11 show, many possible layouts of the Service Domains can be defined to help group and highlight different properties and associations between Service Domains.

We mention two of these additional draft layouts for explanatory purposes only:
- **Arranged by organizational unit** – in this layout Business Areas and Business Domains have been specified in a way that aligns to the possible divisional and operational units of a typical bank. BIAN will be working on more formal approaches to defining standard organization-oriented landscape views for different types of banks. These views are intended to support a higher-level business model analysis.

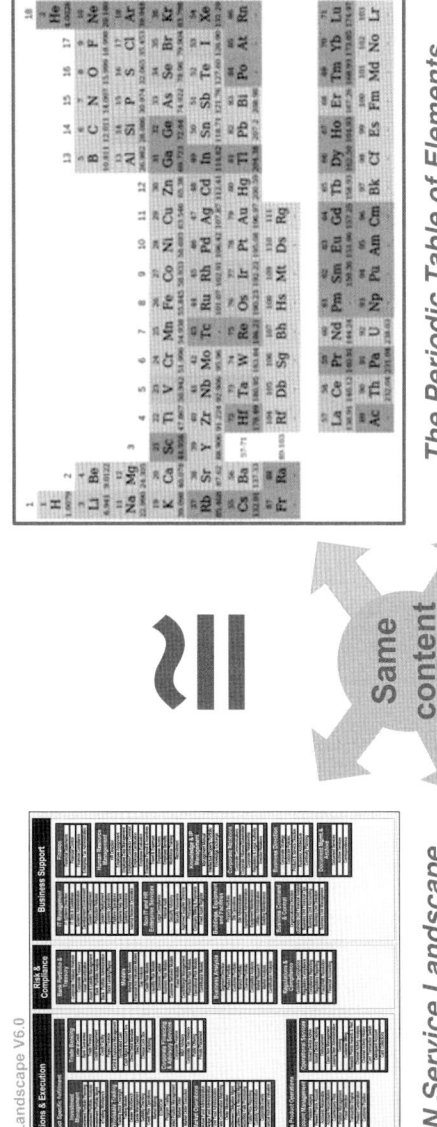

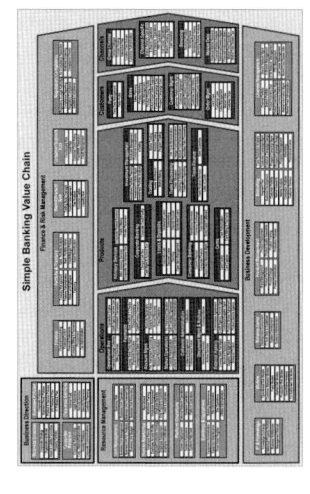

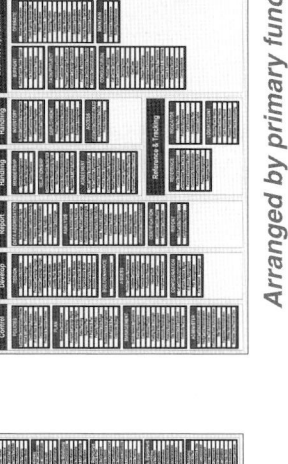

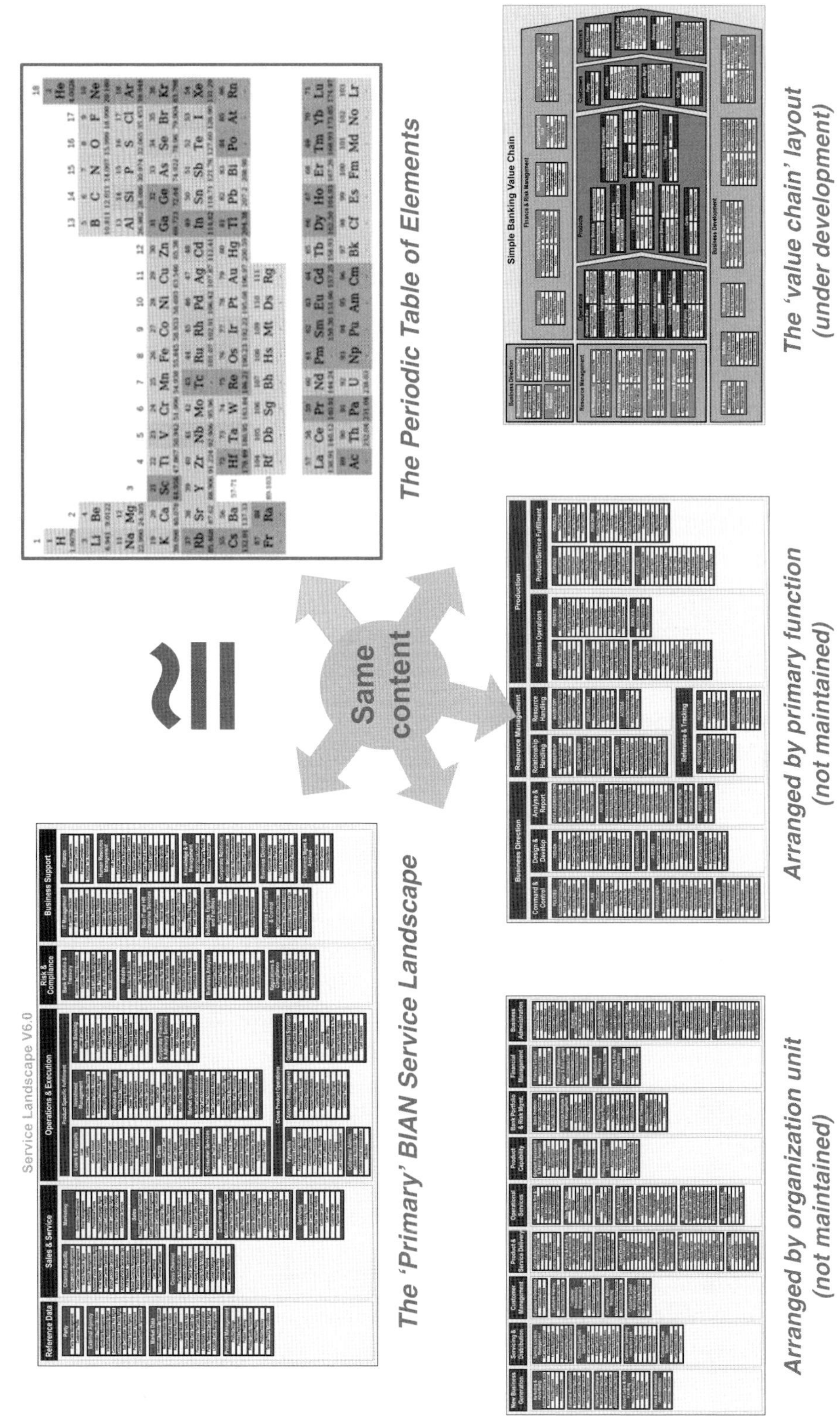

Figure 11: Periodic table and different BIAN Service Landscape views

- **Arranged by functional pattern** – in this layout, the Business Areas and Business Domains cluster the Service Domains based on their associated Functional Patterns (the BIAN Functional Patterns have been refined in BIAN Release 6.0 since this example was developed). This is a type of grouping that could help match Service Domains to shared/common technical platforms and applications. Other application-oriented groupings that help relate Service Domains to suitable application partitions will be evaluated in future releases of BIAN.

4.3 THE BIAN SERVICE DOMAINS

The elemental building block of the BIAN Service Landscape is the BIAN Service Domain. The BIAN standard semantic Service Operations at the heart of the BIAN standard are each uniquely associated with a Service Domain. The specification of the Service Domain and its Service Operations is intended to be generic or 'canonical', meaning that its business role or purpose can be consistently interpreted in different banks, see figure 12. This capability is critical in the definition of an industry standard.

The BIAN Service Domain is a generic business capability building block. It is the elemental building block of the Service Landscape. The Service Domain offers and consumes services in the execution of business. These services are the industry standards that BIAN seeks to define and which are characterized by:
- **Unique business purpose** - has sole responsibility for fulfilling a specific and discrete business purpose.
- **Elemental** - it is not an assembly of other Service Domains.
- **Collectively comprehensive** - all possible business activity can be modeled using Service Domains.
- **Control Record** - the Control Record reflects its business role or purpose (does something to something).
- **Full Lifecycle support** - it is responsible for all possible states of its Control Record.
- **Single or multiple instances** - can have a single active instance or multiple active instances of its Control Record (e.g. a single business unit plan, or multiple customer accounts).
- **Short or long life-span** - its life-span can be short or long lived (e.g. a customer interaction or a product design).
- **Service-based** - all possible business activity can be modeled as a pattern of service interactions between a suitable selection of Service Domains.

4.3.1 The Service Domain Control Record

A Service Domain 'Control Record' is used to track each singular instance of the execution of a Service Domain's business purpose or role. BIAN defines the role of a Service Domain as the business capability needed to be the combination of some type of influence or control that is exerted over a particular business entity or object (asset). For

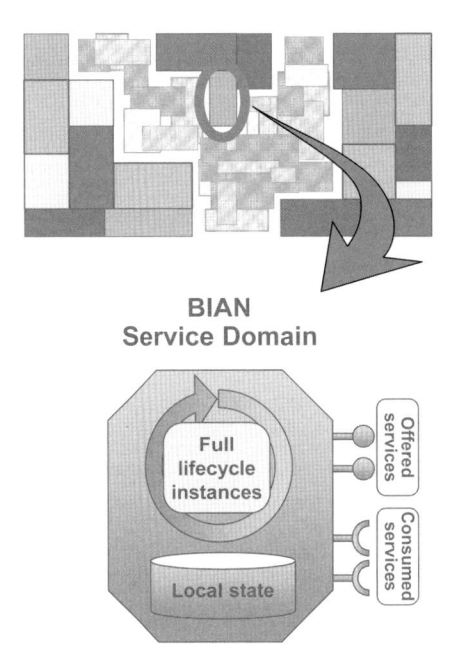

Figure 12: Key properties of BIAN Service Domains

example, applying a contractual agreement to a customer relationship, or executing the operational schedule for a piece of equipment.

To identify elemental and discrete business capabilities, BIAN has used a simple hierarchical decomposition of the possible assets or entity types (both tangible and intangible) that may be found in a bank. BIAN has also identified a finite number of actions or functions that may be performed on those assets/entities to extract commercial value from them – these are called 'functional patterns'. Each BIAN Service Domain has the same design property: its business purpose or role combines the execution of one dominant functional pattern on instances of one type of asset or entity.

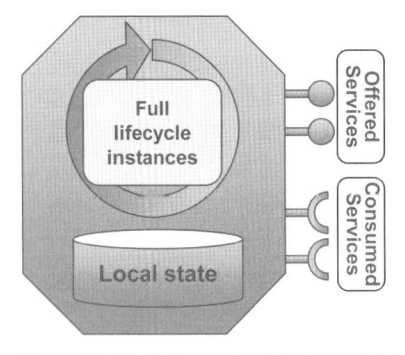

Figure 13: Clarifying points for determining the correct scope

Furthermore, the Service Domain is responsible for exerting this business control for the full 'lifecycle'. For example, an 'Agree Terms' functional pattern can be applied to an instance of the intangible asset type 'customer relationship'. The associated Service Domain 'Customer Agreement' is responsible for the initial set-up and maintenance, supporting any updates and access to the customer agreement, all analysis and reporting up to and including the customer agreement's final termination.

4.3.2 Rightsizing the BIAN Service Domain

A more complicated design consideration relates to the 'right-sizing' of a Service Domain's capability. The critical requirement is that the scope of its capability is 'elemental' in nature. If a Service Domain is an assembly of many business capabilities, then different combinations of these capabilities may be relevant in different deployments and any attempt to define a canonical specification of its behavior and service boundary is quickly compromised.

In practice, BIAN has found that there is a point in decomposing business activity where there is a transition from business functions possessing a unique 'business context', to be a utility in nature. When the business role/purpose of a Service Domain is matched to a business function at the threshold of retaining unique business context it is found in practice to be an elemental business capability building block. The concept is fully explained in the following chapters. A simple example is used here to help clarify the idea for context.

The following considerations help to ensure Service Domains are correctly defined and scoped:
- **Elemental lifecycle** – the set of Service Operations associated with a specific object must identify a meaningful lifecycle with states that are recognizable for the business. In particular the states and state changes should be triggered by meaningful business events (such as a product bought) and not be technical or implementation-specific processing considerations (such as 'update customer address').
- **Uniqueness of lifecycle** – during the analysis it may come to light that the lifecycles of the object instances of two or more Service Domains are highly similar. This is most likely to occur when the object has been decomposed to too low a level. Service Domains applying the same set of Service Operations to their associated object types will be fulfilling essentially the same business role and the Service Domains can be combined into a single Service Domain applying the same set of Service Operations to the higher order (grouping) object.
- **Role diversity** – Service Domains performing the same set of Service Operations on different objects have distinct business roles due to the different purpose/value of the underlying object instance that is acted on (e.g. planning for a customer relationship is distinct from planning for a marketing campaign and so two different Service Domains are required).

The area of customer management clearly combines a broad range of business capabilities. Within customer management, one of many finer-grained capabilities is the handling of customer agreements - as already mentioned. To test whether this is a capability found at the 'finest level of detail that retains unique business context,' the customer agreement handling capability can be broken down further into its constituent actions/capabilities.

This decomposition results in actions/capabilities such as reviewing, classifying and filing documents and maintaining customer details that may not be uniquely associated with handling a customer agreement. Such fine-grained actions could be performed in many areas of the bank and so are more utility in nature. Handling customer agreements is therefore confirmed to be a correctly scoped, elemental business capability building block for a 'right-sized' Service Domain.

4.3.3 Translating BIAN Service Domain designs into software specifications

The BIAN standard is a 'business architecture' level perspective defining the discrete business capabilities that make up a bank and the operational service exchanges between them that are defined in semantic terms. These high-level generic business designs need to be translated and extended in implementation. They need to be matched to the specific scope and layout of an enterprise and then the high-level business behaviors that define functional requirements must be extended in detail and realized by systems operating in a range of very different technical environments.

In summary, the semantic descriptions of the role of the Service Domains, togther with the Service Operations that they call and consume, define logical functional boundaries and interfaces that can be mirrored in the underlying systems architecture. When the underlying systems are aligned in this way, the benefits of service-based design outlined at the outset of this document can be realized (including optimized performance, improved interoperability, better resource leverage and greater operational solution reuse).

The practice of retaining Service Domain boundaries in the derived software design is an important aspect of implementing a service-oriented architecture. It has no obvious equivalent in conventional process-based design, where business functionality is typically decomposed to a fine-grained and tightly coupled sequence of tasks that can be automated and run as a repeatable script or production process.

In contrast, applications aligned to the BIAN service-oriented design retain the coarse-grained functional boundaries defined by the Service Domains. Top-level application modules match the Service Domain scope, encapsulating its specific business role, providing service-based access to its capabilities and delegating services to other Service Domain aligned applications as needed.

In more advanced technical environments (such as the 'cloud') the service execution can be event-driven, asynchronous and loose-coupled, supporting a highly adaptive, flexible and effective operating model. In less advanced technical environments the standard can be used to eliminate overlaps and complexity in the application portfolio and rationalize interfaces, often leveraging client/server and enterprise service bus (ESB) technologies.

4.3.4 The BIAN Service Domain specification

The BIAN Service Domain specification extends the high-level definition captured at the Service Landscape level (and described earlier in this section). In addition to this general definition, the Service Domain specification sets out the functionality required to support the Service Operations offered and consumed by the Service Domain, and descriptions of the Service Operations themselves.

The functional description is limited to what is needed to detail externally visible behaviors. BIAN does not attempt to fully specify the internal working or functionality of the Service Domain in any detail. BIAN defines 'What' a Service Domain does by detailing the services it offers and consumes. BIAN does not attempt to define 'How' a Service Domain fulfills its purpose, providing only a very limited but sufficient description of its internal operation as necessary to highlight those services it needs to call on from other Service Domains.

In earlier releases of the Service Landscape, reference has been made to Service Domain 'responsibility items' (as defined in the BIAN metamodel). Each responsibility is related to a Service Operation in one of three ways:
- The responsibility item handles a Service Operation offered by the Service Domain.
- The responsibility item delegates activity to a different Service Domain by calling on its Service Operation(s).
- The responsibility item describes additional activity associated with the handling of either an offered or called Service Operation when required for definitional clarity.

The third type of responsibility item is used sparingly where key steps/decisions in the internal business logic need to be explained in order to justify the inclusion and clarify the specific business context for offered and consumed services.

Since BIAN Release 5.0 the main attention has been on expanding the Business Scenario coverage, linking Service Operations to Business Scenarios and providing a further definition of the Service Operation content. As with earlier releases, no specific consideration has been given to the use of the responsibility item to represent the internal working of the Service Domain.

Note: at this stage a more simple and informal template can and has been used on deployment projects to summarize the desired functionality of the Service Domain for both reference and comparison purposes. This is called the Functional & Non-Functional Feature template.

The responsibility items for a Service Domain are organized into four 'responsibility item types' that have been refined based on practical experience. They define the type of access or action performed through the associated Service Operation. With BIAN Release 5.0 the same categories were used to classify the business events associated with a Service Domain and may be used in the future to categorize Service Domain functional properties.

The names of the responsibility item types have been simplified with BIAN Release 6.0 though their definitions have not been amended:
- **Initialize & Register now 'Origination'** – offered Service Operations associated with setting up, verifying and/or registering a new occurrence of the Service Domain's Control Record.
- **Invocation & Execution now 'Invocation'** – offered Service Operations associated with the Service Domain performing tasks on an active or established Control Record instance(s) in response to an external request.
- **Maintain & Analyze now 'Delegation'** – delegated Service Operations called by the Service Domain to enable it to fulfill its business role.
- **Report & Notify now 'Reporting'** – offered Service Operations associated with providing scheduled and ad-hoc reporting, or providing subscription-based notifications to Service Domains.

For BIAN Release 6.0 the model has been extended with a Business Capability Model, more detailed service connection descriptions, a Business Object Model and linkage to the ISO 20022 Standard Message descriptions.

4.3.5 Service Operation details

The most important aspect of the Service Domain specification is the semantic definitions of the Service Operations that it offers and consumes. A Service Domain's use of delegated service calls to other Service Domains provides additional insights into the internal working of the Service Domain. With the expansion of the Business Scenarios with BIAN Release 5.0, the Service Operation profile of the Service Domain is expanded by providing examples of called and delegated Service Operation use. With BIAN Release 5.0 the Service Operation profile has been defined for a significant proportion of the Service Landscape in candidate form. The BIAN Metamodel Release 6.0 introduced the notion of *behavior qualifiers*, which qualify (i.e. refine) the generic behaviors defined for a service domain. It also introduces the notion of *behavior qualifier types*, which classify behavior qualifiers. Furthermore, the Metamodel now supports the definition of service operations based on behavior qualifiers; such extended service operations are refinements of the pattern-generated, generic service operations that BIAN introduced starting with v4.0, and are an important part of BIAN's efforts to publish semantic APIs.

The structure and content of a Service Operation is described in in Chapter 5 within the context of business behaviors modeled using Business Scenarios. Briefly, the specification captures in semantic terms the key types of information that are exchanged and also defines the nature of the operational dependency between the involved Service Domains.

4.3.6 The BIAN Business Scenario

The BIAN Business Scenario is not actually a component of the BIAN standard as it does not represent a canonical design. However, it is included in the BIAN Framework because it provides a powerful mechanism to illustrate by example the roles and interactions that the Service Domains support. Without Business Scenarios to provide explanatory context it can be very difficult to relate individual Service Domains and their Service Operations to the business activities within an enterprise.

The BIAN Business Scenario is a very simple depiction of how some suitable selection of BIAN Service Domains might work together for any identified business event. It is used to help visualize the roles and Service Operation exchanges of the Service Domains involved. It defines an archetypal flow but is not required to be complete or exhaustive. Nor does a Business Scenario prescribe a specific start or end, or indeed the sequence of flow – it merely needs to contain sufficient activity to provide context for the Service Domain interactions that are of interest.

BIAN has used Business Scenarios internally to help identify and specify Service Domains and their Service Operation interactions. As just noted, some specific constraints have been applied to what is included in a Business Scenario and some formality has been developed to the terminology and descriptions of Business Scenarios to support their use as a reference mechanism to access the BIAN standard.

The key changes and additions to the Business Scenarios included in BIAN Release 6.0 are as follows:
- A Business Scenario captures the response associated with a 'business event'.
- A Business Scenario documents the response to that event by a single 'primary' Service Domain and captures only the first order service exchanges with that primary Service Domain and any other Service Domain.
(Note that some earlier Business Scenarios included limited second and higher order service exchanges in a nested model of business activity, however these more complex representations are being discontinued as of Release 6.0 and onwards as they can breach SOA encapsulation principles. (Second order activity can be captured as a separate related Business Scenario with the targeted Service Domain acting as the primary Service Domain.)
- A Business Scenario will typically follow a simple flow – some other Service Domain invokes a service of the primary Service Domain or the primary Service Domain initiates action due to some internal timetable or trigger. The primary Service Domain

will then delegate to one or more Service Domains as it completes its response to the business event.
- In some cases, there may be an anticipated pre or post event trigger to another Business Scenario to model a linked process but this association between Business Scenarios is not mandatory and indeed does not occur too frequently in the model performed analysis to date.
- A standard naming convention and definition has been adopted for the Business Scenarios to facilitate access/reference.

The BIAN Business Scenario is captured and referenced using tools. In conjunction with BIAN Release 5.0, BIAN created a tool called the WorkBench, to capture the Business Scenarios in a structured way. In the past a PowerPoint format was used, as shown in figure 14.

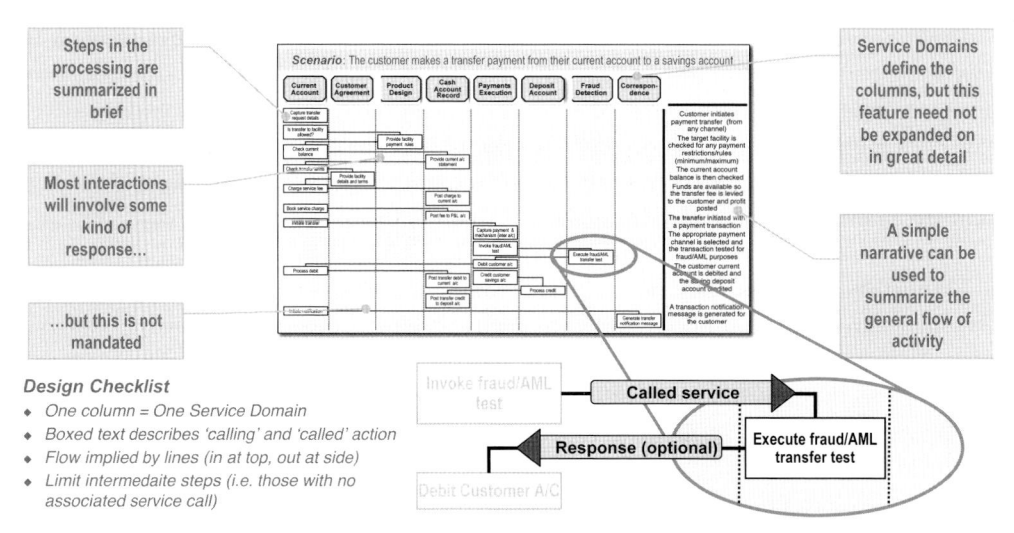

Figure 14: Simple Business Scenario with rules

The flow of activity in the diagram reads from top to bottom. The role of a Service Domain and the actions it performs in the specific Business Scenario are captured in a single column. The arrows connecting between columns indicate a Service Operation between the two corresponding Service Domains.

With the Release 6.0, the scope of the Business Scenario is limited to a single business event as handled by a primary Service Domain. As noted this view is necessary to ensure business activity is correctly modeled as a loose-coupled network of collaborations between Service Domains rather than imposing a lengthy fixed sequence or process flow. This does mean, however, that to properly represent complex business activity a collection of related Business Scenarios may be needed where a single more complex scenario had been used in the past.

BIAN has expanded the tooling used to develop Business Scenarios to better enable the selection and browsing of the Service Operation connections between Service Domains in order to support the representation of complex business activity.

The Business Scenarios provide a visual representation of how Service Domains might collaborate in response to some business need or activity. They clarify the different roles of Service Domains by example. The simple format is intended to support discussions with business practitioners, avoiding the need to explain complex underlying technical design considerations. The scenario view defines an archetypical flow, the sequence as represented can change in practice, some interactions might be obsolete, and others might be missing. Essentially itis intended to provide an effective environment for practitioners to highlight key requirements and to discuss the considerations that need to be captured in the definitions of a Service Domain's Service Operations.

A second format for the Business Scenario is that the one that is captured in the BIAN UML repository, as shown in the diagram below.

Service Operations revealed in the Business Scenarios can be identified by four standard types of behavior. It is possible that more than one type of interaction can apply to an interaction in a Business Scenario, depending on how the scenario might be implemented. BIAN recognizes the following standard types of behavior:

- **Request & Hold** - implies that a response from the called Service Domain is expected quickly. The calling Service Domain is likely to wait for this response and then move on to the next task in hand as a single thread of activity.
- **Request & Monitor** - implies that the response will not be quick to arrive, typically because some work needs to be processed by the called Service Domain before it can react. E.g. a request for information has to be sent to the customer and their response is likely to take some time. The calling Service Domain needs to set up some mechanism to receive the response when it comes (or to chase it up if it doesn't) but in the meantime it will pause or conclude the current thread of activity and move on to something else.
- **Hand-Off** - implies that the calling Service Domain has no further interest in the outcome of the requested action. For example, a Service Domain may ask another Service Domain to perform some task such as send correspondence to a customer, but it assumes this is done correctly and has no further interest or involvement. Once the Hand-Off service interaction has been called, the calling Service Domain assumes the requested action will be performed and can either conclude the activity thread or move on to the next step as appropriate.
- **Make Announcement** - is where one or more Service Domains establish in advance an interest in a notification from the Service Domain of some event or new business information. For example, Service Domains may request that a Product Fulfillment Service Domain notifies them when a product goes into default. When the condition is met, the 'subscribing' Service Domain(s) are notified as appropriate.

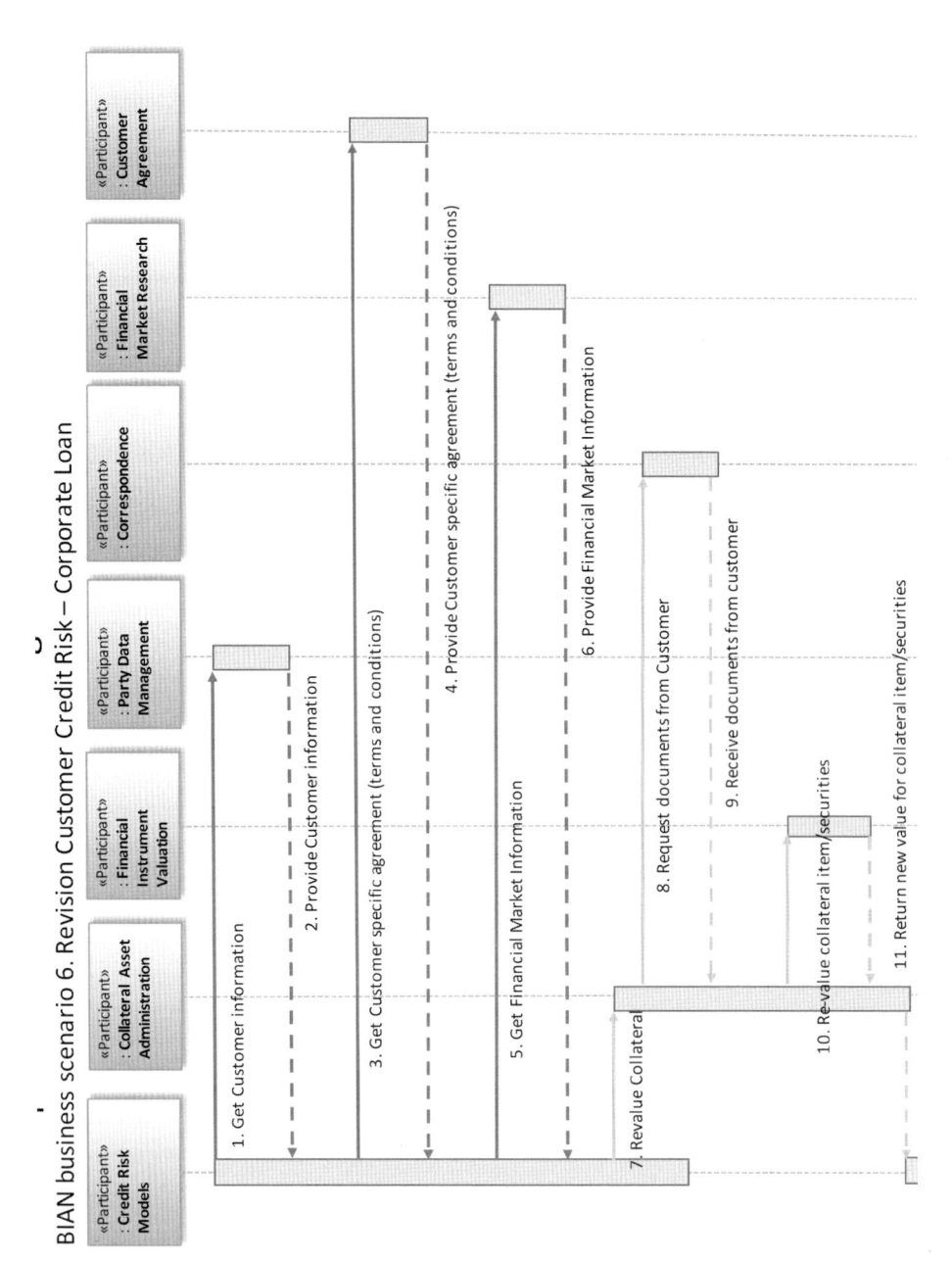

Figure 15: Example Business Scenario in MagicDraw

In practice it has been found that different combinations of these interactions can sensibly apply in different deployment situations for the same Service Operation. As a result, the classifications provide little insight and, at worse, can be misleading. They have been discontinued with the Release 6.0 and the associated implementation considerations moved to the appropriate guidelines for interpreting the model in solution design and deployment.

The scope of a Business Scenario can be compared to that of a conventional high-level Business Process with one key difference. Both describe action steps and some implicit flow of control, but the Business Process does not formally divide functionality between discrete service-based partitions (Service Domains) unlike the Business Scenario.

Presenting Service Domains in the context of a familiar business operation using the Business Scenario format makes the service-based designs easier to understand. Furthermore, presenting different Business Scenarios - each involving a common Service Domain - can help to reveal how a service-oriented architecture can be used to define highly re-usable and leveraged operational capabilities.

4.3.7 Wireframe models

With the BIAN Release 5.0 the use of Wireframes was greatly expanded and the Wireframe view itself made more formal. A Wireframe Model pulls together a related collection of Service Domains and documents the established Service Operation connections between them. These connections can be demonstrated using one or more Business Scenarios. There are many different reasons a collection of Service Domains may be 'clustered' in a Wireframe model.

For Release 6.0 a collection of Wireframe models has been developed for the most active Working Groups to provide a framework for developing a comprehensive collection of first order Business Scenarios.

The Wireframe is a static model, showing the Service Domains and (all pertinent) available connections. Conversely a Business Scenario is a dynamic model that shows the temporal pattern of a collection of interactions that are triggered by some business action or event.

A Business Scenario can be overlain on the Wireframe diagram as shown in the example in figure 16. The Wireframe shows the Service Domains and major Service Operations available for handling the external connection to the SWIFT network and a payment Business Scenario is mapped over the framework.

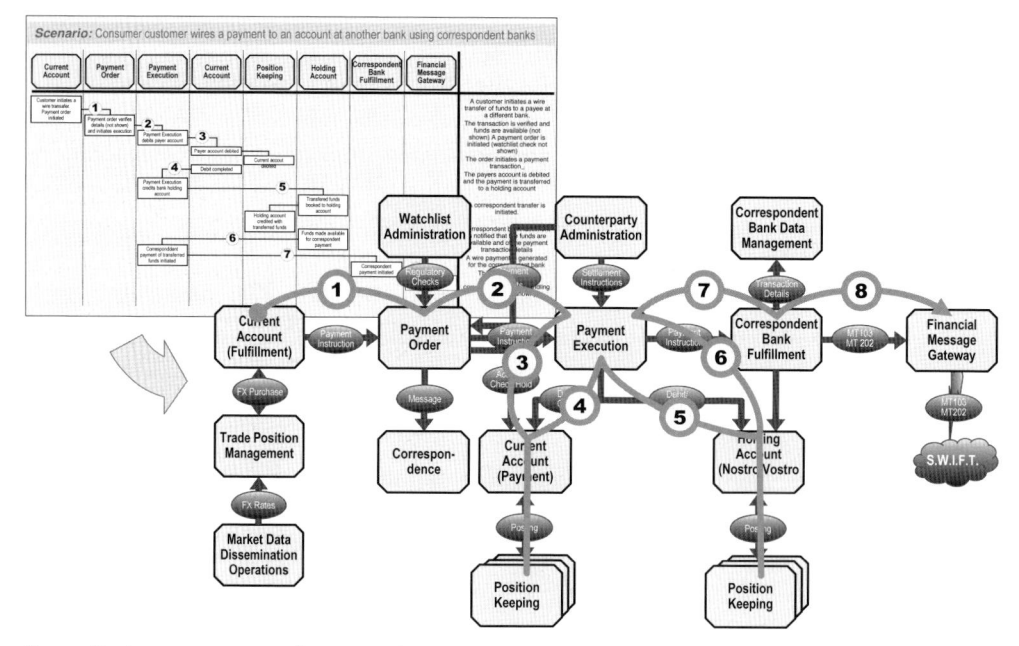

Figure 16: A payment transaction mapped on a Wireframe view

As noted with Release 6.0, the informal Wireframe model shown in figure 16 has been refined in several ways:

- The point of contact on the Service Domain aligns with five points that reflect the type of Service Operation interaction. These are described in the diagram in figure 17 that shows how different Service Operation action terms align to the called and offered service connections.
- A point to note is that service connections to the left and right sides of the Service Domain act on existing instances of a Service Domain's Control Records, i.e. these services act in a steady-state configuration. Vertical connections result in the creation of a new Control Record instance and/or termination of an existing Control Record instance.
- The ellipses on the service connections refer to the associated action term for the Service Operation.
- The protocol for the connections is that the arrowhead points to a called Service Domain. If the call has a dependent response the root of the connection has a circle connection.

Figure 17 shows the five connection paths related to a mortgage loan. Due to the multitude of connections the Wireframe view can quickly become complex.

4   The BIAN Service Landscape

The Figure shows the main offered and called service operation connections for the Mortgage Loan fulfillment Service Domain

Offered services | Delegated/Called services

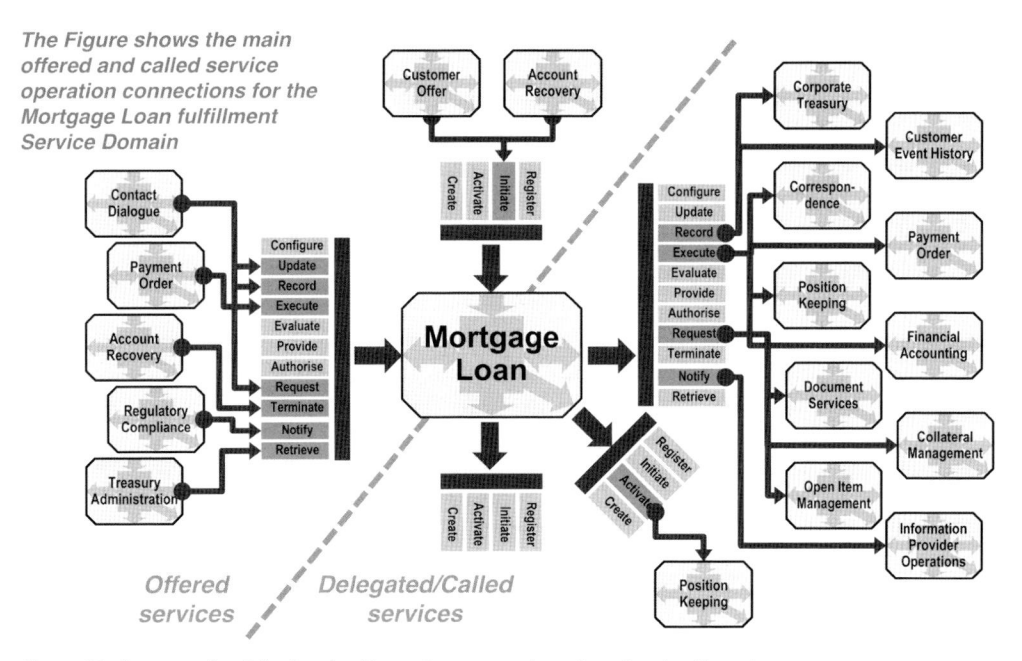

Figure 17: An example of the Service Operation connections for a Service Domain

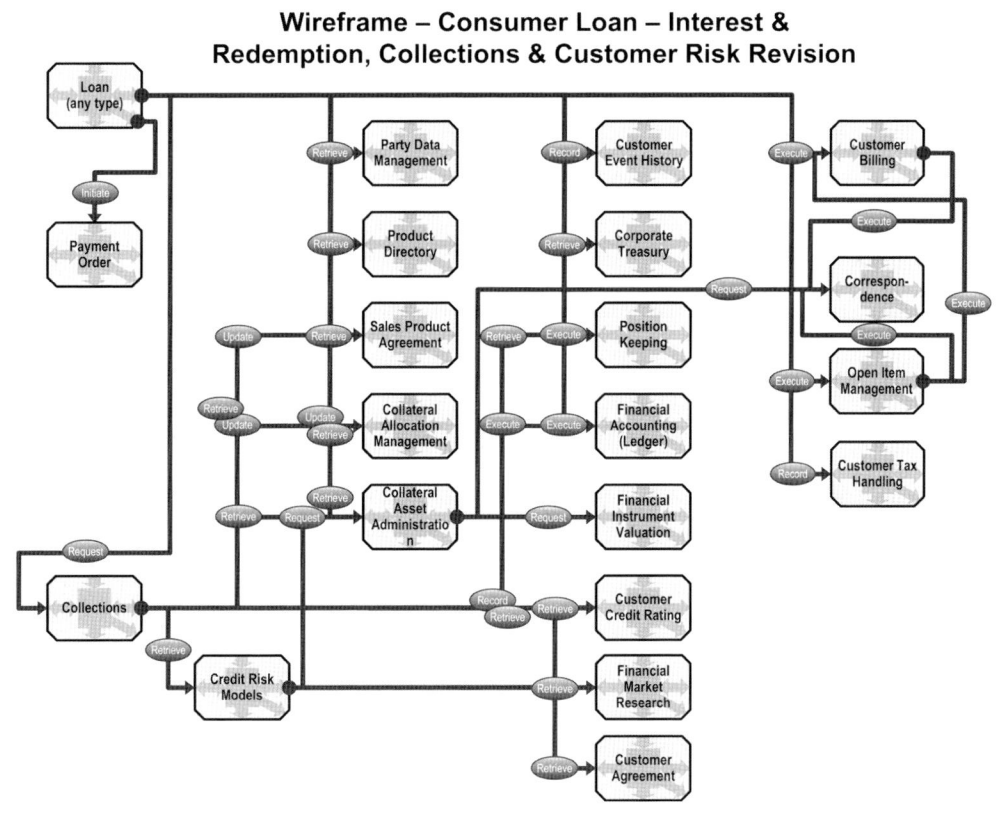

Wireframe – Consumer Loan – Interest & Redemption, Collections & Customer Risk Revision

Figure 18: A Wireframe showing the main Service Operations for a collection of Service Domains

4.4 THE EVOLVING BIAN FRAMEWORK

The BIAN Association strives to continually expand and refine the content of the BIAN Framework. As it does so, the number of Service Domains covered may increase and additional detail will become available in terms of Service Operation definitions and coverage. This is in addition to the standard design specifications (Service Landscape, Service Domains and Service Operations).

The BIAN Association aims to publish an updated version of the Service Landscape twice a year. The most recent version of the Service Landscape includes approximately 300+ BIAN Service Domains with 2,000 default Service Operations for all of them and some 1,000 example Business Scenarios that have been linked to the available Service Operations. We have also added 25+ semantic API definitions and are aiming to grow this number significantly with the upcoming releases.

For the Service Landscape 6.0 there are several degrees of completeness applied to the Service Domains and their Service Operations. These are tracked and reported against the overall Service Landscape. A key activity in moving to BIAN Release 6.0 is to raise the level of completeness from candidate to the Working Group 'reviewed and approved' state for as much of the landscape content as is possible. With the new approach and tooling support it is likely that there will be a continuous flow of new content for the model. BIAN will determine the best release schedule for making this content available within the membership and to the broader public in the future.

Candidate	Defined	Complete
A Service Domain is positioned in the Service Landscape with a completed entry in the underlying Excel definition spreadsheet. Key design details are captured in the spreadsheet. Narrative example of use (NB, not a completed business scenario). Initial mapping to exisiting and/or proposed Working Group.	The Service Domain has been included in at least one Business Scenario and its associated offered and delegated Service Operation calls have been fully specified and assured in the associated Service Domain template.	A comprehensive collection of the service operations offered and called (delegated) have been specified and quality assured. Note that all possible service operations will never be defined, comprehensive here implies that service operations that cover all mainstream uses of the Service Domain are supported for the full lifecycle of its focus object and likely range of reporting needs.

Figure 19: Levels of completion of Service Domains

The current levels of completion related to Service Domains and Service Operations are:
- **Candidate** – a Service Domain is positioned in the Service Landscape with a completed entry in the Repository.
- **Defined** – the Service Domain has been included in at least one Business Scenario.

- **Complete** – a comprehensive collection of the Service Operations offered and called have been specified and quality assured.

4.5 STATEMENT OF COVERAGE BY THE BIAN STANDARD

It should be noted that the Service Operations defined by BIAN aim to reflect the mainstream behaviors of a Service Domain that would be common in the majority of deployments. The way that some Service Domains operate in practice will evolve. New differentiating features may be developed by advanced organizations that, in time, may be adopted by the mainstream. Furthermore, location variations may be required to deal with considerations such as geopolitical requirements and variations of operational scale. The purpose of the BIAN Service Domain partition is to define the core working of a discrete and generic business role. It recognizes that there may need to be site-specific adaptations and refinements in deployment, but the implicit service boundary/role should be stable regardless of these local enhancements.

In the future BIAN will consider ways that it can capture and share prevailing practice details for Service Domains which will include implementation level detail that may also highlight optional features such as those just described. These informal design details will not be part of the formal standard but will be used to help adoption amongst the membership and beyond.

PART III

5 How to apply the BIAN standard

■ 5.1 INTRODUCTION

The BIAN standard defines generic business capability building blocks (Service Domains) and their semantic Service Operations. In order to map these standard designs to a specific organization they need to be selected, adapted and assembled to match the operational scope and structure of the organization and its underlying business applications. BIAN's high-level conceptual definitions must then be mapped to more detailed implementation-level technical designs. This presents initial guidelines for applying the BIAN designs in different business and technical environments.

This document has been revised to reflect deployment insights gained, up until the Service Landscape Release 6.0.

■ 5.2 BIAN'S ALIGNMENT TO TOGAF

Appendix 2 elaborates on the synergies of using BIAN in combination with TOGAF, by looking at TOGAF as the overall framework for architecture work and at BIAN as a pool of industry-specific architecture deliverables. Based on this, BIAN deliverables are related to the TOGAF framework.

As to be expected, the BIAN deliverables have much ground in common with the TOGAF framework. In general, BIAN provides content in a specific structure. When applying TOGAF in a financial services environment, BIAN content speeds up the work and improves quality. On the other hand, TOGAF facilitates architecture development work by providing a structured approach and a complete structure of relevant artifacts. Hence, TOGAF adds value to the BIAN deliverables especially in terms of the project approach and capability to perform, as well as by providing generic technology architectures.

Appendix 2 also describe how BIAN deliverables can be used as input for the different phases of TOGAF's ADM and how they influence the way of working within each phase.

They also relate the BIAN deliverables and philosophy to some specific guidelines and techniques that are relevant when applying the ADM cycle. Later, we map the BIAN deliverables on the TOGAF Content Framework and thus provide insight into which areas BIAN adds architecture content. The final section positions BIAN deliverables in the enterprise continuum to better understand the nature of BIAN deliverables in this respect.

TOGAF Reference Models and the TOGAF Architecture Capability Framework are not covered here. This is because TOGAF Reference Models only relate to technology architectures, whereas BIAN only provides Business and Information Systems Architecture deliverables. With respect to TOGAF Architecture Capability Framework, BIAN does not provide deliverables related to establishing and operating an architecture function within an enterprise.

For a further description on how to use BIAN in the TOGAF ADM phases we refer to Appendix 2.

■ 5.3 MAPPING BIAN TO OTHER INDUSTRY STANDARDS (E.G. IFX, ISO 20022)

A 'Capstone' Project with Carnegie Mellon University supported by PNC Bank and BIAN developed a repeatable approach for mapping BIAN Service Operations to the message specifications in IFX and ISO 20022. The findings are fully documented in a report that is available on the BIAN website. This work built on an earlier joint project between BIAN and IFX that explored the ability to map BIAN Service Operations to implementation level message standards and is also documented and available at the BIAN website.

Both initiatives followed a similar general approach to mapping messages to the BIAN Service Operations. This used the standard design structure of the Service Domain and its associated Control Record to narrow in on possible matches. In the CMU initiative the standard Service Operation 'action terms' were also used (these were not available for the earlier exercise). The main steps in a repeatable mapping approach (that combines both efforts) are described below. Note that it may help to refer to the descriptions of Service Domains and Service Operations in Section 4.3 to fully understand the explanation:
- **Business Scenario Selection** – a suitable collection of BIAN Business Scenarios is used to agree the business context for the mapping. From the Business Scenario views the target Service Domains and their associated Service Operations are isolated.
- **Service Domains and their Control Records are identified** – for each involved Service Domain, the associated Control Record is used to identify the primary asset type/entity acted on by the Service Domain.

- **Asset Type aligned message selection** – candidate messages are selected from the target message standard based on matching the primary asset type to their data/object model. In general terms standards such as IFX often define and categorize messages that provide access to data views of major business objects. An example object would be a customer (relationship).
- **Functional Pattern-based filtering** – the second facet of a Service Domain's Control Record is its 'functional pattern'. This can be used to further filter the selected messages and/or messagecontent based on a sub-set data view of the asset type. Continuing with the example of the customer relationship, BIAN defines a Service Domain that applies a functional pattern 'Agree Terms' to the customer relationship. This can be used to narrow the customer relationship messages and details of interest to just those associated with their contract.
- **Mapping Action Terms to matched messages** – BIAN Service Operations use one of a predefined list of action terms. These action terms can align to the types of messages in the target standard.
- **Matching message payload** – the final step uses the semantic content descriptions of the BIAN Service Operations and matches this with the payload of the candidate messages to further filter out messages and message content.

The steps described above may be applied in different combinations depending on the target message standard being mapped. Practical experience to date has confirmed that the semantic descriptions of the BIAN Service Operations are adequate to support a fairly rigorous mapping to established message standards.

■ 5.4   OTHER MAPPING CONSIDERATIONS

BIAN currently maintains a comprehensive UML Metamodel of its designs. This is an extension of the established ISO 20022 model. The BIAN Metamodel is fully documented in the BIAN Metamodel guide that is available on the BIAN wiki. The BIAN model is maintained in a UML-based repository that allows members to download the content into their own tooling environments with limited adaptations.

BIAN's policy is to align with prevailing industry standards where possible to avoid creating duplicate/competing definitions. This includes adopting naming conventions/notations and aligning with the most popular tooling when this is possible. Where there are competing standards, BIAN will attempt to reconcile or at least document incompatibilities.

BIAN is currently evaluating the following standards and supporting tooling/techniques to improve alignment:
- Open Notations: ArchiMate and possibly SoaML;
- Open reference models: TOGAF, SOA, RefArch, BIZBOK;
- Vocabularies/Ontologies: ISO 20022, OMG/FIBO.

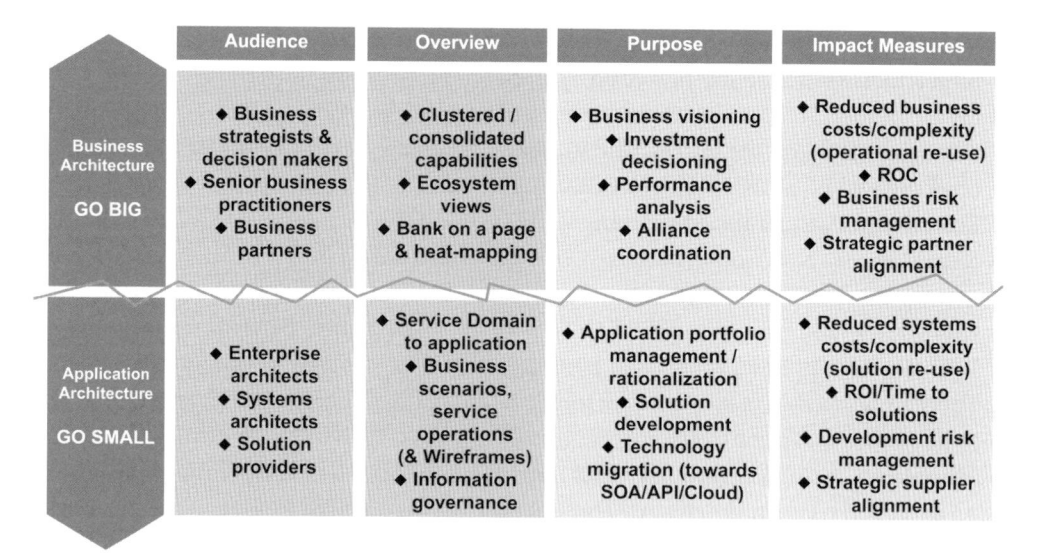

	Audience	Overview	Purpose	Impact Measures
Business Architecture **GO BIG**	◆ Business strategists & decision makers ◆ Senior business practitioners ◆ Business partners	◆ Clustered / consolidated capabilities ◆ Ecosystem views ◆ Bank on a page & heat-mapping	◆ Business visioning ◆ Investment decisioning ◆ Performance analysis ◆ Alliance coordination	◆ Reduced business costs/complexity (operational re-use) ◆ ROC ◆ Business risk management ◆ Strategic partner alignment
Application Architecture **GO SMALL**	◆ Enterprise architects ◆ Systems architects ◆ Solution providers	◆ Service Domain to application ◆ Business scenarios, service operations (& Wireframes) ◆ Information governance	◆ Application portfolio management / rationalization ◆ Solution development ◆ Technology migration (towards SOA/API/Cloud)	◆ Reduced systems costs/complexity (solution re-use) ◆ ROI/Time to solutions ◆ Development risk management ◆ Strategic supplier alignment

Figure 20: Other mapping considerations

Others may be added to the list based on the recommendation of members of the BIAN Association.

5.5 TRANSLATING BIAN 'DOWN THE STACK'

Before briefly considering three different technical environments, there are some general comments as to how the BIAN high-level conceptual designs can be interpreted 'down the stack' for the supporting application and infrastructure levels.

5.5.1 Translating at the business architecture level
At the business layer Service Domains discrete operational partitions are defined that we also refer to as Business Capabilities building blocks.

5.5.2 Translating at the information architecture level
This sub-section briefly summarizes how business information and the underlying data representations are scoped and handled in the BIAN service-based design. First, it is necessary to clarify how some terms are used here:
- Business information – refers to business concepts and details that can be described in simple narrative terms. Business information defines what needs to be known to describe something, or in order to outline some necessary action.
- Semantic vocabulary – BIAN maintains a vocabulary of key business information terms that defines their meaning and relates them to equivalent or similar terms in other selected industry standard vocabularies.
- Business object model – BIAN is currently developing a business object model that is cross-referenced to the industry standard ISO 20022 model. The BIAN BOM provides

a more detailed decomposition of the business information governed by each Service Domain and made available through its Service Operations.
- Data/data structure – refers to a machine-readable data representation of one or more business information terms. Note that a data view is typically far more detailed and that there may be many competing data views/formats for the same business information term.
- Information/data scope – defines the extent or boundary of the context for which the definition of a business information term and/or its associated data representation is valid/agreed.

These definitions are needed to explain a useful property of the BIAN service-based design with respect to information and data governance. In a more conventional process view of business activity the scope of the information referenced (and any underlying data representations) typically spans the complete end-to-end process. Consider for example a mortgage application and fulfillment process. When the customer first completes the application form they will provide details about themselves, the mortgaged property and agree the payment terms and conditions that apply. This information will be referenced and updated and transactional activity logged through all subsequent stages of processing until the mortgage is finally repaid. It is hard to identify any specific stages in the processing of the loan where any aspect of the associated business information may not be needed for some reason.

These business information requirements will be translated into more detailed data structures and elements for the supporting mortgage loan processing business application. As (for the sake of this example) the complete end-to-end mortgage process is supported by one business application, the same data views of the business information can sensibly be adopted by all users/interested parties. In summary, in conventional process-based solutions the scope of the business information tends to be broad and the mapping to the underlying data structures is the same for all interested parties.

It is obviously very sensible to be able to support broad access to common business information and to have widely applied data standards. However, in practice this is not always easy to achieve across application portfolios that may combine many bespoke developments and different commercial packages. It is even more difficult to coordinate between different enterprises. It is therefore interesting to note that these two properties – broad scope and common data definitions/mappings can sometimes be relaxed to some extent in service-based designs.

Consider the scope of business information in service-based design using the example of a month-end credit card billing process. In that process each Service Domain will retain control over the Control Record instances that handle the fulfillment of its business function for the full lifecycle. For example, Customer Agreements maintain the customer's agreed terms and conditions from start to finish. The only information exchanged with other Service Domains is extracted reference views of the agreement (and perhaps some control-related requests).

It is possible to determine for each Service Domain what portion of the business information that it uses to support its role needs to be externally visible and what portion of that business information relates to specific internal processing that can be hidden or encapsulated away from all other Service Domains. In the example of the Customer Agreement there is a limited public view of the Customer Agreement and a more complete array of business information needed to set-up, verify and maintain the agreement behind the scenes.

The scope assessment of the overall business information can therefore be divided into public business information for which the definition needs to be agreed by the parent/owning Service Domain and all other Service Domains that may access its services, and the more comprehensive internal business information that only needs to be seen/accessed by its 'parent' Service Domain.

The next step is to consider the required degree of precision with which a business information item is mapped to a representative data structure. This consideration is rarely exposed in more conventional process-based designs but is an important property of Service Operation exchanges. The concept can be clarified using two examples at either end of the resolution spectrum.

A Credit Card Fulfillment Service Domain needs to post the transaction details for a card transaction against the transaction journal (maintained by the Position Keeping Service Domain). It is obvious that every field (amount/date/currency/account number etc.) needs to be strictly defined in machine readable, formatted fields.

At the other end of the range, Campaign Execution has identified a new prospect who is not currently a bank customer and wishes to notify Prospect Management to follow up. In this situation there are many possible ways (information items) to identify the individual and to describe the new business prospect. Furthermore, the precise data formatting of the underlying data fields can be more loosely matched. It does not matter if one side of the exchange doesn't capture middle names or has different address field lengths. Sufficient information can hopefully be exchanged to have a good chance of making the business connection.

In summary there will be many Service Domain exchanges that require similar levels of consistency to data scoping and formatting rigor to the more conventional process-based implementations. But there are areas of the Service Landscape where the scoping of shared business information definition and values is reduced to a significantly more focused 'public' semantic vocabulary. Also, where differences exist in the internal data representations of these semantic business terms in the respective applications of the supporting Service Domains this does not constrain their ability to exchange services.

These information and data properties are a key aspect for achieving loose coupling between service-based capabilities in highly networked technical environments such as the world wide web, the cloud and, most recently, through mechanisms such as application program interfaces (APIs).

An additional observation can be made with respect to business information governance. The BIAN Service Domains are defined to represent non-overlapping business capability partitions that collectively cover all possible aspects of banking. Each Service Domain has a defined Control Record that represents the information used to manage one instance of the Service Domain performing its role for a complete lifecycle. It follows that the business information associated with the collection of one or more Control Records for a Service Domain (and any derived analytical views) is also discrete and that the combination of these discrete information partitions covers all possible business information.

As a result, the Service Domains can be used to define business information partitions that can then be used to scope out business information and the underlying data governance responsibilities for the Service Domain's supporting applications. Note that this partitioning of the business information and its supporting data views does not preclude that one Service Domain may require access to the data governed by another Service Domain. This information will be accessed through appropriate Service Operation exchanges and the retrieved information, once interpreted as necessary, becomes information that is owned and governed locally.

Another possible situation is that two Service Domains may govern discrete business information that happens to share a common data representation and even the same current value. For example, the Customer Agreement Service Domain may maintain a name and address for a contract that has the same format and value as the mailing address maintained by the Correspondence Service Domain. Though they may use the same data format and even have the same value, these two data items represent different business information as they have different contexts, meaning and purpose.

It is for the above reasons that the BIAN Business Object Model is being defined with a structure that aligns with the Service Domain Control Records.

5.5.3 The Control Record can be modeled
The business information view of a Service Domain's Control Record can be modeled using any suitable entity or object data approach to define its structure and content. Such a view is used to help define the information payload of a Service Domain's Service Operations. In earlier releases, prior to BIAN Release 6.0, BIAN defined a standard

collection of types of information that might make up the content of a Control Record based on the Service Domain's functional pattern. This generic list provides a checklist from which a suitable selection can be made and adapted for each individual Service Domain.

In most cases the Service Domain's Control Record defines a single 'primary' object or entity with a potentially complex make-up of more detailed elements that can be represented in a conceptual data model. With BIAN Release 6.0 an additional design property has been used to specify a Service Domain – the 'behavior qualifier type'. The behavior qualifier type indicates how the functional pattern of a Service Domain can be broken down into finer elements. Based on this decomposition a more detailed structure of the function and data can be derived. The way behavior qualifiers have been defined and applied is explained in more detail in a later section of this publication.

In addition to the higher-level of specification for the Service Domain, BIAN has also started to define its own Business Object Model, linked to the ISO 20022 industry standard. The BIAN BOM aligns to the Service Domain Control Records and provides a significantly higher level of specification of the associated business information than available in previous releases. The BIAN BOM is being expanded to cover the BIAN Service Landscape.

For some Service Domains the underlying information model can have a more complex structure than others. This is particularly the case where the Service Domain handles asset types that include some form of relational/hierarchical property. Examples of Service Domains that have an embedded hierarchical property are:
1. Service Domains for a legal party (a legal entity can be made up of other legal entities);
2. Service Domains for a product (a product can be an assembly of other products);
3. Service Domains for risk management service (risks can be composite views of other risks).

Service Domains with a hierarchical structure require additional Service Operations to manage the internal hierarchical relationships. For example, in the case of the Service Domain 'party', there is one Service Operation to add a new party and then an additional service to add a new party relationship.

5.5.4 Translating at the application level
There is a detailed list of the different ways in which a BIAN Service Domain partition can map to the underlying business applications and their constituent application modules. Points of clarification to add here are:
- A BIAN Service Domain may align to a single business application; several Service Domains may be covered by a business application, or a single Service Domain may be supported by a collection of business applications.

- It is more likely that at some level, an application module within a business application will align most closely to a Service Domain.
- It is not necessary that the mapped business application or application modules are implemented with a service-enabled external interface. The exchanges can be realized by many types of technical exchange mechanisms.

The main purpose of the Service Domain is to define a logical capability partition that can be used as a pattern to better structure the application logic so that it avoids fragmentation and duplication and improves encapsulation. Some examples of the way the Service Domain concept can be leveraged at the application level include:

- **Specialization** – because the Service Domain supports one 'elemental' capability, its implementation can be optimized for that specific behavior. Conversely more complex designs that support multiple behaviors are often forced to adopt technical and operational compromises.
- **Externalization & Re-use** – the Service Domain design partitions make it clear when actions should be delegated to other specialized Service Domains ('externalized') – allowing the Service Domain to focus on its own specific role and for greater re-use of functionality between Service Domains. This important concept is explained in more detail with examples later in this section.
- *Service Enablement* – though it is not mandatory, it is anticipated that the Service Domains are typically implemented to act as service centers in a service-oriented architecture (SOA). The many advantages of SOA are well documented elsewhere.
- **Loose Coupling and Multi-Threading** – features typically associated with SOA. The Service Domain partitions are well suited to an implementation where the required collaborations between Service Domains are fully asynchronous and defensive (i.e. handle delayed/erroneous responses). Also, where the Service Domain can handle multiple concurrent streams of activity.
- **Encapsulation** – because the Service Domain's business role is discrete, and it performs its role from start to finish for every occurrence, the partition tends to 'encapsulate' business information and logic. The Service Domain can 'hide' complexity that is not relevant to those that consume its services. This property is particularly useful for highly distributed environments like the cloud.

Finally, because the business role addressed by a Service Domain is enduring, it is often possible to build out and integrate the capabilities of a Service Domain incrementally. It may also be able to add new capabilities as new practices evolve without destabilizing established services, extending the shelf-life of business applications significantly.

5.5.5 Translating at the infrastructure level

A Service Domain and its mapped application module(s) can be further related to the supporting technical infrastructure. For simplicity in the explanations that follow it is assumed that a single application module has been mapped to the associated Service Domain. Furthermore, BIAN is developing a Vendor Agnostic IT Model, or Reference

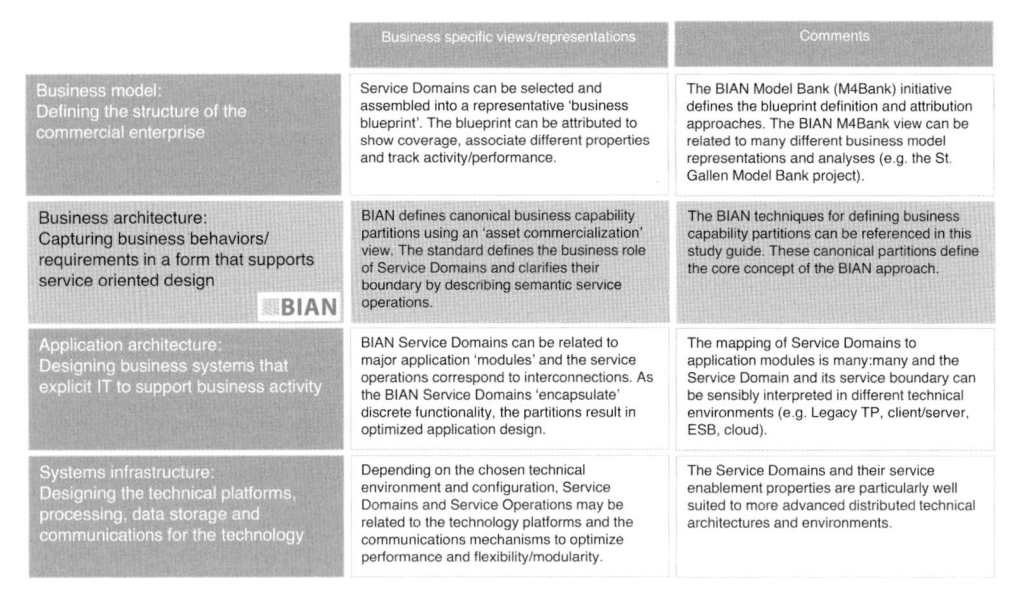

	Business specific views/representations	Comments
Business model: Defining the structure of the commercial enterprise	Service Domains can be selected and assembled into a representative 'business blueprint'. The blueprint can be attributed to show coverage, associate different properties and track activity/performance.	The BIAN Model Bank (M4Bank) initiative defines the blueprint definition and attribution approaches. The BIAN M4Bank view can be related to many different business model representations and analyses (e.g. the St. Gallen Model Bank project).
Business architecture: Capturing business behaviors/ requirements in a form that supports service oriented design	BIAN defines canonical business capability partitions using an 'asset commercialization' view. The standard defines the business role of Service Domains and clarifies their boundary by describing semantic service operations.	The BIAN techniques for defining business capability partitions can be referenced in this study guide. These canonical partitions define the core concept of the BIAN approach.
Application architecture: Designing business systems that explicit IT to support business activity	BIAN Service Domains can be related to major application 'modules' and the service operations correspond to interconnections. As the BIAN Service Domains 'encapsulate' discrete functionality, the partitions result in optimized application design.	The mapping of Service Domains to application modules is many:many and the Service Domain and its service boundary can be sensibly interpreted in different technical environments (e.g. Legacy TP, client/server, ESB, cloud).
Systems infrastructure: Designing the technical platforms, processing, data storage and communications for the technology	Depending on the chosen technical environment and configuration, Service Domains and Service Operations may be related to the technology platforms and the communications mechanisms to optimize performance and flexibility/modularity.	The Service Domains and their service enablement properties are particularly well suited to more advanced distributed technical architectures and environments.

Figure 21: The association between the BIAN standard and prevailing model views

Application Architecture, where Service Domains are mapped to a proposed Application Module, which is planned for BIAN Release 7.0.

Each Service Domain will have its own non-functional profile in terms of its data storage access and processing requirements that need to be supported by the technical infrastructure. Most technologies provide comprehensive instance partitioning facilities/virtual machines so that multiple Service Domains and their associated application modules can operate independently on the same platform. This allows for Service Domains/application modules with similar operating profiles to be supported on shared technical infrastructures with the required performance profile.

Some optimization options can be considered for supporting the communications traffic between application modules as represented by the high-level Service Domain Service Operations. Where the volume and frequency of the exchanges is modest, most data exchange/communications mechanisms can be considered according to the technical environment.

Where the exchange is high volume/high frequency, it is possible to configure the infrastructure to facilitate the exchange. For example, the logical service exchange between two discrete conceptual functions as represented by Service Domains can be mapped to a shared database with each having controlled access to their respective views of the data. In practice this would eliminate the need for a physical service-based data exchange to realize the conceptual service interaction. Other technical communications options may be found.

5.5.6 Translating summary

The mapping of Service Domain conceptual designs down the stack is summarized in figure 22.

The Service Domains are discrete and measurable capabilities, and investment at that level can be related to the underlying applications and technologies.

At the Business layer, Service Domains define discrete operational partitions:
- Unique, discrete business capabilities;
- Act as operational service centers;
- Business performance related directly to business needs and priorities.

At the Application layer, requirements map to major application modules:
- Service Domains align to major application modules;
- Business information needs mapped to data use;
- Operational services mapped to A2A messaging/ interfaces;
- Orchestration related to different solution architectures.

At the Communications & Infrastructure layer, applications map to supporting platforms:
- Communications technology;
- Processing centers;
- Data storage.

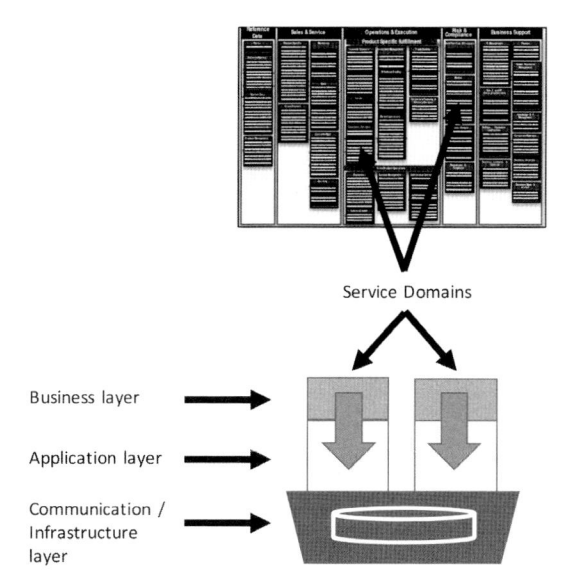

Figure 22: Mapping Service Domains down the stack

5.6 APPLYING BIAN SERVICE DOMAINS IN DIFFERENT ENVIRONMENTS

5.6.1 Using BIAN specifications as a high-level implementation design

The high-level semantic BIAN designs can be extended and interpreted to help define systems requirements that are sufficiently detailed to support the initial stages of solution implementation. The BIAN standard is a business architecture level model view that defines a type of service-oriented architecture (SOA). A SOA captures the business activity as a collection of collaborating operational service centers. It might be expected that the only type of systems architecture that could be linked or derived using the BIAN model would correspondingly be service-oriented. Though there are several significant operational advantages in service-based systems design, the BIAN business architecture provides valuable insights and design structures for most of the prevailing technical environments found in banks.

This section addresses the considerations and approaches for interpreting the BIAN standard in solution design and implementation. It is structured into a number of sub-sections as follows:

- **SOA – benefits and externalization** – there are benefits for adopting service-based designs at the technical systems level and at the higher business architecture level defined by BIAN – these are outlined. The benefits can be associated with the degree or level to which the service-oriented concepts are adopted in the application architecture. We informally consider three stages/levels of adoption. These levels are used to explain an important BIAN concept of 'externalization'.
- **Business to technical architecture – mapping Service Domains** – the BIAN Service Domain is a conceptual design of a business capability that is defined in terms of its business role/purpose and the Service Operations it offers and consumes. This 'business capability' building block can be mapped to the supporting business application and systems structures in many ways.
- **Service Domain clusters** – a 'cluster' represents a collection of Service Domains as might map to a business application. Different roles for the contained Service Domains are defined to help manage the service dependencies that define the external boundary of the application.
- **Adding detail to the BIAN business architecture specification** – the BIAN standard and supporting artifacts provide a high-level specification of the core functionality, business information use and Service Operation boundary of Service Domains. These business architecture specifications provide an organizing framework for adding the additional layers of detail needed to specify systems requirements and implementation designs. These layers of detail can be considered in terms of application logic, information/data and communications.
- **Interpreting SDs in technical environments Levels 1-3** – as further described in Section 5.9 we define three informal stages/levels of SOA adoption. These indicative levels have been used to consider how the BIAN standard applies in the three main,

fundamentally different prevailing technical architectures found in most banks today.
- **Point solutions** – finally in this section we set out the general steps that can be followed when leveraging the BIAN business architecture in the context of a 'point solution'. This includes describing some working templates and model views that have been used in recent BIAN implementation projects.

5.6.2 Service-oriented architectures and the benefits of 'externalization'

The benefits of adopting service-oriented architecture (SOA) approaches in systems design and implementation are, in general, well understood and documented. The generally accepted benefits and those more specifically addressing the BIAN approach are summarized here to provide some general context.

The general IT systems-related benefits for adopting SOA, as described in detail by The Open Group, can be paraphrased as follows:
- **Service** – the adoption of services in the systems architecture can improve information flow, help expose embedded functionality and offer greater organizational flexibility.
- **Service re-use** – service-based software leads to lower software development and management cost.
- **Messaging** – has a wide range of positive impacts including configuration flexibility, better monitoring and intelligence, greater control and security.
- **Complexity and composition** – services can simplify software, supporting more complex, adaptive and more easily integrated solutions.

The SOA benefits described by The Open Group relate to the impact on the development, performance and fit-to-purpose of software solutions. BIAN applies the SOA concepts at the level of business architecture – defining the operational capability partitions and interactions that make up the bank rather than the specific mechanics of their supporting systems. Some of the key business architectural design properties that BIAN implements include:
- **BIAN Service Domains are discrete** – the business role/purpose of a service partition is unique, non-overlapping and discrete.
- **BIAN Service Domains are collectively comprehensive** – BIAN seeks to define a complete set of service partitions. All possible financial services activity can be modeled using the identified Service Domains.
- **BIAN Service Domains are 'elemental'** – the Service Domains support a single business purpose. They are not made up of smaller Service Domains; instead they form a 'peer set'.

Because of these specific operational design properties, the BIAN SOA provides additional opportunities when used to better align the underlying business applications:
- **Operational re-use**: the unique operational capabilities of individual Service Domains can be widely accessed across the enterprise, increasing operational

capability re-use, concentrating scarce and/or specialized resources and improving resource utilization/leverage.
- **Increased operational flexibility**: as more business capabilities are made available through shared services, changing business needs can more readily be supported through service realignment/re-use. In time these might, in some cases, be offered by external parties.
- **Reduced business information inconsistencies and fragmentation**: the SOA partitions act as the single source for the business information that they 'govern'. This property is used to reduce inconsistency and fragmentation.
- **Performance optimization**: each service partition fulfils a narrowly defined business purpose so that its internal capabilities can be optimized for that specific behavior.
- **Support for distributed systems solutions** – because the Service Domains define discrete business capabilities that fulfill the full lifecycle of their role, they define highly encapsulated entities. These partitions are well suited for distributed environments such as the cloud where shared databases are not always a practical option.

The building block of the BIAN SOA is the Service Domain – it is a conceptual specification of a functional partition. A critical aspect of the Service Domain's definition is to clearly distinguish between the functions that it performs directly (using its own internal capabilities) and those functions for which it still retains the ultimate responsibility but that it relies on other Service Domains to execute through making delegating service calls. The general design approach to determining what should be delegated is referred to as 'externalization' within BIAN.

5.6.3 Defining BIAN's concept of 'externalization'

Externalization is a consideration that is particular to service-based design where each service center has a unique and narrowly defined or 'elemental' business role. It then delegates a potentially wide range of activities to other service centers with their own functional specializations. Externalization refers to the decision as to what the service capability does itself and when it necessarily calls on the services of some other specialized capability (Service Domain).

In summary, a Service Domain's business purpose or role is characterized by its 'Control Record'. The Control Record is a 'pattern' that combines a type of asset that is then acted upon in a specific way (to gain some commercial benefit). For example, the asset could be an employee and the action performed could be to assign work to that employee. The associated Service Domain then covers the processing logic and governs the business information needed to handle all instances of its Control Record through the full lifecycle. In this case, to make, track and report on all employee task assignments.

To fulfill its business role, a Service Domain may need to call on a wide range of other specialized Service Domains for many different reasons. Continuing with the example of an employee assignment, it may be necessary to check the employee's qualifications

5 How to apply the BIAN standard

for a proposed assignment. Employee certification is a different specialized function and so the assignment Service Domain would delegate the employee's certification assessment to another Service Domain – i.e. the certification function is 'externalized'.

The called Certification Service Domain might simply track employee qualifications or may go further and actually assess the employee directly. The calling assignment Service Domain does not care how the called Service Domain reaches its conclusion, it only needs to know if the candidate employee is suitably qualified.

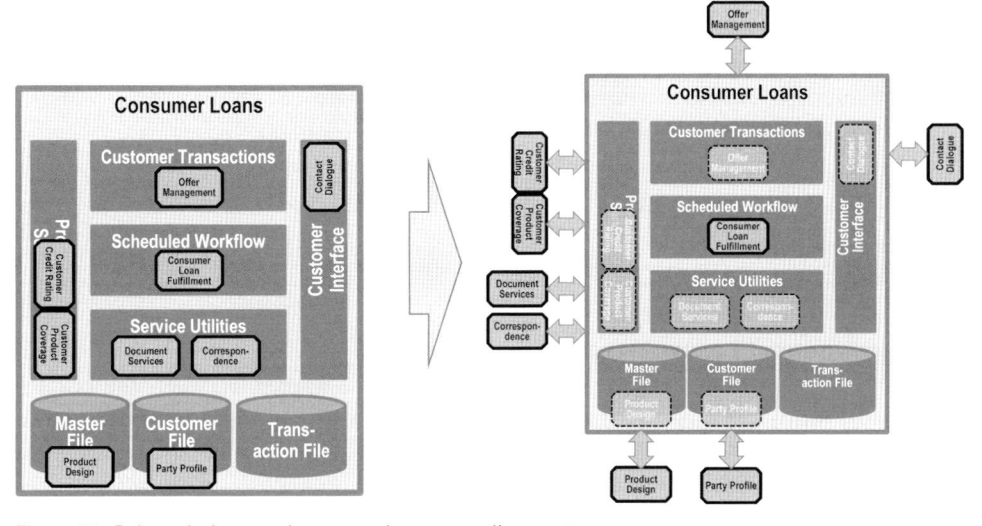

Figure 23: Point solutions environment: Legacy re-alignment

As shown in figure 23, the BIAN Service Domains are used to re-allocate legacy systems functionality to create service components in line with business capabilities and thereby reduce functional duplication and fragmentation.

In this example eight out of the nine 'modules' are not Consumer Loans-specific and can be externalized in generic components that can also be used in other core financial services processes.

There are some key considerations and possible differences between the concept of externalization in service-based design and the more conventional sub-routine or utility calls often found in process-based design:

- **Responsibility allocation** – responsibility is specifically allocated with an externalized service call as follows: the responsibility for confirming that the call is appropriate in the first place, subsequently making the call, accepting and acting on the result remains with the delegating Service Domain. The responsibility of the called service provider is only to deliver to the actual or implied service agreement.

Assigning responsibility in a delegated exchange is an important aspect of service design and is necessary to protect the principle of encapsulation and to ensure service integrity. A service provider can only control the delivery of the service offered. They must make clear the nature of the service they offer in order for the service consumer to make an accurate decision on the suitability of the service for their need. The consumer then retains responsibility for that selection decision.

For example an individual who uses a taxi service to get to the airport can reasonably expect that the taxi is well maintained and fueled up. But what if the traffic is particularly bad, or the taxi gets involved in an accident or the taxi suffers a flat tire and the individual misses the flight? Applying the definition of externalization, the fault for missing the flight would lie with the decision to use the taxi service (with insufficient contingency) and not with the taxi service provider.

The allocation of responsibility for utility calls in process-oriented design is not necessarily so explicit. Users and usages are not as well assigned (if at all) as they are in the service-based model.

- **Business information/data access** – for a delegated service, there is an implicit assumption that all information/data that needs to be agreed between the parties in order to fulfill the service exchange is contained in the messages underlying the exchange. Conversely with process/utility calls there can be assumptions made that there is some shared/global database with common data definitions, available to all, that will support this and any necessary interaction.

  Note: this description only considers the service exchanges involved in the transaction itself. It does not address another implicit assumption that the participants in a service exchange are suitably qualified to perform their role. For example, in addition to the individual service call there will need to be coordination between the involved parties to ensure that they both have in place the necessary security policies and governance mechanisms.

- **Functional scope** – the Service Domain designs have well defined procedures to specify the functions or capabilities that are performed directly by the Service Domain and those that are to be supported elsewhere and accessed through delegated service calls (externalized). The discrete non-overlapping properties of the Service Domains provides a comprehensive and robust framework for defining the required internal/contained and external functionality. As noted at the start of this section, the internal functionality needs to support the full lifecycle of the Control Record. Any function, information and action that does not have some aspect of the Control Record as its subject should be externalized.

In conventional process-oriented design, the definition of utilities and other shared resource access is determined primarily by implementation considerations and feasibility – there is no high-level design partitioning discipline that enforces the correct scope of any particular functional 'module'.

The description of externalization so far has been applied to the Service Domain partition. In simple terms the functionality contained within the Service Domain needs to be limited to the logic needed to address the lifecycle of its Control Record instances/subjects directly. Any other functionality should be external, i.e. accessed through delegated services from some other suitable Service Domain. The concept of externalization can also be applied at a higher level as described in the following subsection.

5.6.4 Externalization in business application design

The concept of externalization and delegation can be applied at the higher business application level. The mapping of the Service Domain capability partitions to the scope of business applications is addressed more thoroughly later in this section, but at this point it is sufficient to consider that a stand-alone business application (such as a loans processing application) will typically contain the functionality represented by several Service Domains. The externalization assessment can then be used to determine whether this function should be supported by an embedded internal capability or by an external shared service capability. In this context, external means externally accessible. In implementation there are different options for achieving this that are explored under the topic of Service Domain 'clusters' later in this section.

An example helps to clarify how the Service Domain roles can be used to define clear boundaries for the functional partitioning (externalization) of business applications. Consider the design of a new business application for processing product offers made to existing customers – an 'offer management' application. Functions that are integral to the 'offer' include selecting the right product, making the necessary disclosures, and negotiating any customer-specific terms and conditions before final agreement is reached. This is then followed by the associated product contract set up and the product's fulfillment processing.

As well as steering the customer through the offer decision-making process, there may be additional related tasks involved. For example, capturing and verifying customer details, assessing their credit worthiness, obtaining an underwriting decision and other approvals, confirming the offer meets the bank's requirements (eligibility checks), addressing any possible regulatory limitations (suitability checks) and handling background document and correspondence exchanges.

In a process-based implementation, the boundary between the processing logic and data requirements of the newly developed offer management application, and where the new application will need to interface to existing systems, will usually be determined by the feasibility based on the state of the legacy environment. It will depend on the availability of viable interfaces to the legacy systems; and the associated integration costs will be justified in terms of data and production consistency. In this example, the external facility most likely to be referenced will be that of customer information. It is probable that most of the other functions listed will be supported by solutions built within the new product offer system. Even in the best-managed and architected application environments, there is likely to be some duplication of function and data in the newly developed application.

In a BIAN service-based design, every one of the items listed in the above example represents a delegated function that should be externalized. One core Service Domain is responsible for orchestrating the offer process itself and, in doing so, it delegates to a wide range of other specialist 'Service Domains' that may support or influence the offer 'decision'.

It is not necessary, or indeed likely, that a new offer management application could be built where every one of these discrete delegated Service Domain functions is supported by an external call to some existing legacy system. The design requirement is, however, that every Service Domain capability *could* be supported by such a service call to another application.

By structuring the application logic into discrete service-enabled partitions, a decision can be taken in each case as to how they are best implemented in this specific deployment environment. The implications for business application design and operation are far reaching. In later sections of this chapter, three stages of adoption or alignment to the principle of externalization are described.

As noted, the concept of Service Domain 'clustering' also applies when mapping BIAN to business applications. With clustering, some simple operational roles are defined for the Service Domains within a cluster aligned to a particular application. The concept is outlined in Section 5.6.7.

5.6.5 Business to technical architecture – mapping Service Domains

The BIAN SOA defines discrete business capability building block as Service Domains. The Service Domains are usually considered to operate as service centers – operational capabilities that provide (and consume) business services from other operational capabilities. At the business architecture level, the Service Domains can be used as the elemental blocks for building different views of the business enterprise that are then utlised for different types of planning and analyses.

The Service Domains define partitions of the application logic and information/data that need to be reflected in the solution's technical architectures. The way that the Service Domains map to the technical architecture will vary for different technical environments, broadly reflecting different 'levels' of service enablement. In the light of this, the mapping in three different technical environments is considered below. However, before looking further at this mapping, some more general statements are needed as to how the logical partitions defined by Service Domains line up with the business applications/systems in general.

As noted earlier, in Section 5.6.4, 'externalization' of a stand-alone business application will typically have functionality that is represented by a collection of several Service Domains. This is not always the case; indeed, the mapping between Service Domains and a business application can cover every possible combination.

It is possible in cases where Service Domains can potentially combine many different technically supported tasks (such as product design or financial modeling) that the implementation for the Service Domain could include multiple (small or highly specialized) business applications. Sometimes a Service Domain will map neatly to a single business application. The most common situation, however, is where a business application has a functional scope covering multiple Service Domains.

Figure 24 illustrates three mapping arrangements. It is used to identify the service support issues when the mapping used is not the more convenient one-to-one option that is shown in the middle of the figure. The other two options shown are:
- **Many to one (many-to-one)** – when multiple business applications support the scope of a single Service Domain, the issue is the support for Service Operations that rely on information or functionality that spans the business applications – where is the necessary consolidation of the activity performed.
- **One to many (one-to-many)** – when a single business application covers the role of multiple Service Domains, the issue is whether all of the Service Operations across all of the constituent Service Domains can be accessed externally (functionality can often be embedded/integrated in a way that compromises its ability to act as a discrete service center).

In all the mapping options described so far, the service boundary of the Service Domain and the business application are 'aligned' meaning that a business application is fully contained within the scope of a Service Domain, or that a Service Domain is fully contained within the boundary of a business application. The case when they are not aligned is when the same Service Operations for a Service Domain somehow straddle two or more business applications. In this case there will need to be duplicated/redundant logic in more than one business application and, as a result, the discrete/non-overlapping principle behind the BIAN service-based design will have been violated.

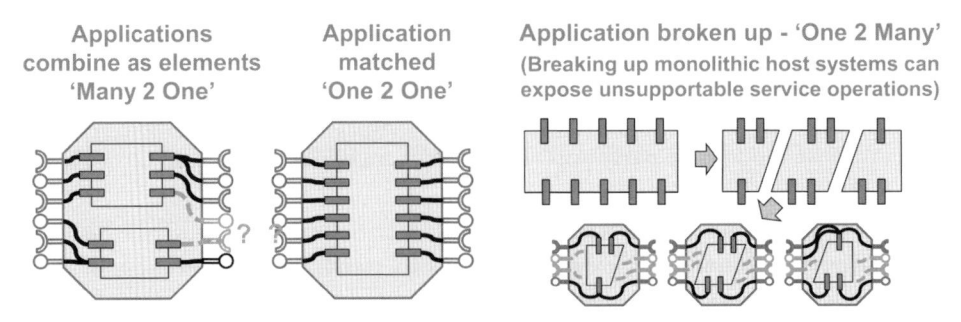

Figure 24: Mapping business applications to Service Domains

5.6.6 Business architecture versus systems architecture views of a Service Domain

The mapping arrangements described so far assume that the business application performs a discrete business role (and can therefore be mapped uniquely to one or more Service Domains). When considering the scope/mapping of application logic, there are two situations where the relationship between the logic supported by the software components and the discrete business capabilities of the enterprise is not directly and uniquely resolvable. These situations are:

1. The application module is a 'utility' function that can be used in many different contexts. Each instance of use is completely independent/unaware of other instances. For example, a 'library' of complex algorithms could be coded and reused in many different applications supporting many different Service Domains.
2. The application module provides a 'common solution' that can be configured to support the needs of different business functions. An example would be in the area of product fulfillment. There could be a collection of products such as different types of loans that are captured as discrete business capabilities at the business architecture level (and so would have different Service Domains). But in operation they have very similar behaviors such that an application solution built for one could be reconfigured and redeployed to support the others. As with the utility function, each application deployment is functionally independent/unaware of other deployment instances.

This mapping of utility and common solution application modules to Service Domains is shown schematically in figure 25.

The use of shared utility and common solution application modules is an important aspect of effective software development and deployment. The use of these kinds of application module can be properly represented at the system architecture level. It is however not an aspect of the business architecture representation because the business architecture level intentionally shows only discrete business capability building blocks. These building blocks may be supported by any appropriate combination of application modules including unique logic, re-using utility elements or employing a configured instance of a common solution.

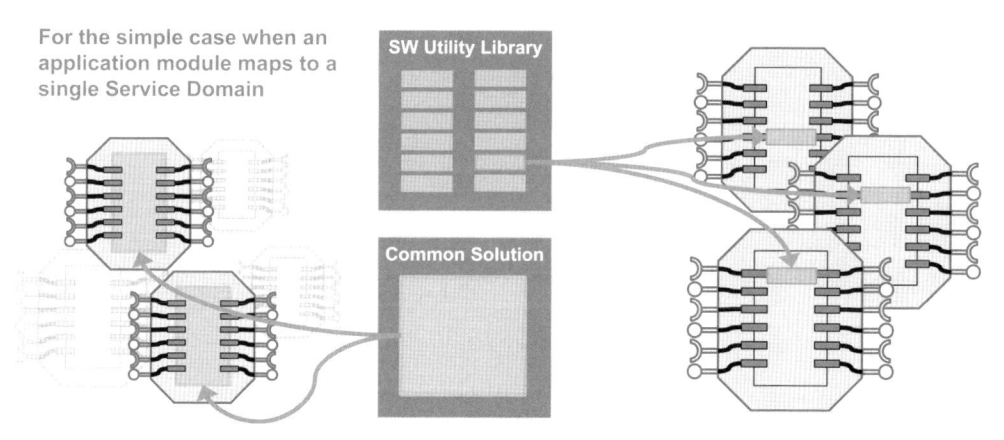

Figure 25: Aligning utility and common solution application modules to Service Domains

The tracing of utility solution elements and the possible scope of common/shared solutions can be overlain on the business architecture representation. Where there is a common pattern to this, the mapping can be a useful guide for application development. Figure 26 shows how utility and shared solution options might be related to a BIAN business architecture model.

5.6.7 Service Domain clusters

The clustering of Service Domains could be used to define groupings that correspond to an organizational 'segment' as defined in TOGAF, such as a business unit, profit center, division or enterprise. They can also be used to define a grouping that maps to the functional scope of a business application or production system. This second type of grouping is considered here.

The mapping options just described relate BIAN Service Domains to discrete conceptual application partitions, recognizing that there is not always a simple one-to one association. Service Domain clustering take this one step further by taking into account considerations when the logical/conceptual design must be translated into a physical implementation design.

The BIAN Service Domains each represent a discrete, non-overlapping business capability building block. In theory (and in some technical environments) each Service Domain could be implemented as a stand-alone application and all business activity could be supported by service collaborations between these distinct applications. In practice of course, most conventional business applications combine the capabilities of several Service Domains as an integrated business solution. The reasons for integrating capabilities together in such a package include performance, operational coherence and integration considerations.

The reasons for combining capabilities into an integrated application are not addressed in this publication. However, for a cluster of Service Domains in a business application,

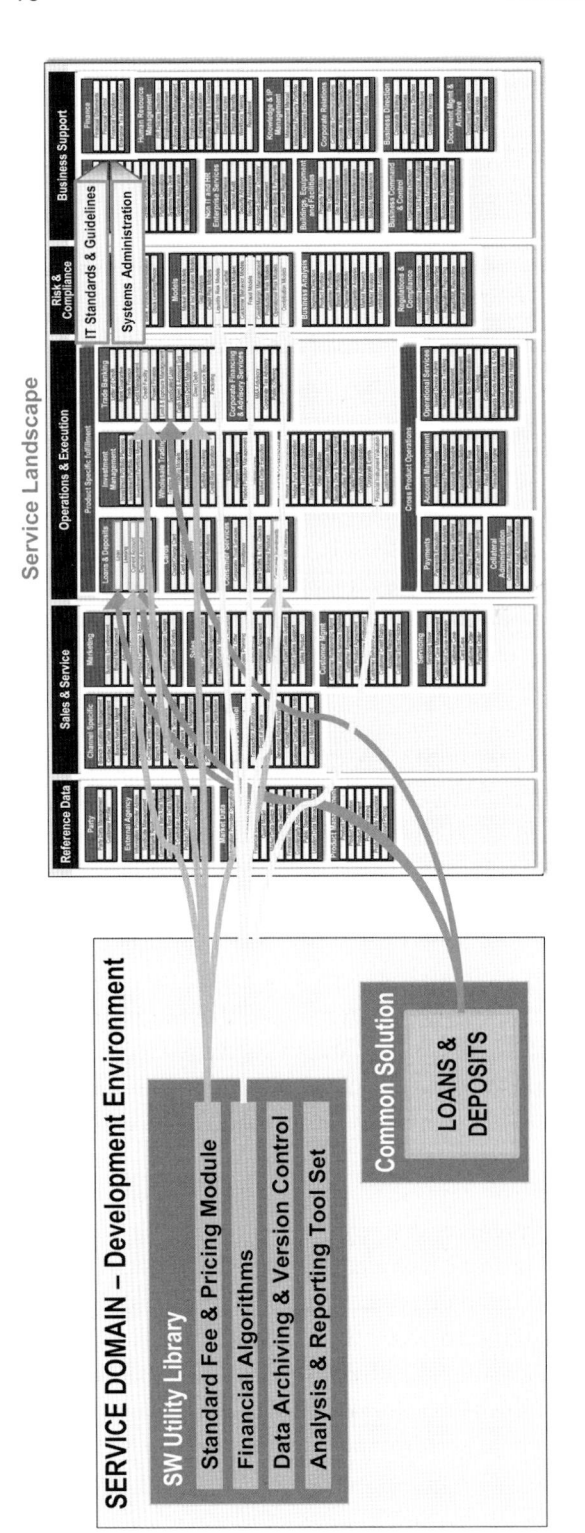

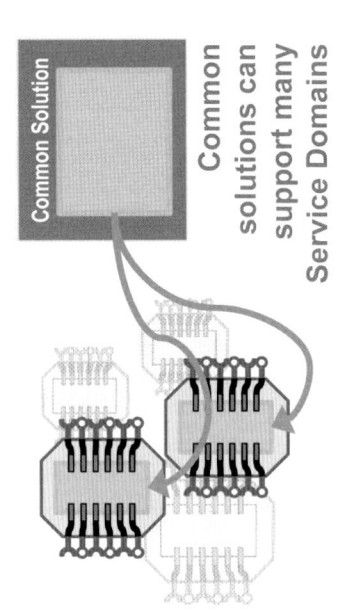

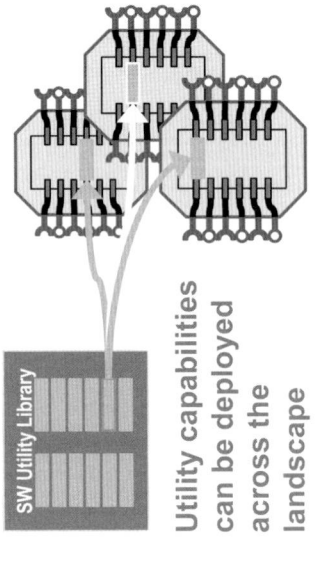

Figure 26: Mapping Service Landscape with shared and common solutions

it is necessary to define 'roles' that explain how the individual Service Domains relate to the broader application portfolio. The Service Domains tend to play one of three roles in the context of the overall enterprise systems portfolio, as defined below.

Service Domain roles within a cluster are:
- **Core** – the Service Domain exists only in the business application represented by the cluster. All reference to this Service Domain must be supported by the external service boundary of the cluster. (As must all of its delegated Service Operation dependencies.) The Service Domain Current Account Mortgage Fulfillment would be a core Service Domain in the Current Account Mortgage Processing Application cluster.
- **Proxy** - represents a capability that is likely to be repeated in other clusters and is included in the cluster to provide a local 'view'. In such a case it could be the master version, meaning all other instances need to reference this instance for their needs, or it could be a slave, meaning it needs to synchronize with the master instance elsewhere through suitable 'background' services. SD Party Data Management could be a slave proxy Service Domain in the Current Account Mortgage Processing Application cluster.
- **Utility** - the cluster contains a non-unique instance of the Service Domain. Where this local instance operates in a fully standalone manner, it does not need to synchronize or even be aware of other similar Service Domain instances elsewhere (as the Proxy role needs to). Position Keeping (the transaction journal) is a utility instance in the Current Account Mortgage Processing Application cluster.

When Service Domains are grouped into a cluster, the external boundary of the cluster can be defined by referencing the available Service Operation connections between any of the Service Domains within the cluster and the surrounding Service Domains with which they interact. For Proxy Service Domains, additional external connections are needed to ensure their synchronization with other copies of the Service Domain maintained elsewhere.

An example of a business application cluster is shown in figure 27 (note that only a sample of Service Operation connections and surrounding/referenced Service Domains is included for simplicity).

5.6.8 Mapping implementation level functionality to a Service Domain
The BIAN Service Landscape provides high-level descriptions of the BIAN Service Domains and their Service Operation exchanges. Beyond the formal content of the standard, the Business Scenarios also provide examples of how the BIAN Service Domains may collaborate in different situations and, over time, BIAN will develop and provide other example views to assist with the adoption of the standard.

Key:

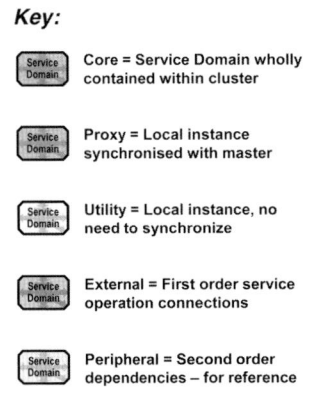

- Core = Service Domain wholly contained within cluster
- Proxy = Local instance synchronised with master
- Utility = Local instance, no need to synchronize
- External = First order service operation connections
- Peripheral = Second order dependencies – for reference

Figure 27: Example cluster for a retail financial services business application

The content outlines the mainstream business operational features and exchanges at a high-level. The intent is to define clear functional partitions/boundaries in a way that is implementation-independent and unambiguous. The descriptions should be interpretable for any prevailing technical environment and they should be sufficiently detailed for the capability partitions to be consistently interpreted between different deployments.

The Service Domain boundaries can then be used to align and arrange application logic into discrete (non-overlapping) functional partitions with clear interfacing requirements that are well suited to service enablement in a SOA. The high-level semantic BIAN definitions clearly need to be extended to provide the necessary software implementation-level detail.

In this section, three main ways of extending the content are described:
- **Service Domain functionality** – BIAN does not define the internal functioning of a Service Domain but the functional scope can be inferred from the business role/purpose, Control Record and service boundary. This outline functional description can be extended using functional and non-functional checklists
- **Service Operation** – the BIAN Service Operations provide a semantic description of the exchange dependency between two collaborating Service Domains. This definition can be extended in two key ways – 1) the information content can be defined in more detail by mapping to underlying message exchanges; and 2) the protocol or orchestration of the interaction can be defined in terms of the structure/choreography of the dialogue.
- **Semantic APIs** – the BIAN Service Domains and Service Operations can be used as a basis for defining high-level standard application programming interfaces (APIs).

A fourth way in which the Service Domain specification can be extended is the definition of the business information (and associated data representation) governed and referenced by the Service Domain and its Service Operations. BIAN is continually developing the business information model view of Service Domains and populating a business vocabulary that is integrated with the BIAN content repository.

5.6.9 Possible Service Domain functional specializations

When interpreting the high-level BIAN designs there will often be a need to add or make amendments to handle site-specific variations before additional detail is mapped to the structures. These variations may be required to deal with considerations such as local geo-political constraints, aligning with legacy systems' behaviors, supporting unique differentiating business practices and/or technical environment implementation features. Whatever the reason for these specializations, if the core role and purpose of the individual Service Domains remain intact, the anticipated benefits of the BIAN SOA standard will be realized.

When adding or refining a Service Domain it is important to consider the Control Record. When adding detail and/or local specializations it is vital that any changes still align to, or relate to, the role/purpose of the Service Domain as reflected in its Control Record. As previously mentioned in the discussion on 'externalization' in Section 5.6, all Service Operation fulfillment, internal functional features and associated business information use need to relate directly to the Control Record.

In the case of Service Operations and the linked messages underlying the requested action, the information content needs to pertain to the definition of a Control Record instance and, if appropriate, initiate some action that relates to its lifecycle behavior. Any extensions to the business information definitions and associated data structures should also relate to the structure and content of the Control Record without changing its basic scope or definition.

5.6.10 Extending the functional definition of the Service Domain

The BIAN definition of a Service Domain considers the internal functionality to be that of a 'black box' – BIAN does not attempt to specify any internal working patterns or architectural structures. BIAN merely clarifies at a high-level what business functionality it should contain to fulfill its business purpose and what business functionality it may need to access by way of delegated Service Operation calls to other Service Domains.

The main reason that BIAN does not expand upon the Service Domain functionality as part of the canonical standard is that BIAN's focus is to help improve interoperability between business capabilities rather than the effectiveness of those capabilities themselves. As a result, the standard only seeks to formally define the service exchanges that connect the business capabilities. To achieve this, it is only necessary to outline the purpose/role of a capability partition and to be able to explain/match its offered and consumed services.

Though a limited definition of the Service Domain functionality is sufficient to specify its Service Operation use, it has been found that more detailed functional descriptions are very useful to implementation teams using the standard. The improved descriptions are needed to ensure that the teams correctly interpret the Service Domain functional partitions. But as the internal workings of the Service Domain can change and evolve, any more detailed functional descriptions are not canonical. Instead they only provide some prevailing examples as a guide.

The limited functionality description provided for the BIAN Service Domain can be easily expanded upon using the simple mechanism of a 'checklist'. The checklist provides a simple structured framework to list the prevailing functional and non-functional properties that might be expected to be in place for a Service Domain (or more precisely the business applications supporting the activity scoped out by the Service Domain). The checklist includes the main prevailing features and can optionally include sub-structures to list more specialist features aligned to requirements such as:
- **Geopolitical requirements** – specific traditions and laws/regulations;
- **Advanced levels of sophistication** – advanced practices yet to become standard;
- **Scale/segment** – different properties that might apply to types of financial institution or specifically to large enterprises.

The BIAN Association does not currently maintain feature tables for the Service Domains. Like Business Scenarios, the feature tables are not canonical and only provide example content. Furthermore, the functional feature lists can be expected to change as new practices emerge. This publication only describes the structure and use of feature tables as a tool. It is anticipated that banks and solution providers will develop and maintain their own feature tables as they deem necessary. The BIAN Association may consolidate and make available example feature tables for Service Domains in the future if this is found to be useful.

When developing the feature lists for a Service Domain, the same externalization tests already described for specialization should be applied to the content. Essentially all listed functionality should be directly relatable to instances of the Service Domain Control Record and its lifecycle behaviors.

When considering the fit of a functional feature to a Service Domain it can help to consider the Service Domain in the context of one or more Business Scenarios. It is often easier to confirm the decision to externalize a function (that does not relate to the Control Record of the considered Service Domain) if the correct location for the functional feature can be assigned to some other Service Domain.

5.6.11 Mapping Service Operations to messages
BIAN Service Operations describe a high-level dependency between two Service Domains. They describe the exchanged business information and may refer to services/

actions that are requested. The BIAN Service Operation does not define the protocol or choreography of the exchange as this is typically implementation-dependent.

In Release 6.0, BIAN has defined types of information that are maintained by a Service Domain and that can be referenced in the payload of called Service Operations. The different types of information are described in more detail in Section 5.7.1. In this section the general steps taken in a procedure that can be used to map the Service Operation to underlying machine-level messages are initially described.

Note that one Service Operation could be realized by a simple 'handshake' exchange or could result in a complex iterative exchange of underlying messages. In this context, a message defines the (machine readable) data content exchanged in appropriate detail. Furthermore, a service exchange may involve some combination of:
- The movement or assignment of some facility or resource;
- A free-form person-to-person dialogue/negotiation;
- 'Structured' information exchange, person-to-machine and machine-to-machine.

As BIAN's focus is on improving application-to-application interoperability, the focus of the Service Operation definition is on the specific content related to the exchange of structured and unstructured information. The use of the term 'structured' here is informal given the ever-increasing ability of technology to infer structure from different information sources.

The term 'message' here refers to standard machine-to-machine data structures that have been defined to support specific application-to-application exchanges. A message may include a combination of individual data items, structured data records and unstructured data. Standard messages have been published by a number of standards bodies. Of particular relevance to BIAN is the ISO 20022 financial services message specifications - since BIAN is built on the ISO 20022 standard. However, it is important to note that published industry standard message specifications will be available only for a small subset of the business activities covered by the BIAN Service Landscape. ISO 20022 is focussing primailely on payments in the 'Bank-to-Bank' and 'Bank-to-Corporates' spaces, whilst BIAN covers all aspects of banking.

The mapping approach described here for available standard messages can be amended and applied to many other message groups. This includes new messages that may be developed, messages that may already be available in proprietary solutions, or messages that may be developed from scratch as required in specific solution developments.

It is also useful to consider the types of information making up a Service Operation. The overall structure and various mechanisms used in the specification of the Service Operation are not important here, what is of interest is how the different types of information content are mapped to the far more detailed data structures and data elements of the message specifications.

BIAN has undertaken several initiatives to explore repeatable ways to map Service Operations to messages. The main goals of these initiatives have been:
- To test the feasibility of the mapping and refine the BIAN Service Operation specification as necessary to support this;
- To provide worked examples that could be applied in targeted solution designs;
- To develop a repeatable technique that can be applied across different available message sets.

The general approach towards developing content is described in more detail below. It has been derived in part from a thorough research initiative performed by students at Carnegie Mellon University in collaboration with BIAN and PNC Bank in the last semester of 2014. The final report for this study is available at www.BIAN.org.

The general mapping approach uses the primary design elements of the Service Domains and their Service Operations. The key aspects are summarized here for ease of reference. It is also worth noting that the general approach defines a complete series of mapping steps. Depending on the way that the target message set is defined and organized, a subset of the steps described may be applicable.

The key BIAN design elements/considerations referenced by the mapping approach include:
- **Service Domain operational behavior** – every BIAN Service Domain has a standard operational behavior – it performs a type of function (as defined by a 'functional pattern') on an instance of an asset type (where an instance of an asset type is some tangible or intangible entity that can be used to generate commercial benefit). It performs this function for the complete lifecycle use of each asset type instance. For example, the Service Domain 'Product Design' performs the functional pattern 'DESIGN' on the asset type 'product/service', (here the term 'product/service' refers to the capacity to support some product/service and the 'asset' is the intellectual property of its specification).
  The full lifecycle for the instance of a product design spans the initial identification/ registration of the design specification, through all specification/update cycles and usage scenarios, and ultimately through to the final termination/archiving of the design.
- **Functional pattern** – BIAN has identified a number (18) of generic commercial behaviors (see figure 32 in Section 5.8) that are applied to different asset types in the execution of business. For example, for an asset such as an ATM network there are several applicable unctional patterns that represent the things done to maintain and leverage this resource for commercial advantage. These include managing/ configuring, operating, maintaining and analyzing the performance of the ATM

network. As noted, each Service Domain's behavior is characterized by one functional pattern.
- **Asset type** – BIAN has used a simple hierarchical decomposition technique to identify the full range of tangible and intangible assets that may be found in any bank. BIAN has also refined techniques to determine the correct level of granularity to perform this type decomposition to identify Service Domains that are elemental in their role. As already noted, each Service Domain's behavior is specified to combine its functional pattern with the full lifecycle 'processing' of instances of its specific asset type.
- **Generic artifact and Control Record** – the Control Record can be thought of as a mechanism used to track/manage the execution of one occurrence of the Service Domain performing its business role for a complete lifecycle. Continuing the example of the Product Design Service Domain, the Control Record is the 'product design' and the state of each product design specification in use is tracked by its own associated Control Record instance.

  With *BIAN Release 5.0* there has been a slight redefinition of the naming of the Service Domain Control Record. It had been defined to be the combination of the functional pattern with the asset type. Since functional patterns describe a behavior, they typically take the verb form. The generic artifact describes some form of tangible record or document that can be associated with the execution of the functional pattern. For example, the functional pattern 'agree terms' which describes the action of defining and maintaining governing terms has the associated generic artifact of an 'agreement'. To make the Control Record more representative it has been redefined to be the combination of the generic artifact and the asset type.

  BIAN Release 6.0 introduces the notion of *behavior qualifiers,* which qualify (i.e. refine) the generic behaviors defined for a service domain. It also introduces the notion of *behavior qualifier types*, which classify behavior qualifiers. Furthermore, the Metamodel now supports the definition of service operations based on behavior qualifiers; such extended service operations are refinements of the formerly pattern-generated, generic service operations.
- **Lifecycle states** – each Service Domain handles the 'processing' of each instance of its Control Record through its complete lifecycle. For each Functional Pattern, BIAN has identified the main, externally visible operating states that a Service Domain may pass through. These can help define allowed pre- and post-conditions for Service Operations, whilst an analysis of state transitions can be used to confirm that all required Service Operations have been identified.
- **Action terms** – the primary purpose for each Service Operation call can be reflected in its action term. BIAN has identified a standard set of action terms to select from and each Service Operation adopts one of these action terms. In general, each action term defines the kind of operation that the Service Operation makes on one or more Control Record instances, for example activating, updating, requesting or retrieving (reporting) on that instance.

- **Service Operations** – a structured framework/template is used to capture the properties, terminology and content of a Service Operation. This includes four types of input and output parameters that describe the main business information 'payload'.

Four parameter fields are defined for both the call and response services of a Service Operation exchange. As described above, the content may take two forms. Past definitions used filtered checklists to describe the types of information. More recently the use of behavior qualifiers and the BIAN BOM results in more detailed and Service Domain/Service Operation-specific content.

Content for the four parameter fields, both the original checklist descriptions and, in selected cases, the more specific content can be reviewed directly in the UML database or using various BIAN access tools. The structure for this content is as follows:

1. **Identifiers** – information items associated with a Control Record instance that can be used to select/identify that record. For example customer, location, product type, date/time, transaction reference.
2. **Depiction** – a broad range of information content that might be extracted from/recorded against a Control Record instance. The depiction of content information for the checklist-based Service Operations has been categorized into three general types – information items, information records (structured) and information reports (unstructured). For the more specific content being defined now, these general categories no longer apply. The specific information elements each have their own associated information type.
3. **Instructors** – provides control parameters that are used to govern the way the Service Operation is executed. For example they could define the time at which to perform an action and/or qualify the specific type of action to be performed and provide the result of the Service Operation call result if appropriate. (Note: the use of behavior qualifiers described elsewhere to define more specialized Service Operations is an alternative to using an instructor parameter to define the particular request.)
4. **Analysis** – references different historical and analytical views of individual Control Records and the whole portfolio of Control Records that can be maintained by the Service Domain. This analytical information is in addition to the Control Record instance information covered by the *depiction* parameter already described. Continuing with the *customer agreement* example, the Service Domain may maintain and provide, on request, analytical views of the make-up of the complete portfolio of all of the active customer agreements it maintains in terms of their properties, usage and processing status.

The service operations in the BIAN Service Landscape contain descriptions of the parameter content at a level of detail that is intended to define the main information elements required to fully satisfy the purpose of the Service Operation. It does not include any optional, advanced or specialized features that may apply more selectively. It is also only intended to be sufficient for an architect or analyst familiar with the

5 How to apply the BIAN standard   87

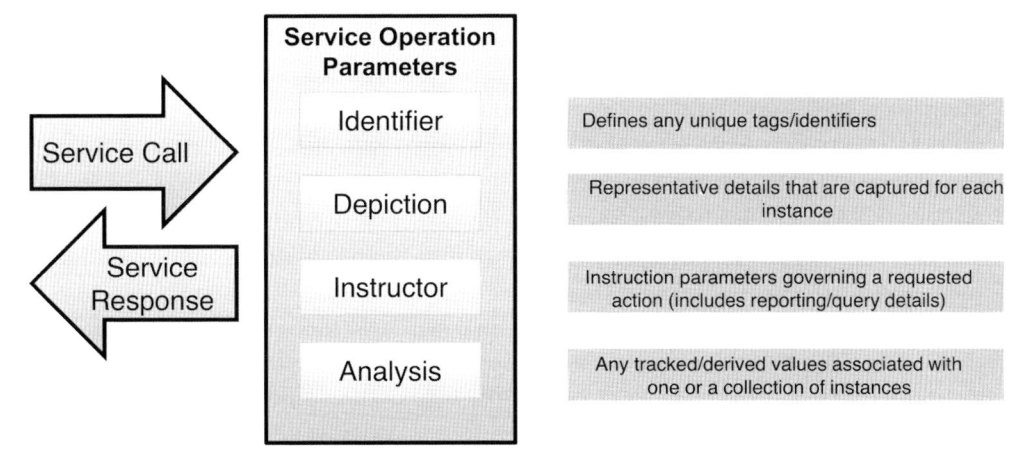

Figure 28: Four types of input and output parameters

subject area to make an unambiguous assessment of the information needs and, where appropriate, be able to map this to underlying systems-readable message specifications. The content does not attempt to be exhaustive/comprehensive as might be expected in training materials for example.

As noted, with the latest Release 6.0, BIAN has started to develop its own business object model (BOM) that is aligned to the Service Domain Control Records and, where appropriate, cross-referenced to the industry standard ISO 20022 model. As the BIAN BOM is expanded, techniques and guidelines will be defined to assist with the information extraction and mapping to Service Operations.

The steps in the general approach reference the different design features of the Service Domains and Service Operations in order to focus on a match between one or more messages and a Service Operation. Different message sets may be organized and specified in ways that relate to only a subset of the steps described.

The general steps are described as applied to an individual Service Operation. As each Service Domain has a selection of Service Operations there may be ways to optimize and extend this approach to match messages at the individual Service Domain level:

- **Step 1 – Asset type to object** – the Service Operation's host Service Domain's Control Record includes the asset type that is acted upon. This asset type can be mapped to the object or data type that is the subject of messages from the target message set. For example, the asset type could be a customer relationship and the associated object is the customer object. The selected messages will contain customer-related data.
- **Step 2 – Functional pattern filtering** – the BIAN functional pattern defines a constrained used of the asset type. This can be used to narrow the scope of the data related to the mapped object and this, in turn, can be used to filter/eliminate the mapped messages. Continuing with the customer relationship/customer object match example, if the functional pattern is 'AGREE TERMS', the customer-related data

can be limited to that directly associated with the details that make up a customer agreement and any message not containing this type of data can be eliminated from further consideration.
- **Step 3 – Action term alignment** – the action term provides a precise definition of the purpose for the Service Operation call (the intended action to be performed). Many messages are similarly associated with intended use/purpose – mapping the action term to this when available can be used to further filter/eliminate candidate messages.
- **Step 4 - Service Operation payload** – the final step uses the semantic description of the business information content of the input and output parameters of the Service Operation. The content is mapped against the information payload of any candidate messages. This is done to confirm that the message contains all key information and may also highlight redundant/excessive data content in the message for the intended purpose of the Service Operation.

The selection and filtering of the messages described above does not take into account any message exchange 'choreography' that may be involved in the Service Operation. The BIAN Service Operation simply defines the main information exchange dependency. In implementation it is clearly necessary to define the nature of the exchange in far more detail. As with the definition of Feature Templates as a tool to support the expansion of the functional definition of a Service Domain, the BIAN Association may develop equivalent tools that can assist with the specification of a Service Operation characteristic for implementation.

5.7 USING THE BIAN MODELS TO DEFINE (OPEN) APIS

The BIAN design approach as outlined is well aligned with API solution development for several reasons:
- Support for emerging industry approaches – two key technology approaches are considered: API development and the adoption of a micro-service architecture.
- Support for industry standards – the BIAN Service Domains and Service Operations present an industry standard definition for the componentization and service enablement of financial services.
- Support for incremental adoption/migration – BIAN-aligned solutions can be implemented and adopted incrementally enabling a prioritized migration from constraining legacy architectures.

5.7.1 Semantic APIs

The BIAN Association has previously published a white paper that describes how BIAN Service Domains provide a template for defining and managing cloud-based services. This can include providing application program interface (API)-based access to these services. The white paper can be found at www.BIAN.org. Release 6.0 includes examples of extended Service Domain definitions that support the use of the BIAN standard to create high-level specifications of open APIs.

A key consideration explained in this white paper still applies for API design. It addresses how access to the services can be controlled. Many banks are looking for ways to move beyond offering 'packaged' products and services to their customers to providing direct access to banking capabilities. This would allow customers and third parties to integrate the bank directly into their operations somehow. Banks wanting to provide external access to their capabilities need to find a way to do this in a more secure manner.

Achieving adequate security spans many levels, including the platform and application access controls (IaaS/PaaS) that are complex but for which solutions and approaches are already available or are rapidly emerging. The aspect that the BIAN Association can provide help with is in defining the allowed use of offered services.

When a bank enables service-based access to capabilities internally (inside the bank) it can ensure that the services are being used for appropriate purposes and by people with the correct access authority. However, when the service is accessed externally, this is far harder to manage. Banks need some way to ensure the services are used appropriately and to do this in a way where every external service access agreement does not need to be specified and implemented individually.

One way to achieve this is to use the role of the Service Domain to define the service access context and use this to control its use. Figure 29 shows an example for a service call to access customer details using the Relationship Management Service Domain to provide the context.

The service API offered could be bundled in a software container with the pre-enabled constrained access to services allowing the external user to then develop their own logic within the container.

The semantic API guidelines presume that approaches like the model bank and clustering have been used to define the broader context for a collection of one or more interfaces that are each defined to be a Service Operation connection between two Service Domains. The guidelines then describe an approach where each Service Operation interface can be defined in the necessary level of detail to implement an application interface.

The guidelines can be summarized in three main parts:
1. A framework describing the range of design considerations;
2. Detailed descriptions of these design considerations including references to established techniques and standards that may apply;
3. A selection of groupings of the techniques as they apply to different types of application interface.

The framework of design considerations defines four categories of design consideration and breaks each of these down into four different types as shown in figure 29.

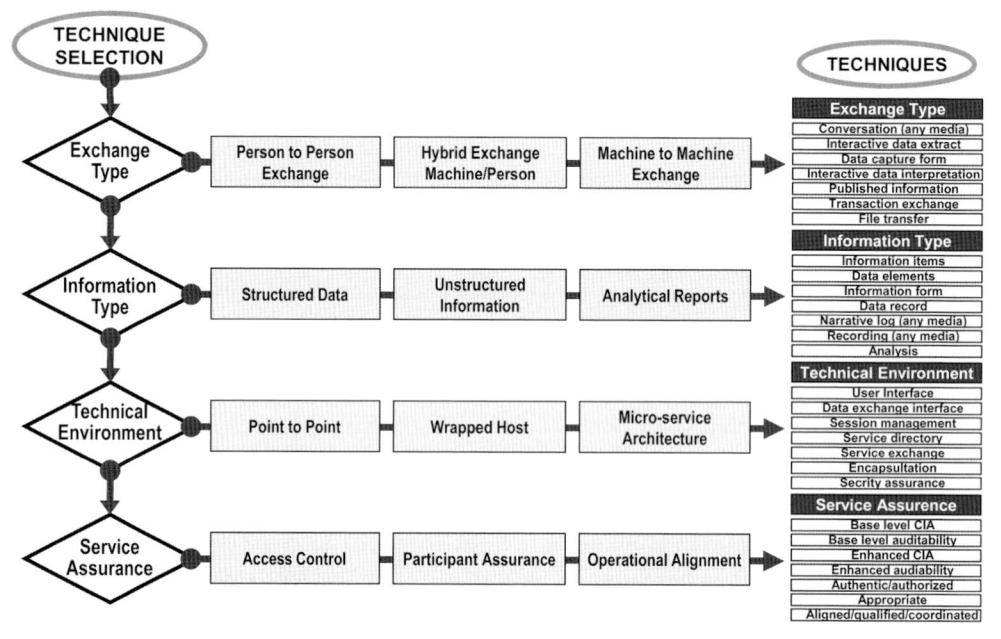

Figure 29: Semantic API design scheme

One of the four categories shown in the scheme requires a little additional explanation here. The 'Information Type' describes the different types of information that can be included in the Service Operation. These types are isolated because the implementation of systems solutions and message mapping has different considerations and approaches for each type:

- **Information items** – refers to single value elements that will typically map to a single data field such as a date of birth or an account balance.
- **Information records** – refers to structured groups of information items, such as might be found in a payment transaction or application form.
- **Information reports** – refers to collections of unstructured information including free-form text or scanned documents/images.
- **Analytical views** – refers to historical and/or analytical views of information that the Service Domain may maintain, referring to individual Control Record instances or to the whole portfolio of Control Record instances that it manages. For example, an average balance or frequency of use/update for a single Control Record and the make-up of different types or states of Control Record in the active portfolio.

The design types are then further broken down to define 28 discrete topics. For each topic we provide:

- A general description including a list of elements that could be included to define an open standard;

- A summary of how the BIAN standard specifically relates to the topic;
- Cross-referenced techniques and approaches that could be used for this design aspect;
- Cross-referenced industry standards that could apply for this design aspect.

The cross-referenced techniques, approaches and standards are not intended to be exhaustive, nor do they always apply in every implementation situation. They provide a guide and BIAN intends to maintain these cross-references based on membership experience and feedback. The complete set of 28 topics is shown in figure 31.

Finally, we use a reference to a case study developed at IBM, a BIAN member, to identify a collection of standard types of interface for which suitable selections of design topics have been selected. These standard interface types make the selection from the 28 design topics easier.

■ 5.8 SERVICE-BASED ACCESS

The next level of the BIAN design outlined here is the definition of the Service Operation exchanges. A Service Domain provides access to its governed information and functions through offered Service Operations. The BIAN Association has defined a standard set of 'action terms' that characterize the range of Service Operation calls, see figure 30.

	Action Terms		Description	Example
Origination	Actions to set-up, establish a new control record instance	Initiate	Begin an action including any required initialization tasks	A payment transaction is initiated
		Create	Manufacture and distribute an item	A new analytical model design is created
		Activate	Commence/open an operational or administrative service	The ATM network operation is actived
		Configure	Change the operating parameters for an ongoing service/capability	The online ATMs in the network are changed to take machines out of service
Invocation	Actions to access/update/influence an established instance	Update	Change the value of some (control record) properties	A customer's reference details are updated with a change of address
		Register	Record the details of a newly identified entity	A new customer's details are captured
		Record	Capture transaction or event details associated with a lifecycle step	An employee logs time spent working on a project against the plan
		Execute	Execute a task or action on an established facility	A payment is applied to a charge card
		Evaluate	Perform a check, trial or evaluation	The eligibility to sell a product is checked against the customer's existing agreement
		Provide	Assign or allocate resources or facilities	A branch requests an allocation of cash for its tellers
		Authorize	Allow the execution of a transaction/activity	Regulatory compliance authorizes a product design feature
		Request	Request the provision of some service	A customer requests that a standing order is set up on the current account
		Terminate	Conclude, complete activity	The use of a product version is terminated
	Delegation – no new action terms apply as the called Service Domains offer the same Origination/Invocation & Reporting options described here)			
Reporting	Actions to extract details and subscribe to updates	Notify	Provide details against a predefined notification agreement	A unit subscribes to update notifications from the customer agreement Service Domain
		Retrieve	Return information/report as requested	An account balance is obtained and a report covering activity analysis requested

Figure 30: BIAN action terms

A selection of action terms and their associated Service Operations is most appropriate for a Service Domain depending on its Functional Pattern. Based on this mapping a default set of Service Operations has been defined for every Service Domain in the

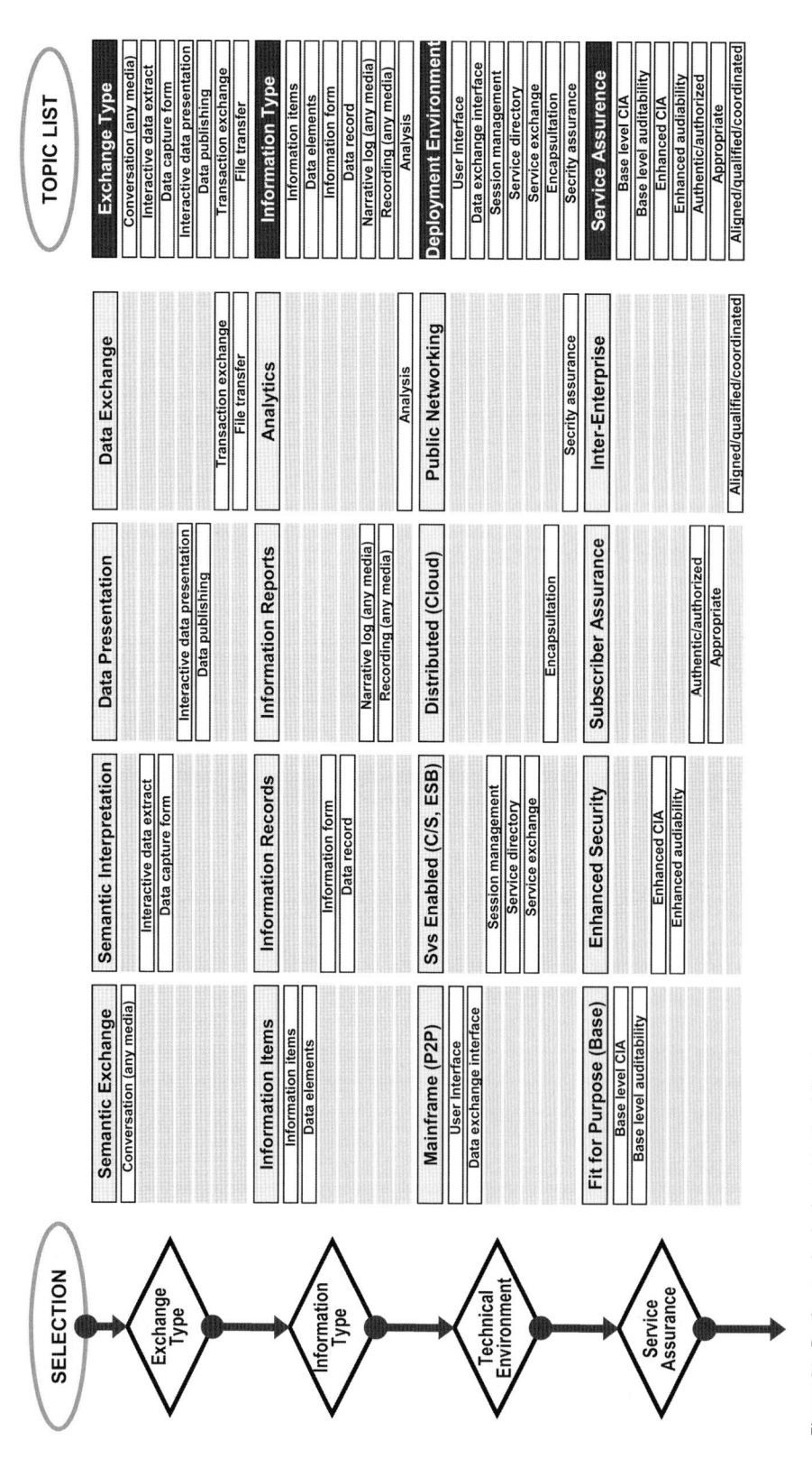

Figure 31: Design topics included in the API scheme

5 How to apply the BIAN standard

TOPIC	Type 1 - Screen based access	Type 2 - File extract	Type 3 - Customer Transaction Request	Type 4 – Automated Transaction Execution
Exchange Type	**Exchange Type**	**Exchange Type**	**Exchange Type**	**Exchange Type**
Conversation (any media)				
Interactive data extract	Interactive data extract			
Data capture form				
Interactive data presentation	Interactive data presentation		Interactive data presentation	
Data publishing				
Transaction exchange				
File transfer		File transfer		File transfer
Information Type	**Information Type**	**Information Type**	**Information Type**	**Information Type**
Information items	Information items			
Data elements	Data elements	Data elements		
Information form	Information form			
Data record	Data record	Data record	Data record	Data record
Narrative log (any media)	Narrative log (any media)			
Recording (any media)				
Analysis				
Deployment Environment	**Deployment Environment**	**Deployment Environment**	**Deployment Environment**	**Deployment Environment**
User Interface				
Data exchange interface				
Session management				
Service directory				
Service exchange	Service exchange	Service exchange	Service exchange	Service exchange
Encapsulation	Encapsulation			
Secrity assurance				
Service Assurance	**Service Assurance**	**Service Assurance**	**Service Assurance**	**Service Assurance**
Base level CIA	Base level CIA	Base level CIA	Base level CIA	Base level CIA
Base level auditability			Base level auditability	Base level auditability
Enhanced CIA			Enhanced CIA	Enhanced CIA
Enhanced audiability				
Authentic/authorized				
Appropriate				
Aligned/qualified/coordinated				

Standard Interface Type/Pattern

Figure 32: Design topics selected for four typical types of exchange

BIAN Service Landscape. The default mapping of action terms to a Functional Pattern is shown in figure 33.

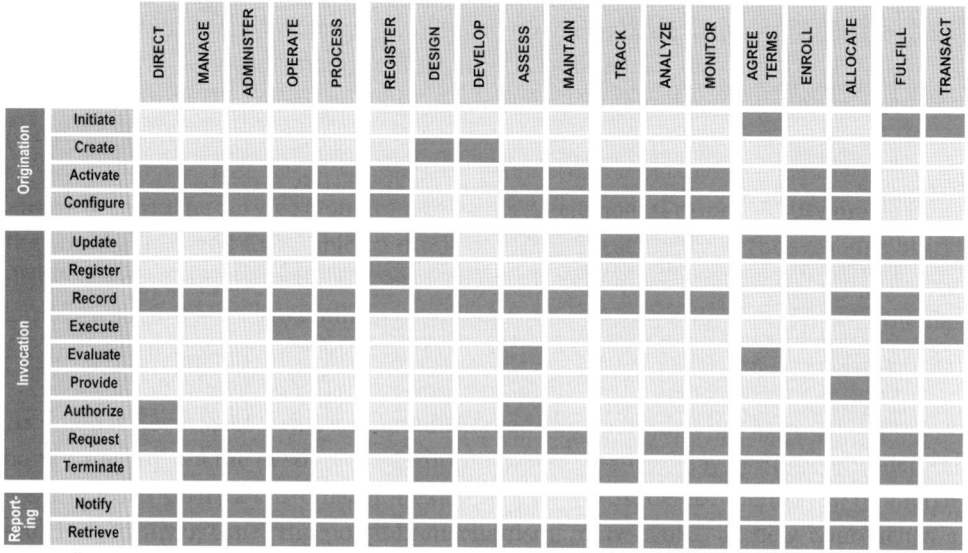

Default service operations mapped to the functional patterns
(Dark grey box indicates a match)

Figure 33: Default action term by functional pattern

As noted, the BIAN Semantic API wiki space should be referenced for more detail on the approach. This space also contains a reference to a case study performed together with PNC Bank and Carnegie Mellon University, describing the creation of APIs in the Payments/PSD2 space. Amongst others, this study resulted in the PNC API Exchange, shown in figure 34.

Figure 34: Example of a BIAN API exchange

5.9 APPLYING BIAN IN DIFFERENT TECHNICAL ARCHITECTURES

The BIAN model defines the capability building blocks as discrete functional partitions that are suited to service enablement. Though it can be highly beneficial to relate the high-level BIAN Service Domains to a service-oriented systems architecture (SOA), this is not mandatory. For explanatory purposes only, we will describe three 'levels' of target technical architecture to illustrate the progression towards a 'pure' service-oriented architecture:

- **Level 1 - Conventional (legacy/core) system rationalization** – in this example the BIAN Service Domain designs are used to assess an existing application portfolio. The Service Domain partitions are used to identify duplication and fragmentation of the business logic and information between the business applications.
- **Level 2 - Host renewal/ESB integration and application/system assembly** – building forward from existing system rationalization and synchronization, technologies such as an enterprise service bus (ESB) can be used to develop shared service capabilities and reduce redundancy across the application portfolio.
- **Level 3 - Loose coupled distributed/cloud systems/APIs/micro-services** – the most advanced use of technology considered is that of the highly distributed internet and cloud environments, where solutions are loose coupled and fully service enabled.

The BIAN Service Domains and their Service Operations collectively represent a complete, organized and non-overlapping description of all of the functional building blocks needed to assemble any financial services business application. The systems support for the Service Domain building blocks and their interactions can be realized in different ways. If the business applications are aligned to the Service Domains effectively then the operational flexibility and efficiencies of a SOA can be realized to varying degrees.

Before describing how the BIAN designs are interpreted in different technical environments, it is necessary to make a distinction between two aspects of business operation that are captured in a Service Domain's specification as these aspects will be interpreted differently. To date, a Service Domain has been described as a business capability building block that performs a business role, engages through its offered Service Operations and may subscribe to services from other Service Domains as needed. This behavior is suitable to describe a service-based implementation but the same business capability building block may also be implemented in a less flexible 'hard wired' technical environment where the connections are point-to-point interfaces rather than being realized being through some flexible service-based mechanism.

The Service Domain can be divided into two components – its functional core and a 'service enabling' wrapper that handles the interactions with other Service Domains as shown in figure 35.

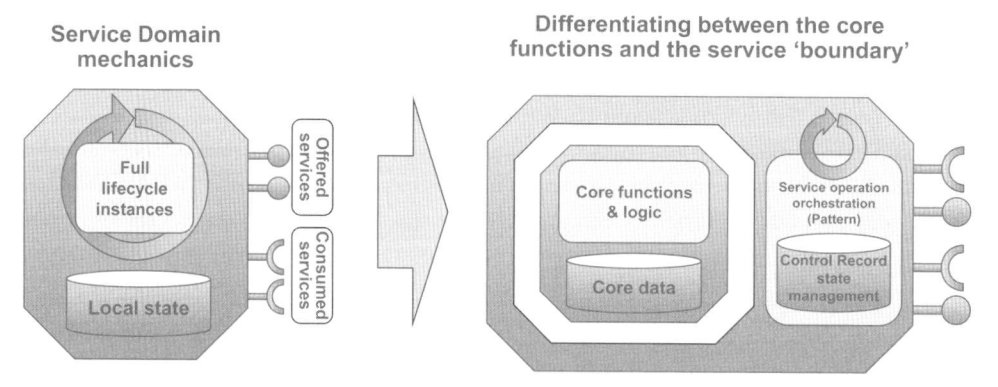

Figure 35: Service Domain broken into a functional core and a service wrapper

This distinction is referenced in the descriptions of the different technical implementation environments that follow.

5.9.1 Level 1 - Conventional (legacy/core) system rationalization

For legacy/core systems rationalization, the Service Domains are used as a stable framework that defines non-overlapping functional partitions which can then be used to map the footprint of legacy/core applications to highlight different shortfalls. The Feature Checklists (described in Section 5.11.4.1) can be used to provide a more detailed functional description of the Service Domains for mapping the existing application portfolio. Only the functional core of the Service Domain is used in this case, there is no assumption that any systems interfaces will be service enabled. The Service Domains are simply used to define the assessment framework.

As shown schematically in the left part of the diagrams in figure 36, most legacy business applications cover the scope of multiple but differing collections of Service Domains and so it is not meaningful to do a direct application-to-application comparison as two applications will typically have different functional coverage. Because the Service Domains do not overlap when the applications are mapped against them, it is possible to do a like-for-like mapping by considering the application coverage for each Service Domain at a time and then consolidating the collection of assessments for all Service Domains in scope for an application to reach an understanding of its long-term role.

This decision can become more complicated since a legacy system will frequently not divide up neatly along Service Domain boundaries. So, if an application is found to be a good fit for some Service Domains and not for others, it may not be possible to retain just the desired elements. The determination must be performed on a case-by-case basis, but the Service Domain framework does at least give a clear indication of where an application has strengths and weaknesses to feed into that selection assessment.

5 How to apply the BIAN standard

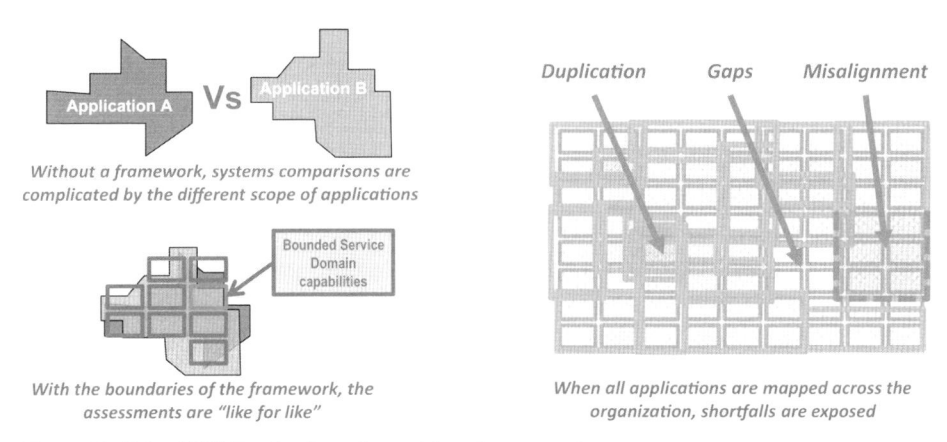

Figure 36: Using BIAN Service Domain partitions for comparisons

The schematic mapping on the right side of figure 36 shows the Service Domains as the background grid and then overlays the functional footprint of the existing business applications. Three different shortfalls are highlighted:

1. **Duplication** – perhaps the most obvious is where two or more business applications perform the role of the same Service Domain. As noted below this may or may not be an issue but at this stage, it highlights potential redundancy.
2. **Gaps** - the Service Domain feature checklist may include functional features that are not currently fully supported, and these will show up as gaps in the mapping. It may also be possible to see which legacy applications are the best candidates for expanding to cover these requirements.
3. **Misalignment** – this is a problem usually suffered by the better business applications. Although they are initially built to support a particular business function, they are subsequently extended into other areas as they offer the easiest/lowest cost solution. The problem can arise that an application designed to support one function becomes compromised when it tries to support many additional and potentially conflicting operational requirements.

The mapping of the application portfolio can provide powerful insights into the overlaps/redundancies in the bank's application portfolio. Most banks suffer from significant levels of redundancy due to a history of siloed implementation and business acquisition activity. Sometimes as systems are replaced, the old systems are not fully decommissioned.

The redundancy revealed by the mapping needs to be evaluated in more detail to determine the extent to which the duplication of functionality and business information leads to fragmentation and consistency issues. This analysis is intended to determine the extent to which the redundancy is causing a 'synchronization' problem across the business. This 'synchronization' issue applies differently to application logic and information/data:

- **Duplicated application logic** – when two (or more) business applications perform the same business function using different application logic this can lead to inconsistencies in operational behavior. This impact can be minimal, or it can expose the bank to significant additional costs, lost income and risk. Different factors to consider in the impact assessment include employee training and productivity, inconsistent customer experiences, operation inefficiencies/complexity, exposure to increased operational risk, inability to track, assess and report on activity consistently, and increased overhead when making changes. There may also be operational synergies/streamlining opportunities that are compromised.
- **Duplicated business information/data** – when two (or more) business applications maintain their own views of the same business information, the synchronization issues are obvious. Changes or updates to information in one place may not be accurately reflected elsewhere leading to errors. Updates may also get lost or overwritten and the ability to consolidate, analyze and react to business information is compromised.

It is possible that two business applications which are found to share a common Service Domain, when analyzed actually turn out to have little or no redundancy because they reference different logic or business information within that mapped Service Domain. They may execute different functions and/or may access different partitions of the business information governed by the same Service Domain. Though this may be the case at some point in time, clearly the extent to which redundancy is found in the application portfolio reflects the extent of the business synchronization overhead that the enterprise must deal with.

The level of redundancy and resulting synchronization overhead can be far higher than might be expected. Most banks are fully aware that they may have duplicated/overlapping business applications, but it is also commonly assumed that these competing systems often address different segments in the main. For example, there may be two customer reference data systems but they each cover different segments, or there may be competing commission systems but they cover different parts of the workforce. Consequently, rationalizing the overlapping applications may appear to offer only limited benefits in terms of reducing the synchronization overhead.

An analysis of the proportion of a typical business application that is likely to be duplicated across the business reveals that the extent and impact of the synchronization overhead (and hence the opportunity for improvement) may be far greater than first anticipated. This analysis was first touched upon in the earlier discussion of 'externalization' (see Section 5.6).

In figure 36, an example has been developed for a notional (fictional) stand-alone loan processing business application. The Service Domains accessed during the on-boarding Business Scenario have been mapped into a simple 'application architecture' (nine Service Domains are involved in the origination scenario). Clearly many more scenarios could be considered to determine a comprehensive collection of Service Domains that would be included in the business application, but this sample is sufficient for the purposes of this exercise.

Finally, a determination should be made for each Service Domain – is it likely that an individual Service Domain will be duplicated in other business applications or is its business role unique to this particular business application? As can be seen to the right of figure 37, eight of nine Service Domains considered are candidates for duplicated use, or 'externalization'.

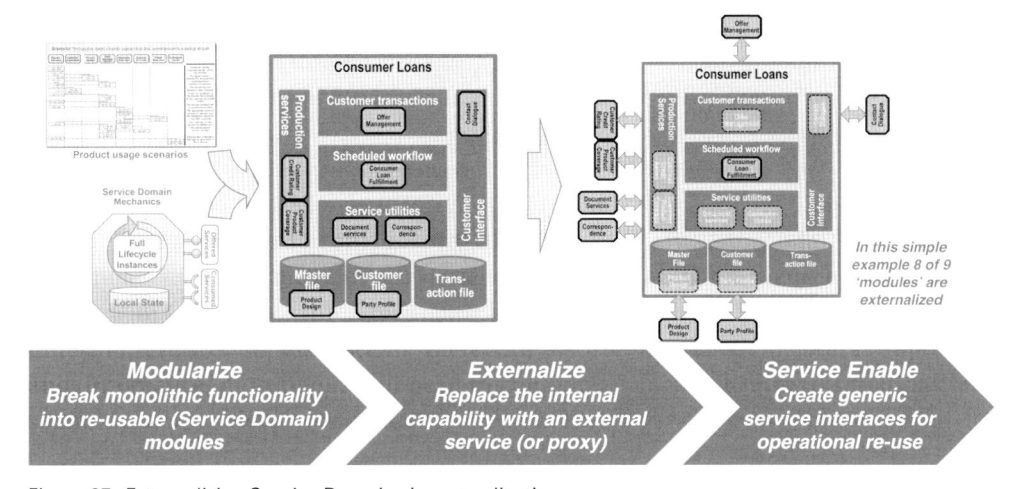

Figure 37: Externalizing Service Domains in an application

The example was not selected to demonstrate a disproportionately high level of redundancy/externalization potential – it is a pattern that is likely to be found for most core/legacy business applications. For some application logic and/or business information, the issue has long been recognized and shared solutions have been implemented to mitigate this. Obvious examples include customer information and relationship management, customer servicing and many shared back-office functions.

The opportunity to reduce the synchronization overhead by developing shared business applications is, however, limited as it typically results in large and complex business applications with extensive connectivity requirements in order to support the different operational needs of many 'subscribers'. For example, consider the implementation of a shared customer reference database to reduce the fragmentation of customer information. Such a business application needs to draw on many sources, provide the many different views of the information and, in doing so, match the operational performance needs for a very wide range of access requirements.

A more promising approach leverages the discrete, non-overlapping properties of Service Domains to specify finer grained shared service capabilities that can help reduce the synchronization overhead and provide the many considerable benefits of operational re-use. This is the Level 2 technical environment described in the next sub-section.

5.9.2 Level 2 - Host renewal/ESB integration and application/system assembly

The second level of technical environment is where existing core/legacy host systems are service-enabled with the intention of supporting shared access to functions and data. Many banks have experience in integrating service-enabling technologies to provide access to their established host systems, such as via an enterprise service bus (ESB). Without any specific organizing blueprint to specify the scope and content of the enabled services the tendency has been to define fine-grained services that provide access to utility functions and/or narrow data sets. These services tend to drive improvements in new business application development by providing re-usable software utilities. There are several limitations with this approach, including:

- **Software re-use versus business capability re-use** - the re-use of a software utility does not always drive through to the rationalization or re-use of operational business capabilities.
- **Complex and unstructured service libraries** - because the services are fine-grained this can lead to large and complicated collections of overlapping services that can be hard to categorize, maintain and reference.
- **Proprietary services** – the defined services often include host application specific/proprietary features that can lock-in legacy systems and compromise the ease of assembling applications using services from different wrapped host sources.
- **Synchronization** – the issue of traceability to function and data, which we highlighted in the prior discussion of application portfolio rationalization, persists if host systems are simply service-enabled with no specific blueprint or design to help reduce any redundancy conflicts between themselves.

The use of the Service Domain partitions as a framework to reveal duplication, along with the associated synchronization issues with overlapping business applications already described, can be taken further with the definition of shared services. The Service Domains define non-overlapping functional partitions that cover all business activity. Accordingly, their associated Service Operations define a comprehensive definition of non-overlapping business Service Operations.

If BIAN Service Domains and their Service Operations are applied to define the service directory for the ESB then their implementation can be used to obscure and, in time, progressively eliminate the redundancy in the application portfolio and greatly reduce the synchronization overheads. In this level of technical environment both the functional core and service wrapper components of the Service Domain specification are used in the solution specification.

5   How to apply the BIAN standard   101

The use of the BIAN Service Domains and their Service Operations to define the service directory for the ESB is shown schematically in figure 38.

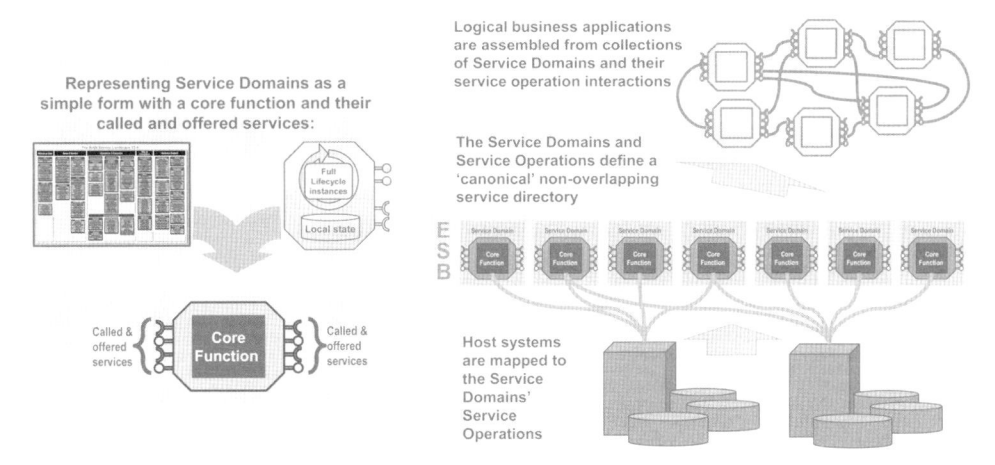

Figure 38: The use of BIAN Service Domains to define Service Domains to define a service directory for the ESB

On the left of the diagram, the BIAN Service Landscape and its collection of Service Domains defines the overall functional coverage, and, on the right, the full collection of Service Operations is enabled through the enterprise service bus. The host systems are mapped to the ESB. These ESB-enabled services can then be 'assembled' to support different business applications.

5.9.2.1   Host alignment
Mapping host systems to the ESB is potentially a very complex undertaking. One advantage with the use of the BIAN Service Domains and Service Operations as the service directory is that the Service Domains are highly enduring and non-overlapping, meaning that it is usually possible to implement ESB services incrementally and have these services adopted progressively across the overall application portfolio.

The selection, prioritization and scheduling of the migration towards ESB-based solutions is an important and complex consideration for any bank. It will need to balance the feasibility, cost and risk of implementation with the anticipated business performance gains. However, the likely benefits in terms of improved operational integrity, flexibility and efficiency should amply justify the required investment in most situations. Conventional project planning and business case analysis techniques can be applied in what will be a site-specific assessment and planning exercise (these are not discussed further in this book).

For this discussion of mitigating considerations, it is assumed that the ESB services are mapped to existing host systems. It is, of course, possible that new business applications could be developed and deployed, replacing existing host systems as part of the migration, or external sources could be referenced from the ESB also replacing existing services as necessary. These options do not change the approach significantly but, for brevity, are not considered here.

The BIAN Service Operations may combine both information access and requests to execute some type of activity. It is clearly important to map the information use and requested activity to the appropriate host capability and, as noted in the previous section, there may be more than one candidate host system to consider. The mapping process is described initially as the steps are applied to a single host system:

- ***Service Domain alignment*** – the business role of the Service Domain is mapped to the host business application, confirming that the business purpose of the Service Domain is properly aligned to, and is covered by, the functionality of the host business application. Note that this association should be based on the functional purpose and not just the profile of business information. It is possible that different business requirements use similar business information. For example, a Service Domain that supports some aspect of marketing may use similar customer information to a Service Domain that supports credit decisioning.
- ***Service Operation alignment*** – once the role of the Service Domain alignment to the host business application is confirmed, the next step is to consider the more targeted purpose of the specific Service Operation. The BIAN Service Operations are defined at a fairly generic/coarse grained level. In some cases it may be necessary to break the individual BIAN Service Operation into a collection of more specialized/finer grained Service Operations prior to mapping to the host facilities. Again, this refinement is not considered here, but the approach followed is the same as for the more specialized/detailed Service Operations.

  The purpose of the Service Operation can usually be inferred from its 'action term', its general description and, where applicable, the Service Operation control parameters. It is necessary to consider the intention of the Service Operation in as much detail as possible from the semantic definition and confirm that the host access is well matched in terms of intent and underlying functionality. For example, a Service Operation intended to obtain the current balance of an account needs to be matched to a host function that accesses the current balance and not the end-of-day balance from the previous day.
- ***Business information alignment*** – the BIAN semantic Service Operation description will usually also contain a comprehensive description of the likely business information exchanged. In some cases, the BIAN Service Operation may also be matched to a more detailed message specification where an industry standard has been defined. The semantic content and/or message definition is used to check that the information content available from the host system is sufficient for the purpose of the service call.

Once the Service Operation is matched to the host business application, the Service Operation fulfillment must be enabled through the ESB connection to the host business application. In the case where some type of action or response is required, the mapping must be made directly to some existing or newly developed host interface. This will often be realized through parameter-based access to the interface. If no suitable interface exists, or there are functional shortfalls, it may also be necessary to front-end the host with some form of compensating capability or enhance the host system itself so that it can fully support the Service Operation.

In the more common case where the purpose of the Service Operation is to exchange business information, the content of the Service Operation needs to be mapped to the data content of the host system, ensuring as noted above that the host data is suited to the purpose of the Service Operation. There are several possible ways that the business information needs and the associated data element set for a Service Operation may map to a host system:

- **Simple match** - the data set matches a single accessible data structure within the host system.
- **Composite match** – the data set can be assembled from two or more accessible data structures.
- **Partial match** – the data set can be supported by an extract from a single available data structure.

For read access, the needs are simple as long as the required information can be matched to available data fields and the access can be handled in a synchronized manner for multiple sources. For updating/recording information on the host business application, a more involved analysis of the integrity of the performed action is clearly necessary.

5.9.2.2 Multiple candidate hosts

The mapping exercise as previously described may be applied to several competing candidate host business applications and a choice between these candidates will then be required. There are several possible options:

- **Master/slave** – one candidate host's business application is selected as the host and any changes/updates are echoed to the other systems in order to maintain consistency across the application portfolio. This synchronization can be a background activity.
- **Shared support** – the same Service Operation may access multiple hosts depending on some further selection criteria. This is a compromise situation where routing logic will need to be built into the ESB environment to determine the target host business application and mask this complexity from the presented Service Operation.
- **Composite service support** – the Service Operation necessarily combines facilities from multiple host business applications. Again, compensating logic will be required in the ESB to coordinate the interfacing and assembly of information from the accessed host business applications, resolving any inconsistencies and overlaps as

may be necessary. This is needed to mask the host complexity from the presented service.

In addition to supporting the compensating logic needed to deal with functional and data shortfalls and coordinating multiple host access requirements, there are several performance enhancements that can be built into the ESB capability, including:

- **Single sign on** – the ESB may be able to manage multiple host sign-on sessions to reduce the connection complexity.
- **Master/slave reconciliation** – the service alignment may help to resolve duplication by identifying suitable master/slave definitions of overlapping host function and data. Capabilities to synchronize between the host systems can be considered to operate in the background host environment.
- **Advance data look-up and caching** – more sophisticated traffic analysis can be used to implement advanced look-up (look ahead facilities anticipating related data sets and retrieving the data in advance to reduce access latency) and data caching, where retrieved data that is likely to be needed again is kept in a suitable caching capability.

The ESB will present available Service Operations that should provide integrated and coordinated support to the application portfolio, see figure 39. The way that these operational services may be presented for consumption varies. They could simply be made available individually to existing end-user applications. In some cases, they could support different application assembly environments that allow for flexible application development.

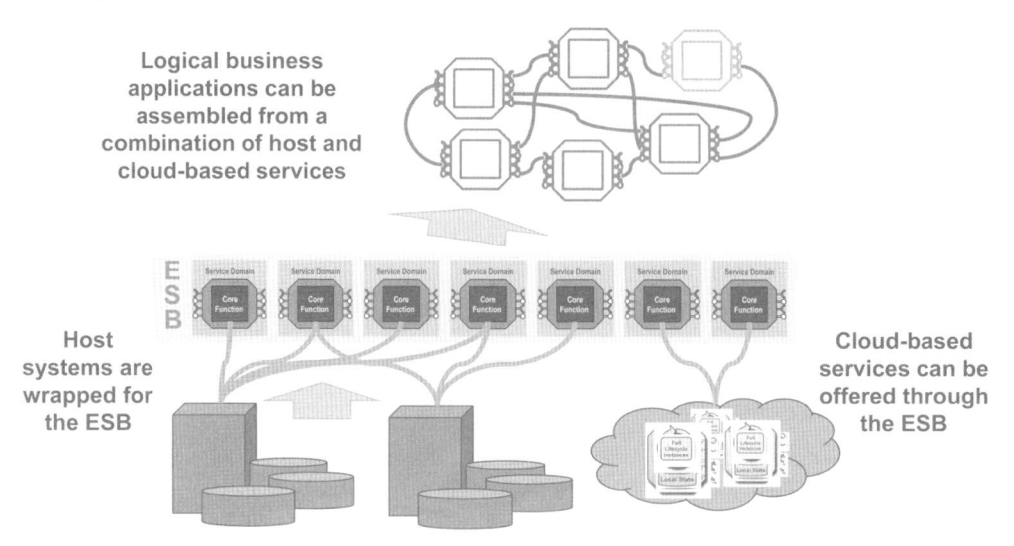

Figure 39: ESB solutions integrating host and cloud-based service solutions

As noted in Section 5.9.2, the ESB mechanism could link to existing host systems or, alternatively, may provide access to other sources, for example external web-based capabilities. An appropriate application assembly environment could support the assembly of business applications that combine wrapped host business applications (perhaps supporting transaction processing) with cloud-based CRM capabilities.

The ESB approach can be used to migrate progressively towards a business application configuration where each operational service is offered by a single source and re-used whenever needed across the overall application portfolio. Such an arrangement would, in theory at least, eliminate operational duplication and maximize business capability re-use.

5.9.3 Level 3 - Loose coupled distributed/cloud systems

The third level of technical environments is the highly flexible, distributed and connective networked platforms such as the Internet and more recently the cloud (here the term 'cloud' includes private, public and hybrid configurations). This level of environment can be considered as a progression from the ESB environment discussed above into something that could be viewed as a 'pure' service-oriented architecture. In this solution the mapped host systems that were presented through the structured ESB are replaced by freestanding, service-enabled business capabilities that are made available to collaborate over the network.

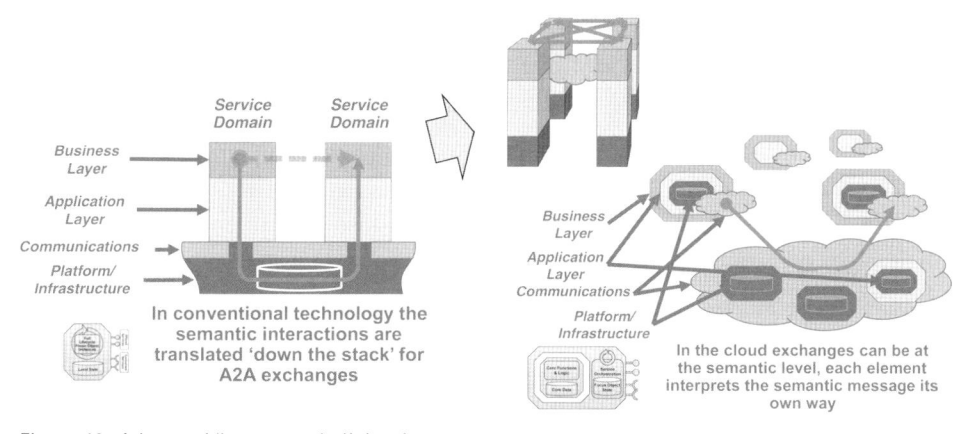

Figure 40: Advanced 'loose coupled' development

Some of the main operating characteristics of this 'loose coupled' highly distributed networked service environment are shown in figure 40 and include:
- **Functional capabilities operate independently** – each capability can act as a freestanding and independent functional 'container' with its own internal processing logic, data storage and state management. It runs to its own schedule/timing, calling services and responding to external events/triggers as it deems appropriate.
- **Communications between capabilities are through service calls** – the exchanges/interactions between the service centers are all via Service Operation calls. These interactions will typically involve the exchange of structured data that can be formatted in one or more data messages.

- **Varying levels of required information precision** – in essence two collaborating service centers may only need to agree/coordinate the meaning of information elements at the more approximate semantic level. This reduces the requirement to adopt common data formats and structures for machine representable data.
- **Exchanges use queue and event-based mechanisms** – the networked service capabilities operate asynchronously. When a capability requests a service from another it can continue with other tasks and monitor for, and act on, the response when received. It should also be 'defensive' - dealing sensibly with delayed, missing or erroneous responses (and requests).

Business execution in such cloud level environments is typically event-driven. Something will trigger an activity in one capability that may then need to call on services from other capabilities. These secondary capabilities referenced in this event may then also call on other capabilities before responding. The processing of the original trigger results in a 'cascade' of possibly 'nested' service interactions across the network until all necessary processing and responses have been completed and the network reaches a new stable state.

The BIAN Service Domains can be aligned one-to-one to the capability 'containers' just described. Both components of the Service Domain specification are used. The functional core defines the role of the container, outlining its required internal features and the service wrapper reflects service enablement within the network (service/state management and directory/connection handling).

The service wrapper handles the necessary logic to ensure that the Service Domain is aware of all other Service Domains it may call on. It also implements the called and offered Service Operations, typically using some form of queue and event management. Figure 41 illustrates an example of a cloud-based implementation.

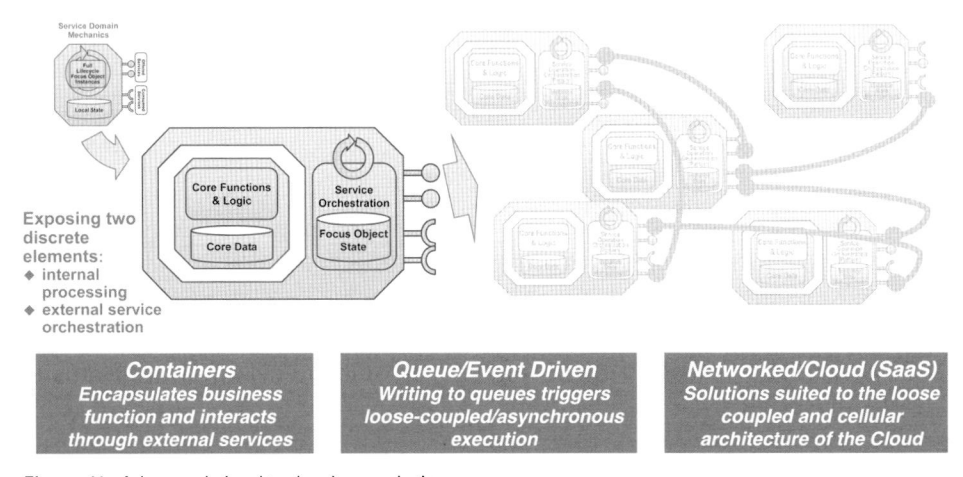

Figure 41: Advanced cloud technology solutions

The BIAN Service Operations define networked 'service containers' representing stand alone business capabilities activated by service calls. Transactions are no longer 'hard wired' but queue- and event-driven as an asynchronous, collaborative exchange of services that could be proprietary or in 'the cloud'.

Note that a service exchange as defined by BIAN may combine the physical assignment/ movement of goods or resources and free-form dialogues between individuals, as well as the more structured exchange of business information/data. The exchanges focus on the exchange of structured (machine-interpretable) information. It is assumed that additional mechanisms will be made available as necessary to accommodate the other forms of traffic (physical distribution and concurrent voice/video channels for example).

5.9.3.1 Service information precision
As noted above, service exchanges in the network require different levels of information precision to be effective. It is an important property of loose coupled networks that can reduce the complexity/overhead of the service connections.

When considering linking capabilities together within an enterprise, the default path is usually some form of shared technical infrastructure. The exchange will typically use existing communication networks (e.g. LAN/WAN) and may also leverage shared database/storage capabilities. In particular the exchange will be realized in a machine-to-machine environment where all data fields adopt a common schema and definition.

As this is the standard technical environment, this approach to making connections may not appear to impose an excessive overhead. But in highly distributed networks where the services can be supported by many different enterprises operating their own business applications and technical platforms, reaching common agreements on data schema and definitions is a significant challenge. Any opportunity to lower this requirement can be highly advantageous.

Determining the required 'precision' for a service exchange evaluates the extent to which a Service Operation can be realized successfully with more approximate information and data definitions. The BIAN Service Operations are defined at the highest level, in simple semantic/narrative terms. It then must be determined for each exchange how far the definition of these business information terms need to be defined and agreed as they are driven down to the far more detailed data structures at the machine-level.

An example can help clarify this concept. Two capability service centers (or Service Domains) that exchange financial transaction data such as product fulfillment and transaction accounting clearly need to have agreed the meaning of the service content with a very high level of precision (amounts, dates, currencies etc. will need to share common data schema and definitions). Elsewhere two Service Domains exchanging marketing insights may share intelligence with a much lower level of precision. A

Marketing Service Domain may identify several prospects and wish to notify a Sales Service Domain. There are several aspects of this exchange where the need for machine-level data precision can be relaxed:

- **Multiple/redundant references** – the service may identify the candidates using several characteristics/properties that can be used in different combinations to allow the association to be made (e.g. name, DOB, address, social security number, internal customer reference).
- **Formatting variations** – the representation of business information elements may be matched in a manner that handles differences (different field lengths/sequencing, missing optional fields, etc.).
- **Different data schema** – the internal data storage for two Service Domains can be different as long as they can both trace their internal data representations to the shared semantic terms with the necessary precision.
- **Acceptance of errors** – it may also be that the service can tolerate a certain level of errors in the exchange – if for example only 99 out of 100 prospects are recognized, the service exchange may still be considered acceptable.

The example highlights that those service exchange situations where reduced precision is adequate are typically in the areas of the business outside of the highly automated transaction processing core. Interestingly these are areas where new business models are encouraging greater collaboration between enterprises, with more banks exploiting specialized third party informational and analytical services.

The mapping of the BIAN standard for cloud-level deployments is summarized in figure 42.

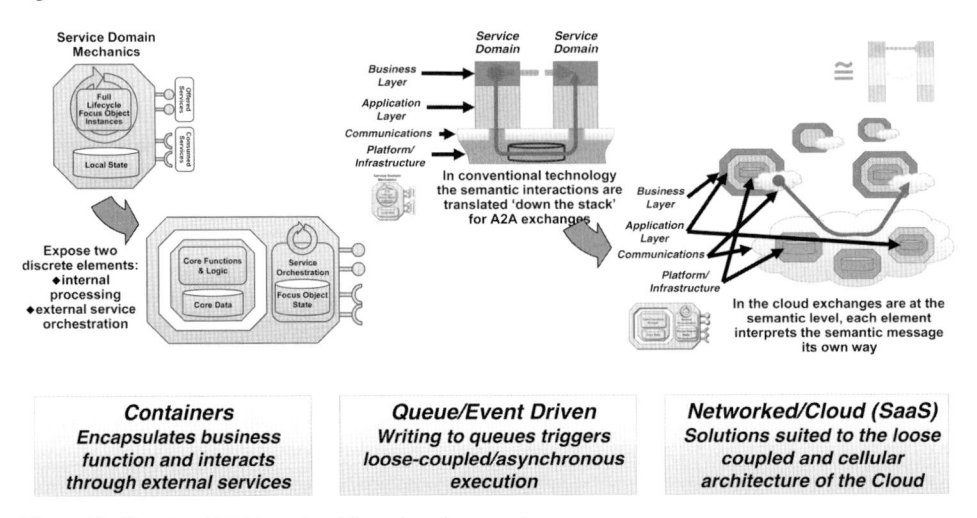

Figure 42: Mapping BIAN to a cloud-based environment

There are already many commercially available cloud-based financial services solutions in CRM and risk management. The operational behaviors enabled by the technology are particularly well suited to the networked/collaborative nature of the operational activities in these areas. It is hoped that the progressive introduction and adoption of the BIAN standard can help to support the development of standard solution designs that will improve re-deployment and integration activities for cloud-based offerings in the financial services industry in general.

■ 5.10 SUPPORT FOR EMERGING INDUSTRY APPROACHES

Two approaches are of interest here. The first is the expanding use of APIs, whilst the second is the growing interest in micro-service architectures.

5.10.1 Application Program Interfaces (APIs)

By definition an API supports a software-based interface with a software application, most commonly from another software application. An 'open' API is a software interface specification that allows an external party to access the bank's software application from their own software application, typically through a managed API environment/platform.

A complete software interface specification needs to consider a wide range of practical implementation issues such as performance, security and technical environment/architecture, in addition to the more obvious function/logic and data/information specifications.

To implement a truly 'plug compatible' software interface, comprehensive specifications must be defined and applied. For anything more than very basic exchanges these specifications will be very complex. Given that these interfaces typically need to relate to existing applications, the specifications will often also include a high degree of proprietary or site-specific detail.

The financial services industry is making progress in defining standard specifications for some of the more common transactional exchanges, in the area of payments for example. But even in these areas where there is a long history of standards-based message interfaces, it is proving difficult to define precise industry specifications that do not require site-specific interpretation and some degree of host software mapping/reworking.

The value that the BIAN model provides with the development of open APIs is in providing an approach by which this specification challenge can be managed, and its implications minimized. By defining a business exchange in terms that can be

consistently interpreted, the BIAN Service Domains and Service Operations help in two specific ways:
1. The service interaction between two Service Domains can be defined in sufficient detail that when used as a high-level specification for an API, the business purpose and key business information exchanged is standardized. Two software implementations mapped to the same service interaction will typically differ in their finer implementation details but if an external user of the service chose to switch between the two suppliers the disruption would be confined to the software in the immediate vicinity of the exchange itself. It should be possible to map the key business information content to the changed data schema. More importantly the main function/logic should be consistent so that any up-stream/down-stream activities at the caller are not significantly disrupted.
2. Because the Service Domain supports a narrowly defined business function and the Service Operations invoke specific responses, the associated messages have highly focused business information content. As a result, the extent of the business information to be mapped (and the associated meaning/purpose of the information) is kept to a practical minimum.

5.10.2 Micro-services

Micro-service architecture has a lot in common with the core design principles employed by BIAN. The Gartner definition of a micro-service underscores this:

"A micro-service is a tightly scoped, strongly encapsulated, loosely coupled, independently deployable and independently scalable application component." – Gartner

Micro-services can be defined at varying levels of detail, indeed the terms *'nano service'* and *'macro service'* are often used to describe finer and coarser grained components respectively. At one level the boundary of a micro-service can be mapped directly to the role of a Service Domain. The functioning of the Service Domain is then the same as the associated micro-service component, and the offered and consumed Service Domain Service Operations define the micro-service boundary.

Because a Service Domain performs a single discrete function and as it handles all instances of its specified business role from start to finish, the Service Domain has very strong function and data partitioning. Furthermore, when a Service Domain is implemented following proper service-oriented design, the service behaviors can strictly enforce encapsulation.

It can be argued that the BIAN partitioning approach defines business components which specifically conform to the goals of micro-service design. The summary table shown in figure 43 outlines how BIAN Service Domains and micro-services can be compared.

Level	Services	Application Integration	
The hierarchy used to build up solutions from elementary components	Defines business capability partitions as discrete and bounded (static) functionality	Defines the exchange of information and actions to support (dynamic) business behaviors	
Elemental Component	The BIAN Service Domain provides a candidate conceptual/logical design for a micro-service. *(Note: There may be multiple physical interpretations of the micro-service design in physical implementation)*	A BIAN service exchange between two Service Domains is an elemental interaction defined in terms of context, purpose & information payload. *(Note: This is a conceptual/logical specification that can be applied to defining and implementing an API)*	*"A microservice is a tightly scoped, strongly encapsulated, loosely coupled, independently deployable and independently scalable application component."* – Gartner
Bundles – initial thinking is that bundles need to be supported at two levels: 1. Business Applications 2. Organizational Entities	Service Domain 'clusters' can be described using BIAN wireframes, business scenarios and more detailed Service Domain & service operation specializations	"API Solution Sets" can combine collections of 'elemental' exchanges as may be required to define internal and external exchanges within and between business applications within an enterprise. Also to provide external access to that enterprise ("Open APIs")	

Figure 43: BIAN Service Domains related to (micro)-services

■ 5.11 USING BIAN SERVICE DOMAIN PARTITIONS TO DEFINE APIS

The BIAN Association recently published a white paper that describes how BIAN Service Domains provide a template for defining and managing cloud-based services. This can include the provision of API- based access to these services. The white paper can be found at www.BIAN.org.

A key consideration explained in the white paper addresses how access to the services offered by the bank can be controlled. Many banks are looking for ways to move beyond offering 'packaged' products and services to their customers and providing some form of direct access to their core financial services capabilities (e.g. payments, cash management, asset and liability management, credit and risk management, financial relationship management). This allows customers and service alliance partners to find innovative ways to integrate the bank's services directly into their operations.

Banks seeking to provide external access to their capabilities obviously need to find a way to do this in a secure manner. Achieving adequate security spans many levels, including the platform and application access controls (IaaS/PaaS). These are both complicated and necessary aspects to address, but solutions are available or rapidly emerging. The security aspect of external service provision that the BIAN standard can assist in is defining the allowed use of offered services in a standard format (SaaS).

When services are consumed within an enterprise it can be assumed and assured that they are being accessed by suitably authorized parties and are being used for appropriate purposes. However, when the service is made available to an external party these constraints are far harder to achieve. It is also desirable to find a way to offer external services in a standard way, so the services can be made widely available under standard controls without the need to implement each external connection individually.

A way to approach this requirement is to use the business purpose/role of the Service Domain to define the Service Operation business context and then utliize this to control/constrain service access. Figure 44 shows an example where the Relationship Management Service Domain is used to provide the business context. The services made available reflect the allowed use for a relationship manager (probably further constrained for an external relationship manager). For example, the 'relationship manager' is only able to access 'their' customers' details and only access (and update) information pertinent to the role of relationship manager. The times of allowed access and volumes/frequency may also be limited to that appropriate for a relationship management position.

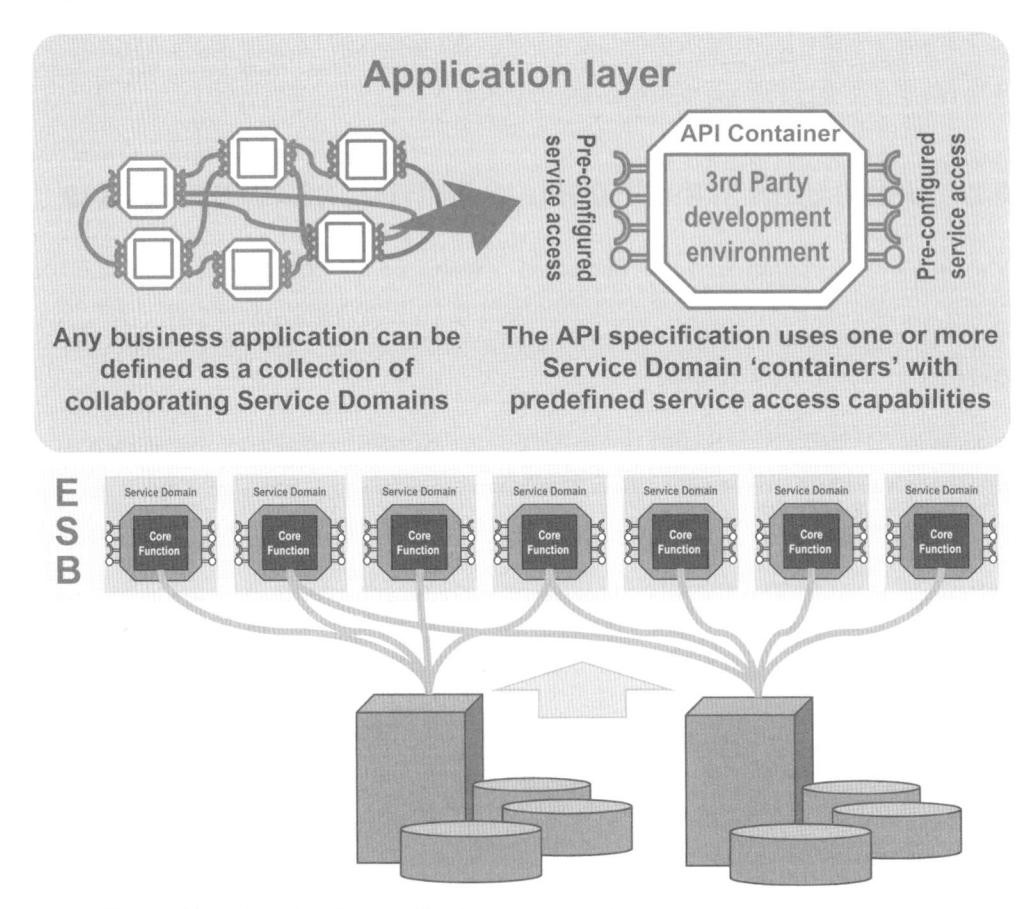

Figure 44: Cloud-based services for a relationship management Service Domain

The role of the Service Domain can be used to constrain access to the ESB services. This approach is well suited to external services and API solutions.

The API container could, for example, be the Relationship Management Service Domain. This container would support constrained access to customer information and product details that would be appropriate for the relationship manager role.

5.11.1 Cross-technical platform solutions

Most banks have application portfolios that combine technologies corresponding to all of the three levels of environment just described. An advantage of the BIAN service landscape it that it can be interpreted consistently in any of these technical environments. The Service Domains define conceptual/logical designs with functional partitions that are the same in each case. Accordingly, the model can facilitate the integration of business applications that may be developed and operate in these different environments. For example, using the BIAN Service Operation standards it is possible to find ways to sensibly integrate external cloud-based services with internal legacy host transaction processing systems.

5.11.1.1 Specifying point solution requirements – accelerator packs
This final sub-section describes the typical steps that can be followed to apply the BIAN designs in the context of a targeted or point solution. The case study project performed at BIAN Association member PNC Bank in cooperation with Carnegie Mellon University of Pittsburgh, provides a particularly good case study that can be found on www.BIAN.org.

Earlier in this section some general descriptions were provided relating to extending the BIAN Service Domain and Service Operation specifications in order to include the additional detail needed to define requirements and support the design and development of business applications. Here some of these 'templates' are described in the context of a typical point solution deployment project.

Many of the templates discussed, when combined with the core BIAN definitions, provide a very re-useable collection of general designs that can be adapted for any implementation. The canonical nature of the BIAN Service Domains and Service Operations ensure that the designs can be consistently interpreted. Solutions targeting a particular area (in the examples included in this section this is the payments function) can be re-applied elsewhere. The working name for the collection of designs covering an area of business operation is an 'Accelerator Pack'. The BIAN Association will develop several accelerator packs targeting different areas of the Service Landscape.

The stages in the point solution approach described here are as follows:
- **Business case** – structured analyses to assess the likely business impact of the solution are used to define the business case for investment.
- **Business Scenarios** – the boundary/scope and main internal activities are captured using Business Scenarios.
- **Wireframe** – the Business Scenarios are used to assemble a 'Wireframe' model that shows the involved Service Domains and primary service connections in a stable framework.
- **Requirements** – the functional and non-functional requirements for the Service Domains in scope are developed. If necessary, the semantic Service Operation

114   BIAN Edition 2019: A framework for the financial services industry

Service Domains define the columns, but this feature need not be expanded on in great detail

A simple narrative can be used to summarize the general flow of activity

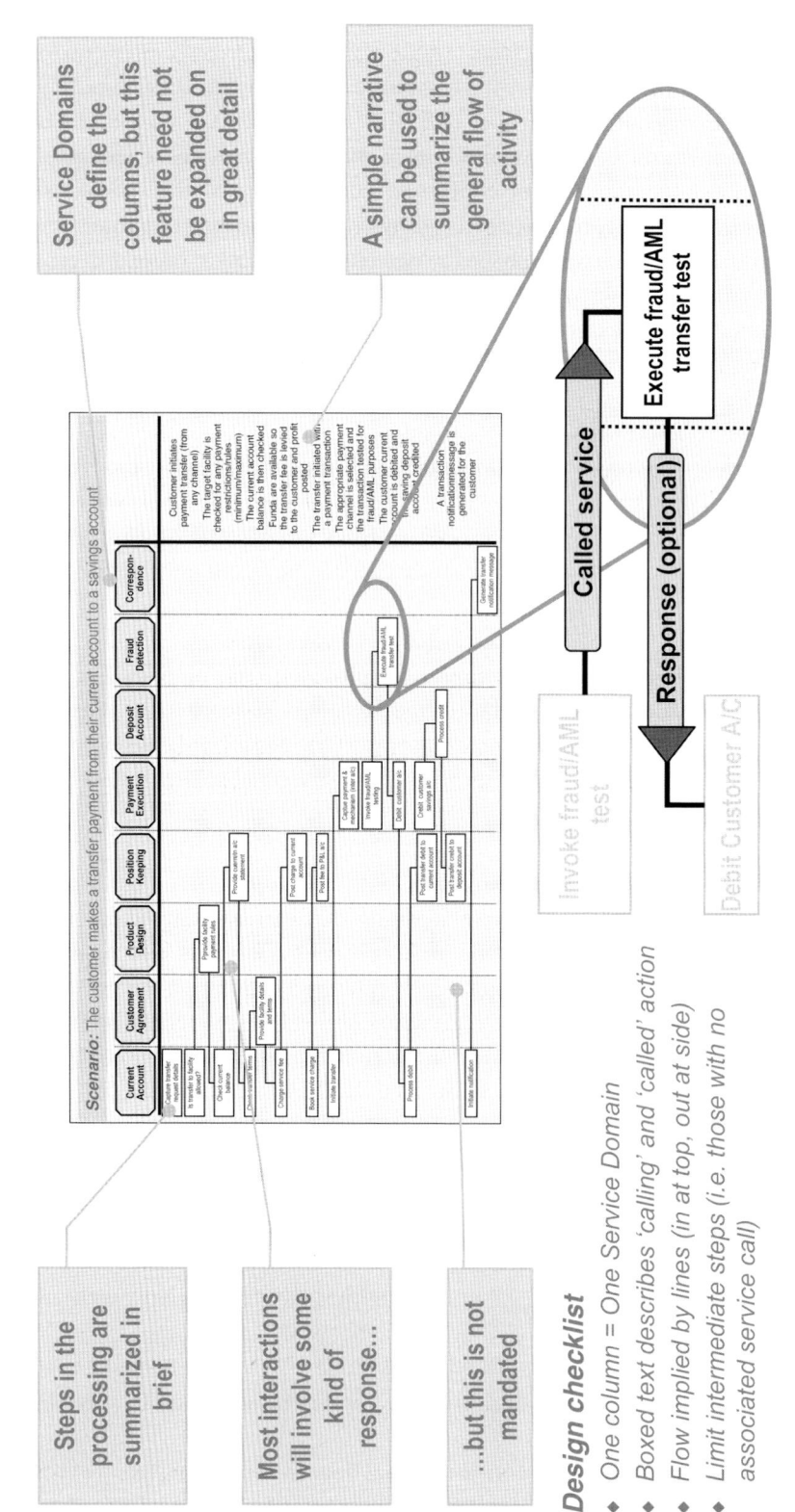

Scenario: The customer makes a transfer payment from their current account to a savings account

Current Account	Customer Agreement	Product Design	Position Keeping	Payment Execution	Deposit Account	Fraud Detection	Correspondence
Capture transfer request details							Customer initiates payment transfer (from any channel)
Is transfer to facility allowed?							The target facility is checked for any payment restrictions/rules (minimum/maximum)
Check current balance							The current account balance is then checked
	Check facility terms	Provide facility payment rules					Funds are available so the transfer fee is levied to the customer and profit posted
	Provide facility details and terms						
Charge service fee			Post charge to current account				
Book service charge							
Initiate transfer			Post fee to P&L a/c	Capture payment & mechanism (clear a/c backing)			The transfer initiated with a payment transaction
				Invoke fraud/AML testing		Execute fraud/AML transfer test	The appropriate payment channel is selected and the transaction tested for fraud/AML purposes
Process debit			Post transfer debit to current account	Debit customer a/c			The customer current account is debited and the receiving deposit account credited
			Post transfer credit to deposit account	Credit customer savings a/c	Process credit		
Initiate notification							A transaction notification message is generated for the customer
							Generate transfer notification message

Steps in the processing are summarized in brief

Most interactions will involve some kind of response...

Invoke fraud/AML test → Called service
Response (optional) ← Execute fraud/AML transfer test
Debit Customer A/C

...but this is not mandated

Design checklist
- One column = One Service Domain
- Boxed text describes 'calling' and 'called' action
- Flow implied by lines (in at top, out at side)
- Limit intermediate steps (i.e. those with no associated service call)

Figure 45: Example Business Scenario with rules

definitions are extended. These define the implementation-level requirements and may include site-specific variations.
- **Solution mapping** – current systems and/or candidate packages and new development options are mapped against the Wireframe and more detailed implementation requirements (aligned to the Service Domains).
- **Customization/development** – identified business application and interface shortfalls are outlined and the resultant customization and development tasks/options scoped out
- **Deployment planning** – finally a phased, multi-threaded migration project is detailed with the necessary business case for investment consideration.

Each of the stages and the currently available templates are now described. As more experience in deployment is gained, the techniques and templates will be refined. The working assumption is that the target architecture for the solution is service-based, as opposed to more conventional process or object-oriented design.

5.11.2 Business case development

Conventional business case development techniques can be used to estimate the financial impact of current shortfalls and anticipate the likely impact on performance arising from the proposed development. This analysis may identify different general categories of business performance (such as productivity, error rates, time-to-market) and compare current and future state impact in terms of measurable cost savings, improved net revenues and reduced risk exposure.

5.11.3 Select and amend Business Scenario(s)

Business Scenarios are used to define the main business events that the point solution will handle; such as processing product fulfillment tasks, handling a customer inquiry, processing a payment transaction. A comprehensive list of required Business Scenarios should be developed to cover the business activities supported by the point solution including any management oversight and reporting activities. An example PowerPoint view of a BIAN Business Scenario is shown in figure 45.

Each Business Scenario has been developed to show the involved Service Domains and the major service interactions between these. Briefly, the approach involves working through an archetypal flow of activity associated with the event, identifying the involved Service Domains and establishing the Service Operation exchanges between them.

In many cases the Business Scenario definition can use the example Business Scenarios that have already been developed within BIAN and that are published along with the BIAN Service Landscape. These examples can usually be adapted as needed to align to the specific business event for the point solution. The Business Scenarios should be walked through with business practitioners to confirm that they collectively cover all the key workings of the target area and, if possible, with application architects familiar

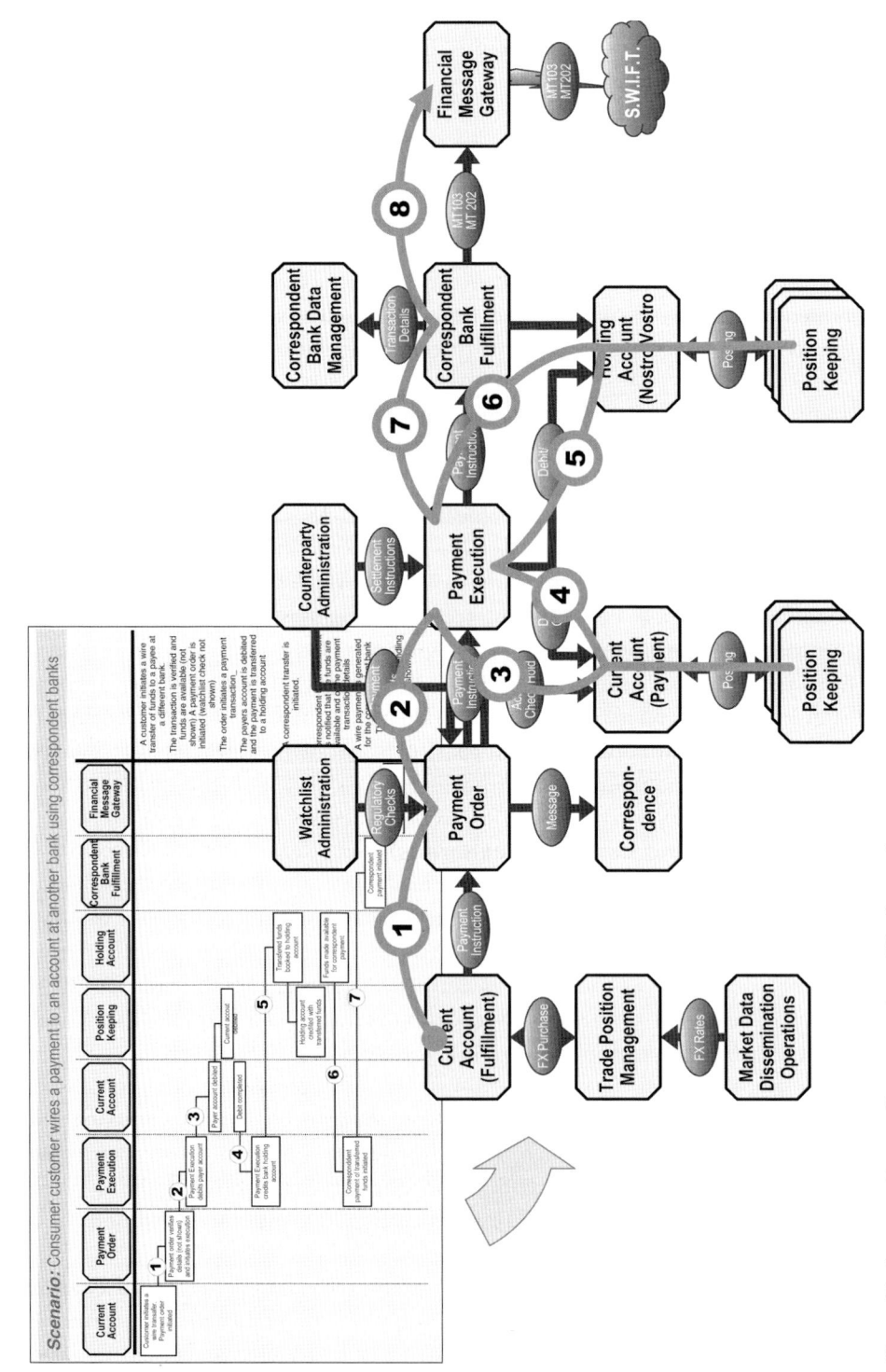

Figure 46: A payment transaction mapped on a Wireframe view

with the BIAN specifications to confirm the Service Domains have been correctly interpreted.

Note: it is possible that the functional scope of a BIAN Service Domain is misaligned for a particular organization. Though BIAN attempts to define canonical Service Domains, there are certain situations where a BIAN Service Domain is either too coarse-grained and needs to be duplicated and specialized, or where two or more Service Domains define excessive detail and need to be concatenated to correctly represent the organization. The resulting amended Service Domains can then be included in the Business Scenarios just as with any other Service Domain.

5.11.3.1 Develop a Wireframe model
The Wireframe model is an informal representation of the Service Domains and the service connections between them for a particular business activity. One or more Wireframe views can be developed to capture the activities covered by the point solution. Unlike Business Scenarios that capture a dynamic behavior such as the sequence of tasks needed to process a request, the Wireframe is a static framework and many possible dynamic behaviors can be traced or overlain on this framework as shown in figure 46 where a SWIFT payment scenario is traced over a Wireframe.

The Wireframe is a good communication device to discuss the functional requirements in general. It is particularly useful to agree the scope of the point solution – the Service Domains (and associated functionality) that is to be supported, those Service Domains with which there is an interface and other Service Domains that are not directly involved but help provide broader context. In figure 47 a comprehensive payments Wireframe shows the core, interfaces and boundary Service Domains.

5.11.4 Define the implementation requirements

The BIAN Service Domain specifications are high-level as appropriate for a business architecture specification. To support implementation activity, far more detailed 'requirement specifications' are needed. Business application requirements can be captured in many different forms. When the target implementation environment is service-oriented, the BIAN Service Domains, Service Operations, Business Scenarios and other related templates align well. In other technical environments that BIAN content may need to be interpreted in different ways. For simplicity, the extensions discussed here are suited to service-based deployments.

5.11.4.1 Feature checklists
The high-level description, Control Record and Service Operation profile of the Service Domain can be extended using a Feature Checklist table. The level of detail contained in the functional feature checklists may vary depending on the deployment options. Where the solution will involve the integration of a commercial package then the requirements need to be at a sufficient level of detail to compare/evaluate competing

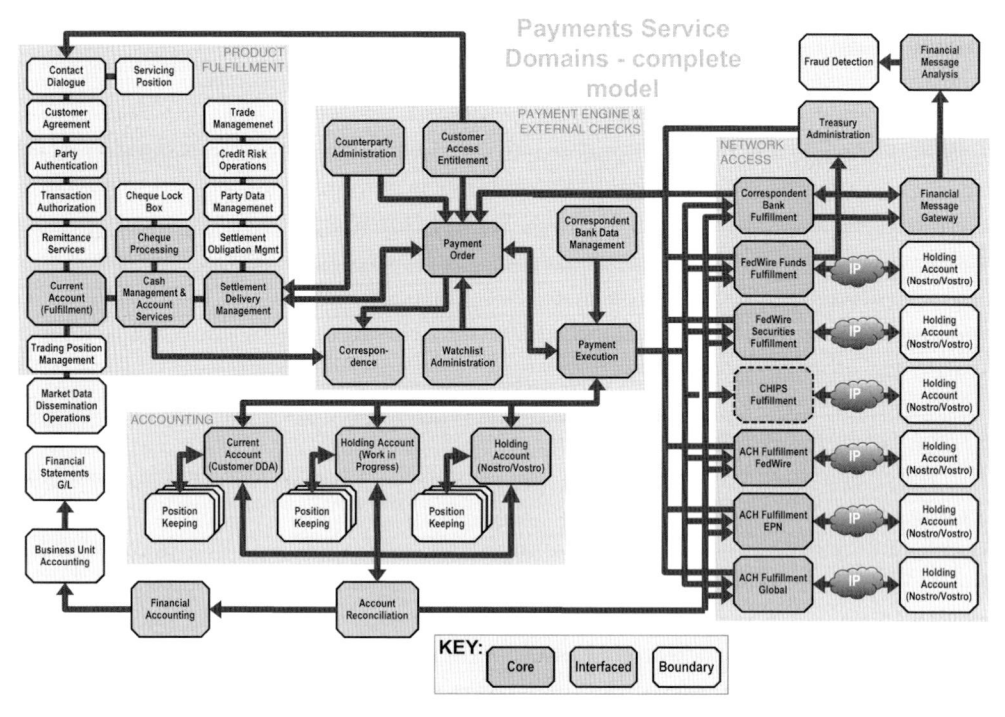

Figure 47: The completed payments area Wireframe (example)

offerings (as might be used in a Request for Proposal or Request for Information (RFP/RFI). If the solution involves a new development or enhancement to existing systems, a greater level of detail is likely to be required.

A simple example of a Service Domain with indicative prevailing functional features as might be defined by a bank for package evaluation is shown in figure 47 for the 'Customer Credit Rating' Service Domain, that is responsible for determining the bank's credit assessment of a customer. The template organizes the functional features under four feature types that are the same as the 'responsibility item types' and 'Service Operation types' BIAN uses elsewhere for consistency. There is also the option to capture key non-functional operational and technical features.

The Feature Checklist table can be adapted to include more detailed specializations that may identify geopolitical, scale- and maturity-specific features. As the example here is for a specific location these refinements do not apply.

5.11.4.2 Service Operations

In addition to expanding the functional feature lists for the Service Domains, their associated Service Operation definitions are used to specify the interfaces or services depending on the technical arrangement. The BIAN Service Operations are intended to include sufficient semantic content to be mapped to the underlying machine-to-machine messages. Where industry standard messages exist, these mappings may be

5 How to apply the BIAN standard

Service Domain: Customer Credit Rating - Maintain and administer the credit scoring for customers based on consolidated internal data and optionally referencing external credit agency insights		
Customer Credit Rating		Feature Description
Feature Types		
Functional	Origination	• Capture new customer details and credit rating requirements (any channel) • Match customer to external credit agency records
	Invocation	• Access to update/change customer credit rating status • Request to update credit score (override schedule updates/maintenance) • Provide insights/notification of customer related activity that may influence credit assessment
	Delegation	• Maintain scheduled and ad-hoc access to credit bureaus/rating agencies • Reference, analyse payment/credit history to influence rating assessment • Reference, anayse product and service activity to influence rating assessment • Execute behavioral models against customer activity to develop credit related insights • Periodic recalculation of credit scores
	Reporting	• Provide access to credit assessment (with sub-set content selections) • Subscribe to credit assessment change alerts • Query customer credit rating details (analyse credit across multiple customers and histories)
Non-functional	Technical Architecture Features	• High performance, highly connected and interactive operational facility
	Operating Features	• Extended hours, 24/7 • Centralized credit scoring funtion • 3rd party service dependency (rating agencies)

Figure 48: Feature list for a Service Domain - Customer Credit Rating

available from the BIAN repository. The approach for mapping the Service Operations to messages was described earlier in Section 5.6.11. Depending on the target technical environment, the BIAN Service Operations can be interpreted as the interface that can be 'hard-wired' or can be implemented as a fully functional Service Operation.

For the Service Domains that are a part of the target solution, all Service Operations as defined for the Service Domain will need to be supported to handle all possible (lifecycle) behaviors. For the services that are accessed by the target solutions, the Service Operations referenced in the range of Business Scenarios define the type of external connections/interfaces needed for the point solution.

As noted earlier, the BIAN Service Operations simply capture the business information exchange dependencies in semantic terms. They do not define in any detail the nature or choreography of the underlying message exchange (i.e. simple one/two-way exchange or lengthy negotiation/dialogue). The requirements specification will clearly need to specify this aspect of the service implementation to help with sizing and designing the external interfaces.

5.11.4.3 Business Scenarios and Wireframes
The collection of Business Scenarios and any derived Wireframe views define examples of behavior that also identify requirements by example. The range of scenarios used to define the scope of the solution is limited to providing the details for the main business events but clearly does not go into a comprehensive set of requirements, for example covering error and exception handling that would be needed for a formal requirements specification.

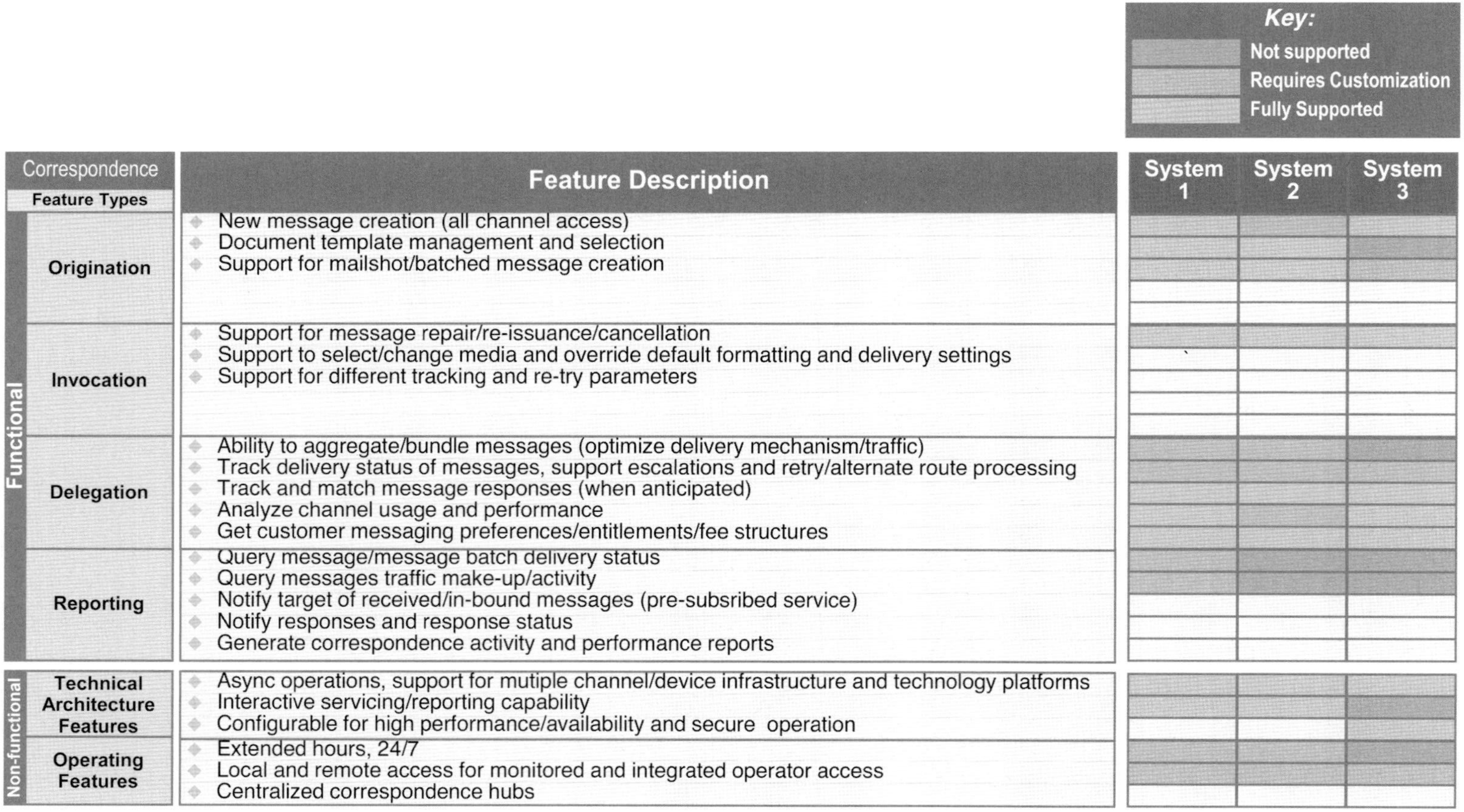

Correspondence

Feature Types		Feature Description	System 1	System 2	System 3
Functional	Origination	◆ New message creation (all channel access) ◆ Document template management and selection ◆ Support for mailshot/batched message creation			
	Invocation	◆ Support for message repair/re-issuance/cancellation ◆ Support to select/change media and override default formatting and delivery settings ◆ Support for different tracking and re-try parameters			
	Delegation	◆ Ability to aggregate/bundle messages (optimize delivery mechanism/traffic) ◆ Track delivery status of messages, support escalations and retry/alternate route processing ◆ Track and match message responses (when anticipated) ◆ Analyze channel usage and performance ◆ Get customer messaging preferences/entitlements/fee structures			
	Reporting	◆ Query message/message batch delivery status ◆ Query messages traffic make-up/activity ◆ Notify target of received/in-bound messages (pre-subsribed service) ◆ Notify responses and response status ◆ Generate correspondence activity and performance reports			
Non-functional	Technical Architecture Features	◆ Async operations, support for mutiple channel/device infrastructure and technology platforms ◆ Interactive servicing/reporting capability ◆ Configurable for high performance/availability and secure operation			
	Operating Features	◆ Extended hours, 24/7 ◆ Local and remote access for monitored and integrated operator access ◆ Centralized correspondence hubs			

Key:
- Not supported
- Requires Customization
- Fully Supported

Figure 49: Mapping candidate systems to the feature list of a Service Domain

Where more detail is required, additional Business Scenarios can be developed, or more conventional requirement definition approaches used, to augment the service-based requirements produced using the BIAN Business Scenarios, Service Domain feature lists and Service Operation definitions.

Taken together, the Feature Checklists, Service Operations, Business Scenarios and other information templates provide a framework for defining the high-level requirements for a point solution. This framework can be expanded adding detail to the Service Domain partitions if the solution is service-oriented, or any other suitable format can be adopted to support the implementation environment as necessary.

5.11.5 Map and assess existing systems/candidate packages

The same mapping and assessment approach can be applied to existing systems and external candidate packages. With existing systems there will clearly be a far greater familiarity with the available features and supported interfaces, and consequently more thorough assessments of the commercial offerings will be required in practice. For simplicity, other than highlighting this need here, no further distinction is made in the approach.

The mapping and assessment of existing business applications and candidate commercial offerings combines several factors:
- **Functional coverage** – how well are the functional needs supported?
- **Service enablement** – how well does the candidate solution align to and support service-based operations?
- **Hygiene factors** – are there any 'deal breakers' that severely constrain the use of a candidate?

5.11.5.1 Functional coverage
The target state defined by the Business Scenarios, Service Domain feature checklists and Service Operations provides a framework against which the 'footprint' and quality of coverage of the candidate solutions can be mapped. As described earlier in Section 5.9.2 considering application portfolio rationalization, Service Domain Feature Checklists provide the primary mechanism to check coverage.

Also described earlier in Section 5.6.8, because the Service Domains define non-overlapping business capabilities, when solution options are mapped to the features of the Service Domains and compared one Service Domain at a time, they provide a mechanism for ensuring comparisons are made considering 'like-for-like' elements.

In figure 48, a simple assessment is performed for three candidate systems (existing or commercial candidates) to determine whether the requirement is either fully supported, can be supported with limited enhancement work or if the requirement is not supported at all.

Based on this mapping the candidate solution with the best initial coverage and least required enhancement investment can be selected. This selection may need to be adjusted as the coverage for all the target Service Domains is considered collectively. A candidate solution will typically span many Service Domains and may be assessed to have different relative strengths making it the preference for some Service Domains but not for others. If the candidate system can't be easily broken up, this limitation may outweigh its relative strengths against more flexible alternatives.

The checklist Service Domain mapping is useful for highlighting specific functional shortfalls, see figure 50. A second mapping using the Wireframe view can be used to expose major overlaps/conflicts and the external boundary interfacing requirements for the point solution at a higher level. This can be a useful discussion framework as it provides a big picture view of the target solution.

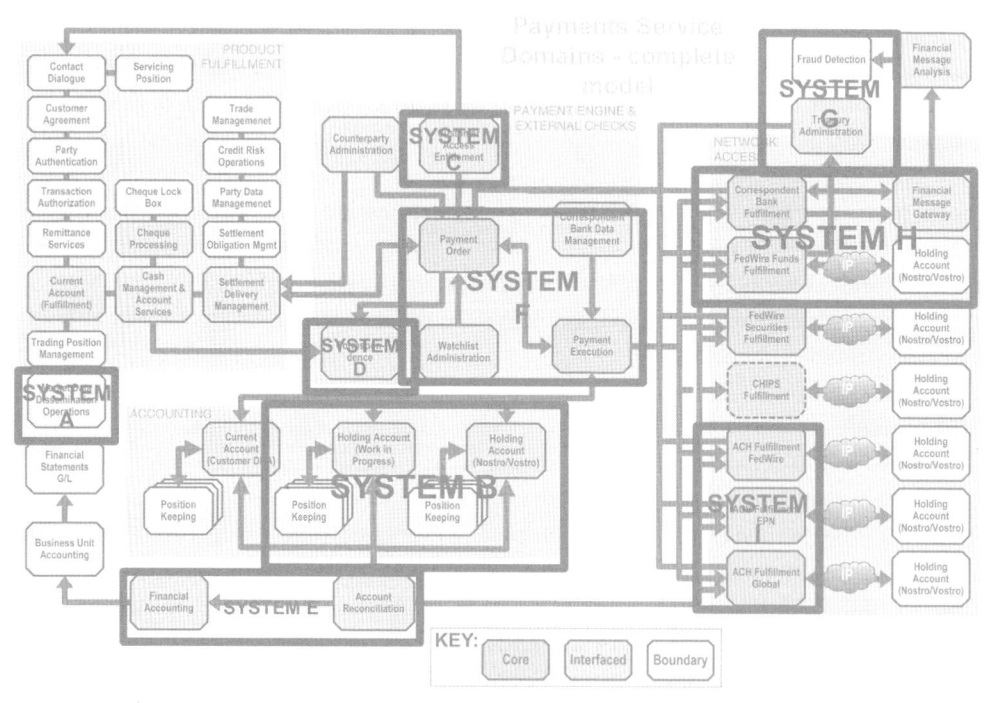

Figure 50: Overlaying current systems on a Wireframe model

5.11.5.2 Service enablement
An additional test for the mapped candidate solutions against the Service Domains considers their 'service alignment'. There are two considerations here, one obvious the other not quite so:
1. **Supporting Service Operations** – do they (the candidate systems) support the required collection of offered Service Operations? Existing interfaces may need to be improved to generalize and service-enable them so that they can be called by any suitable party.

2. **Externalizing duplicated functionality** – considering the delegated services for the Service Domain, does the mapped system make external calls to fulfill these needs, or is the functionality embedded and what would be necessary to externalize this capability when necessary?

The concept of externalization has been described more completely in Section 5.6. With respect to solution selection, the assessment needs to consider the implications with respect to the suitability of the candidate system for the specific point solution requirements. In practice, few solution options will cover the requirements for a single Service Domain, the candidate solution will usually include functionality that relates to multiple Service Domains, some scoped to be a part of the target solution, some that will be external.

It is possible that there may need to be some level of operational compromise because a single candidate system may not be architected in a way that fully supports the potentially conflicting needs of two or more Service Domains within the point solution. It may also not be possible to expose the full range of operational services for all mapped Service Domains within the scope of the point solution if the system has a monolithic (non-modular) internal structure. Finally, it may be difficult to decouple and 'externalize' functionality that is intended to be external to the point solution and supported elsewhere through an external service interface.

Any of these service enablement needs, if not supportable, may compromise the ability to adopt candidate solutions. The assessment can be complex and needs to be done on a case-by-case basis. The Wireframe model described in Section 4.3.7 can be a useful framework to structure this assessment as it provides a stable 'big picture' view where the scoping and integration issues can be captured and discussed.

5.11.6 Candidate system 'hygiene factor analysis'

A final assessment to consider is hygiene factor analysis. This can be useful to quickly eliminate candidate solutions and so greatly simplify the overall selection process. As there are many factors involved in determining the suitability of a candidate solution (functional, technical and operational) it is easy to overlook fundamental flaws in a solution that prevent its long-term use or compromise its strategic value. For example, a system may offer good functional coverage today, but its technical architecture may severely constrain its ability for enhancement or to scale-up to support higher volumes.

In this type of analysis, different criteria are used to compare the suitability of different systems. Based on this analysis, operationally flawed systems that need to be retired are exposed. The system that has the best 'strategic fit' for a Service Domain can be selected and all other systems can be placed on a 'maintenance only' investment diet. An example analysis is shown in figure 51.

Assessment criteria	Assessment description	System 1	System 2	System 3
Functionality	Scope and granularity of functional coverage	5	4	2
Modularity	Ability to partition (modularize) and connect to the application	4	3	2
Ease of Use	Ease of use, as supported by user commentary	4	3	3
Enhance ability	Ability to extend and/or enhance the system	5	3	3
Code Quality	Code base quality and availability of skills utilities to maintain the code	4	4	3
Technical Architecture	Criteria as appropriate – e.g. STP, Analytics, Workflow, Capacity, Interoperability, Real-time	5	3	1
Maintainability	Can the application be maintained and supported in production	4	4	2
Scalability	Can the system handle projected transaction volumes without major reworking	4	4	1
Stability	Is the production system robust	5	3	2
Efficiency	Is the cost of use/transaction cost/performance appropriate	4	4	4
Content Quality	Is the data of appropriate quality (complete/accurate)	4	3	3
Performance/Availability	Does the application meet performance/response expectations	4	3	3
Channel Agnostic	If appropriate, does the systems support different channels/media/networks	4	4	2
Security	Are there suitable access and audit controls	5	3	2
	Overall Rating (worse case)	4	3	1

Key:
1. Incapable of support
2. High cost to support
3. Material cost to support
4. Minimal cost to support
5. Fully meets need

- Can be a foundational system going forward
- Should be maintained until a replacement developed
- An operational risk, should be replaced a.s.a.p.

Figure 51: Example hygiene factor analysis

- The sliding scale can be used to identify the best fit system for a Service Domain.
- A system that scores an exception score on any factor represents an operational risk regardless of its scores on all other criteria and should be retired.
- A system that is not selected as the strategic fit should only be maintained (i.e. no investment to extend the systems), as it will be replaced. All technical alignment and functional enhancement investment should be directed to the strategic/best fit system.

The second point underscores the value of the analysis for eliminating flawed systems. The final point provides an additional important insight. A system that is not seen as the long-term solution but is retained for some interim period requires a different approach towards its maintenance and enhancement investments. With the clarity to focus on one target/strategic solution for each Service Domain, it is often possible to reduce the costs of other systems, investing only to keep them working for the shorter term and avoiding structural or architectural changes given that the system is to be replaced at some point.

5.11.6.1 More general considerations when implementing point solutions
Some more general issues for the adoption and integration of existing or commercial applications into a point solution are, in no specific order:
- Internal versus commercial solutions – the analysis as described above assesses the support for the transactional functions as captured in Business Scenarios. There are many background alignment considerations to add to this when integrating commercial offerings such as alignment to architectural and operational policies and standards.
- External interfaces – the analysis defines a boundary for the point solution based on a robust view of the scoping using Service Domains. In practice, the access to external 'services' may not be immediately available and different approaches can be adopted

to fill the gap. The use of 'proxy' capabilities that compensate for shortfalls in the target legacy environment can be useful as an intermediate solution.
- Operational service re-use – an important by-product of adopting the service-based approach to point solution design is that it helps develop solutions with the potential for re-use.
- Elements of the point solution can be implemented in such a way that their service-based capabilities can be used by other/subsequent solutions.
- External legacy capabilities that are service-enabled to support the point solution may now be accessed in the same service-based manner by other solutions.
- Future proof – for reasons fully explored elsewhere, the functional partitions defined by the Service Domains are enduring/stable over time. With good design (that handles incremental adoption and enhancement) the service-based solutions that are components of the point solution represent re-useable capabilities that similarly have a long shelf-life.

5.11.7 Customization/development

The Service Domain designs, in particular the Feature Checklists have been described in terms of solution selection. It is likely that the same mechanism can be adapted and used to specify enhancement and customization needs and used to track the implementation of these developments. This is a use that BIAN will monitor and add insights to in future releases.

5.11.8 Migration planning

Finally, for this sub-topic we take a look at the issue of migration planning. The point solution assessment will have identified several candidate systems, selected from these and identified shortfalls associated with the involved Service Domain functional areas and their associated service-based interfaces.

The Service Domain partitions provide an opportunity to structure the migration plan by providing functional streams that can be addressed in parallel. One or more associated Service Domains can define one development thread. The service dependencies between Service Domains can also be used to help identify any critical dependencies (pre/post dependencies) between the parallel development threads.

In addition, the Service Domain aligned requirements can be used to identify phases in the migration, where coordinated development across the parallel development threads can provide some meaningful interim phased deliverable. This helps to release benefits in incremental phases during the migration that can offset the overall program investment.

Multi-threaded, multi-phase migration planning is a technique that is widely used. The Service Domain partitions define useful elements in the definition of such a plan.

5.12 SUPPORT FOR INCREMENTAL ADOPTION/MIGRATION

Perhaps one of the most important reasons for aligning to the BIAN standard when developing APIs is one key property of the Service Domain partitioning. This is the fact that the BIAN Service Domains define aspects of financial services that are extremely stable over time. The role or purpose of a Service Domain does not change as business practices evolve.

This is because the Service Domain represents an elemental responsibility or something that the bank needs to be able to do. It does not prescribe how that responsibility is fulfilled. For example, one BIAN Service Domain is responsible for providing customer authentication services to confirm the identity of a customer that presents to the bank for any reason.

As noted in Section 3.6.3 this is a canonical requirement in that it is a function that every bank can agree on the need for. In addition, different banks may use different methods/techniques to verify a customer (for example passwords, device identifiers, biometrics) and indeed, over time, the possible mechanisms may evolve as new approaches are developed.

The way the Service Domain executes its role can vary and may evolve. Also, the patterns of interaction in response to different business events and the thresholds triggering Service Operation exchanges may vary from site to site and over time. But the fundamental role of the Service Domain and where it fits amongst the other Service Domains does not change.

As a result, APIs that are aligned to BIAN Service Domain Service Operation boundaries can be designed for incremental adoption. Some basic services can be supported and adopted in limited situations initially, whilst over time additional services either supporting more complex interactions with existing Service Domains or adding new Service Domains into the mix can be introduced without destabilizing existing capabilities.

By selecting high-value, low-complexity API services at the outset, the business benefits from early solutions can help to fund the overall migration and build momentum for adoption by proving positive business impact as new services are offered over time.

5.12.1 Using BIAN as an API 'inventory'

The BIAN Service Landscape is a reference structure that contains the BIAN Service Domains in a layout intended to help with their identification/selection. BIAN seeks to identify all required Service Domains to support all financial services activity in the financial services industry. Furthermore, by defining the Service Operations offered by each Service Domain, the BIAN Service Landscape represents a complete inventory of service interactions at a particular level of detail.

For this reason, the BIAN Service Landscape can be used as an organizing framework for categorizing/classifying available APIs. By mapping an API to the corresponding Service Operation(s) for the Service Domain in question it can be uniquely classified. As the inventory is populated with references to available open APIs, users will be able to identify potential solutions for specific purposes. As noted in Section 5.6 there is always likely to be implementation and mapping work to do in order to deal with practical aspects of the API implementation, but the addressed business requirement can be well matched.

The scope of an available API solution may map to more than one BIAN Service Operation or may provide a subset/more specialized service. Because the Service Domains serve 'elemental' business purposes and their Service Operations are narrowly defined, the mapping should usually be fairly straightforward.

At this stage very few open APIs have been developed based on BIAN specifications and so it is too early to evaluate how practical and effective the BIAN Service Landscape inventory will be. As an aspect of BIAN efforts to develop semantic API designs, an initial classification of Service Operations that can be mapped to open APIs has been developed.

Firstly a review of the Service Domains was undertaken to give an initial indication of which Service Domains provide function and business information that might need to be accessed externally. The Service Landscape in figure 52 has been color coded to show this classification. Service Domains highlighted in gray represent business functions that provide cross product or utility type services. Service Domains highlighted in darkgrey represent business functions that are specific to a particular product. Note: This is only an initial determination for planning purposes. It is highly likely that other patterns of business behavior will be discovered that may make additional Service Domains of interest.

Every Service Domain has an associated set of default Service Operations. Some of these support internal management command and control type exchanges and these are unlikely to be offered through open APIs. For this reason, they have not been included at this stage. For all other Service Operations, a brief description has been provided so that open APIs can be mapped against the associated Service Domain and Service Operation(s).

These Service Operation descriptions are being refined as BIAN develops extended definitions of the Service Domains. The coverage of the first phase of this design extension is presented in the next sub-section covering 'Wave 1' design deliverables.

Initial Service Domain classification for:

- ~70 Product Related Service Domains e.g. Current Account, Deposits, Collateral Allocation
- ~100 Utility/cross-product related Service Domains e.g. Party Authentication, Interactive Help

Selected Service Domains may offer simple read access or may offer complex array of services to cover external access as appropriate

Key:
- Product: Service Domains that fulfill product-specific activities
- Utility: Service Domains that fulfill cross-product activities

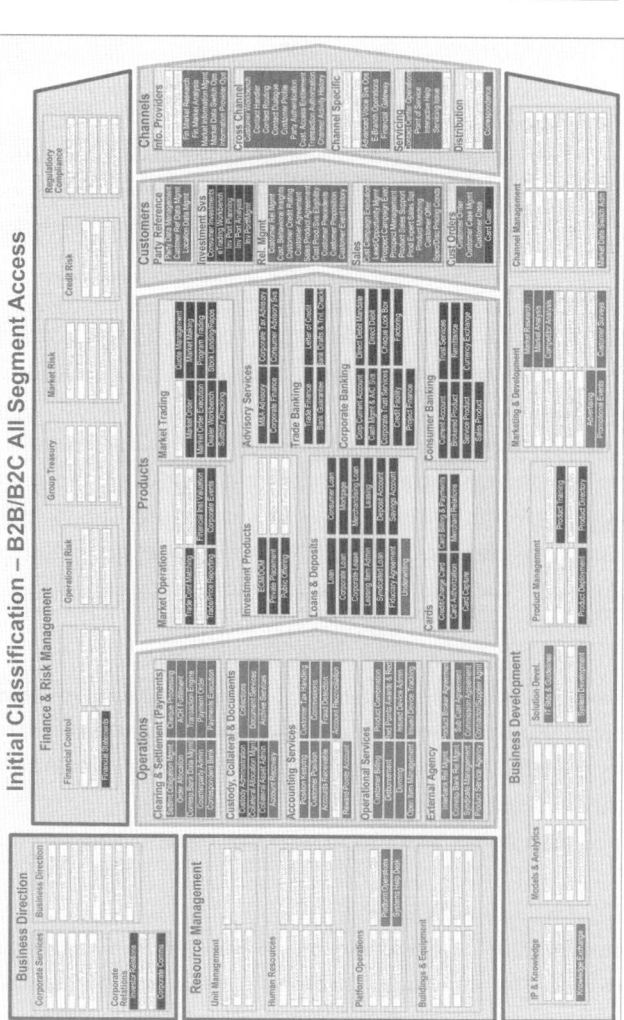

Figure 52: The BIAN Service Landscape – First API Inventory

5.12.2 API inventory

The Board of Directors of the BIAN Association initiated a project in 2017 to identify, describe and build Semantic APIs. In this project four waves of delivery have been identified, based on the BIAN Board's prioritization.

Each of the waves contains specific parts of the Service Landscape:

Wave 1:
- Consumer only;
- Mobile access;
- Simple lending products;
- Payments/PSD2.

Wave 2:
- Retail banking;
- Cards.

Wave 3:
- Product sales;
- Customer servicing;
- Corporate banking;
- Product enhancements (additional features to earlier releases).

Wave 4:
- CRM;
- Advisory services, sales and servicing;
- Investment and trading;
- Wealth management;
- Product enhancements.

Figure 53 shows how Wave 1 is represented in the BIAN Service Landscape.

If we zoom in to Offer Management, we will see a limited set of Service Domains are involved, as shown in figure 54.

Figure 55 shows the Wireframe for 'Offer Management'.

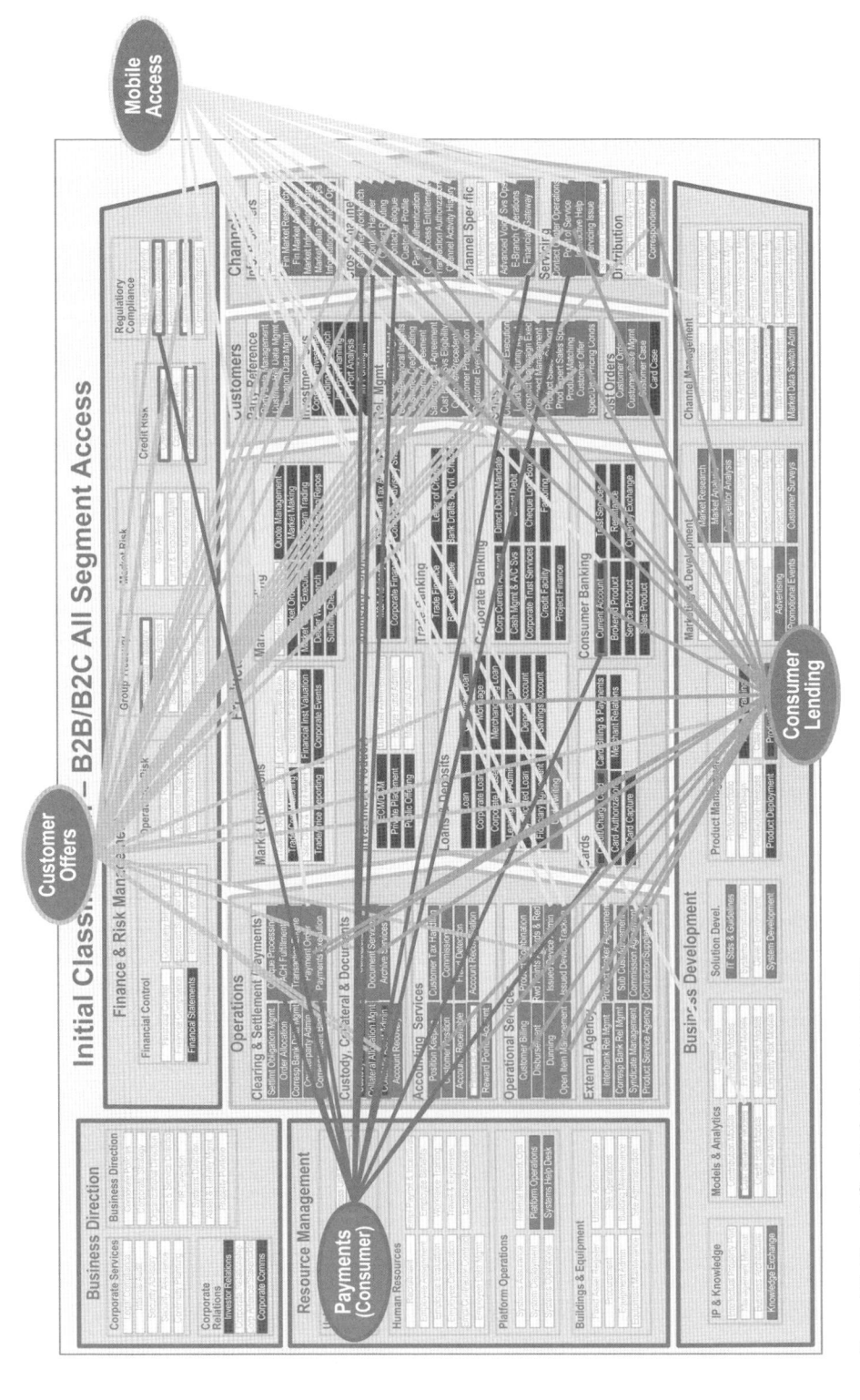

Figure 53: Wave 1, Service Landscape coverage

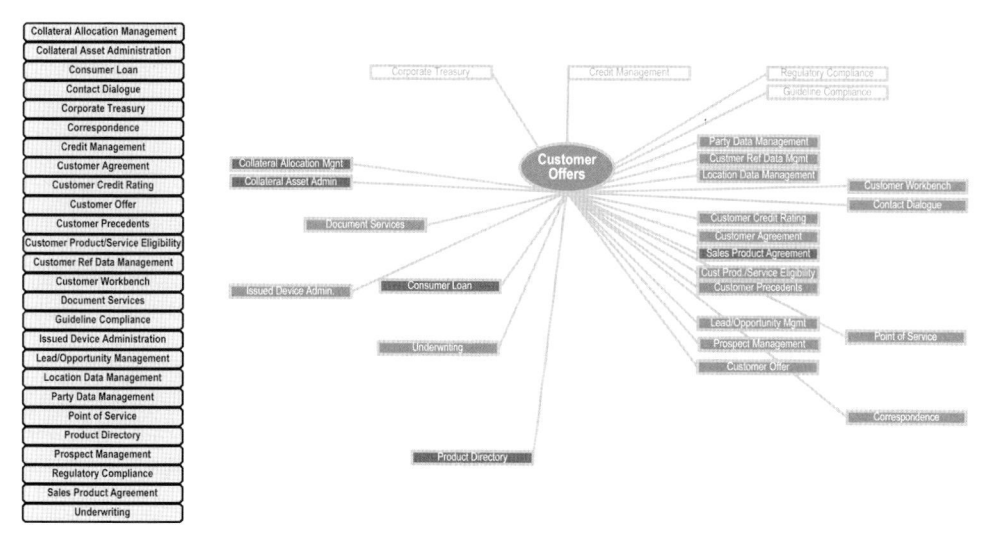

Figure 54: Offer Management – scoping statement

5.12.3 Three levels of architectural alignment

The implementation of open APIs varies greatly depending on the technical approach adopted. BIAN defines three distinct types of technical solutions that correspond to differing levels of sophistication. There can also be hybrid architectural approaches and, in practice, most banks will need to consider a range of technical situations often spanning all three levels for different aspects of their operation.

1. ***Direct to core*** – in this approach basic external access control is handled in the channel (or via some dedicated front-end control mechanism) and the service exchange accesses the host facility directly.
2. ***Wrapped host*** – in this approach access control remains channel-based but the host systems are accessed through a control/wrapping middleware such as an enterprise service bus (ESB).
3. ***Micro-service architecture*** – in this approach the applications are implemented as a network of service-enabled, discrete capabilities that can support external access directly.

The key properties of each level and the business rational for adopting these are summarized in the table shown in figure 56.

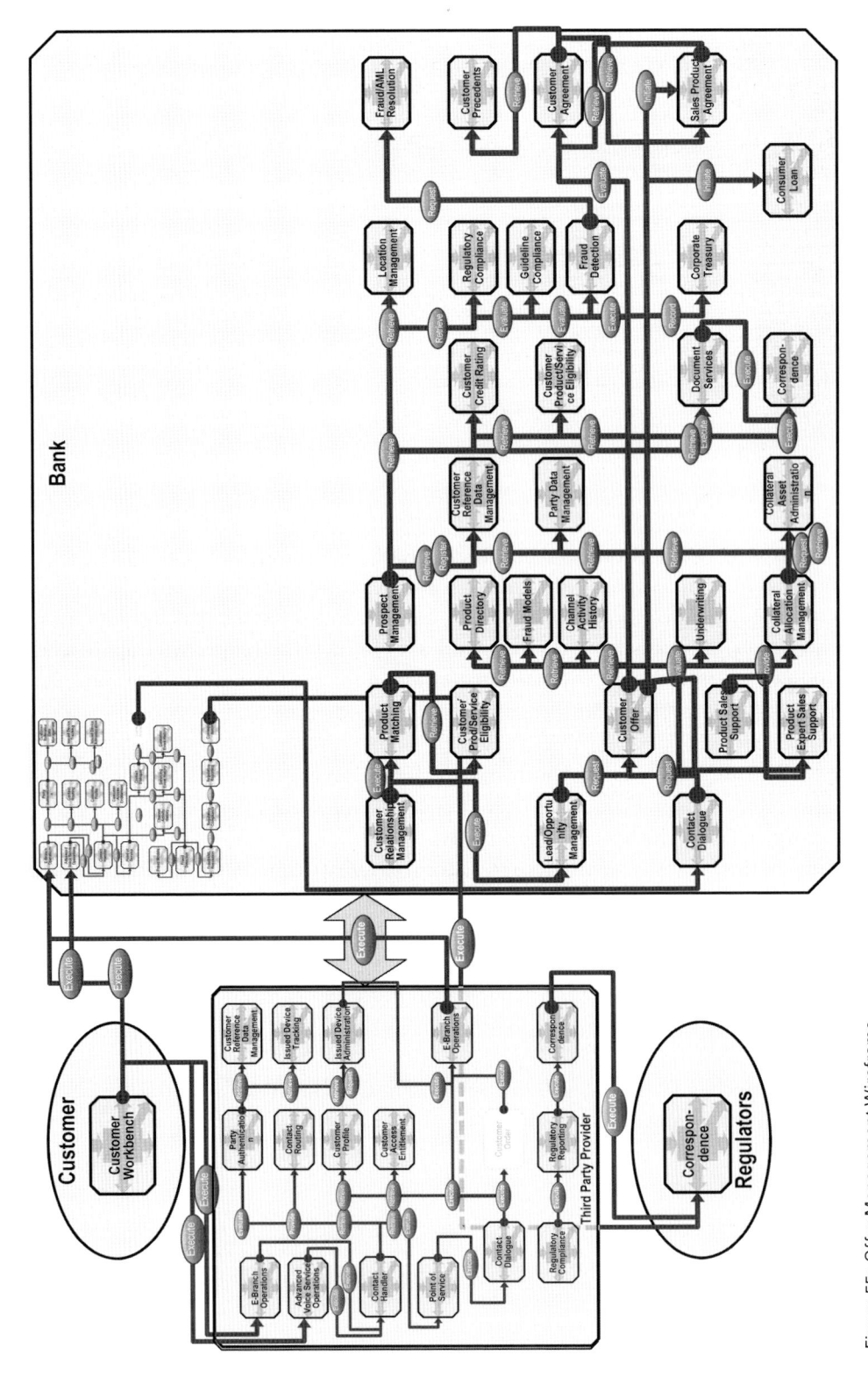

132 BIAN Edition 2019: A framework for the financial services industry

Figure 55: Offer Management Wireframe

5 How to apply the BIAN standard

	Level 1. Direct to Core	Level 2. Wrapped Host	Level 3. Micro-service Architecture
Definition	The API routes direct to the core system providing the service. Intermediate channel based access control and 'buffering' is required	integrating service middleware – a service bus – 'wraps' the host systems. The service bus can offer various host access mitigation capabilities/enhancements	The host services are implemented as loose coupled micro-services with complex interactions supported by sophisticated middleware
API Service description	Read only or simple 'atomic' update transactions supported by a single host system. The solution is likely to be host application specific	Enhanced 'simple access' services aligned to establish standards. Wrapping may enhance service capabilities and some hosts may support more complex exchanges	Support for flexible and complex interactions involving multiple business activities and processing/decision chains
Examples	♦ Retrieve a balance/account statement ♦ Reference a product/service directory ♦ Initiate a payment	Message conforms to industry standards (e.g. ISO20022) ♦ Retrieve a balance/account statement ♦ Reference a product/service directory ♦ initiate a payment ♦ Customer on-boarding/offers	♦ Prospect on-boarding and origination ♦ Customer dispute/case resolution ♦ Customer relationship development/up-sell/cross-sell campaigns ♦ Third party service integration
Business drivers	Provide application-based access to an established/existing type of customer exchange	Provide application based access with a high degree of standards alignment. Mask/augment host/legacy system limitations.	♦ Support sophisticated interactions ♦ Support new business models ♦ Support for 3rd party integration ♦ Leverage advanced technology/architecture

Figure 56: Summary of the API sophistication levels

5.12.3.1 Direct to core

The lowest level of sophistication and the easiest to implement involves constructing a front-end capability to manage external access security and then typically re-package existing host interfaces to support an API. A typical arrangement is included in figure 57. It shows direct customer access to the bank (from an API linked to their personal device) or via a third-party service provider.

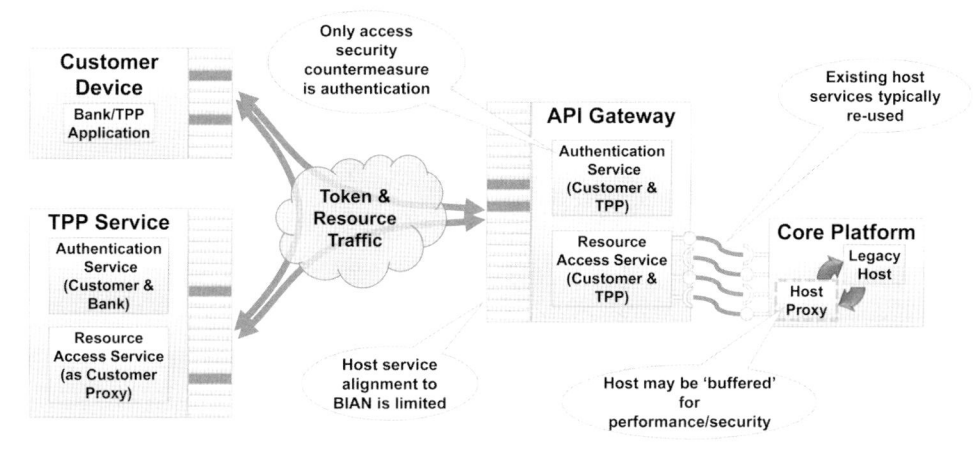

Figure 57: Level 1 Layout

Key aspects of the approach

At this level the changes required to host systems are kept to a minimum but the facilities that can be supported are limited to repackaging existing services that can be accessed through an API front-end platform.

External access control is implemented using access tokens handled by an authentication service capability. Access sessions will typically be limited to single task exchanges that target an individual host system.

Host access may be direct, or host production systems may have a proxy implementation that duplicates aspects of the host system to provide additional access control/security.

API services can be mapped/classified against BIAN Service Domain Service Operations. It is likely however that there will be significant host system-specific features exposed through the API.

Advantages
- Minimal reworking of core production systems – existing external access interfaces can be repurposed to support API access. Solutions can be developed quickly with limited disruption.
- Access control – robust authentication services can be employed to manage external access control independently and with limited disruption to existing production capabilities.
- Basic standards alignment – API services can be packaged/aligned with the BIAN standard to ease future migration to more advanced solution architectures. System/software changes will be needed, but the business purpose of the service will be consistent.

Limitations
- Simple transactions only – the supported services will be simple – read only and/or limited transactional initiation services supported by a single host application access session.
- Limited/no post access transaction tracking - supporting the external tracking of downstream progress of initiated transactions will not usually be possible without significant additional development.
- Authentication only access control – more sophisticated security countermeasures such as behavioral analysis and cross-contact invocation limits/constrains can't be supported.

5.12.3.2 Wrapped host
The second level involves the integration of host access middleware that mitigates host systems shortfalls. The middleware, typically some form of enterprise service bus (ESB) can provide a range of enabling facilities including, as shown in figure 58:
- Host access session man*agement* – supporting host access 'sessions' that can span multiple external access events.
- Data caching – storing frequently accessed host data in memory to minimize host access traffic.
- Host wrapping – adding function and data to mask host system shortfalls.
- Resolve data fragmentation – enforcing master/slave data governance techniques within the application portfolio.
- Advanced look-up – using access patterns to anticipate needs and obtain host data in advance to minimize host access latency.

- Transaction persistence – provide facilities to track customer 'transactions' between contacts and potentially transactions spanning multiple systems.

Again, customer access can be direct or via a third-party service provider and front-end authentication is the main security countermeasure.

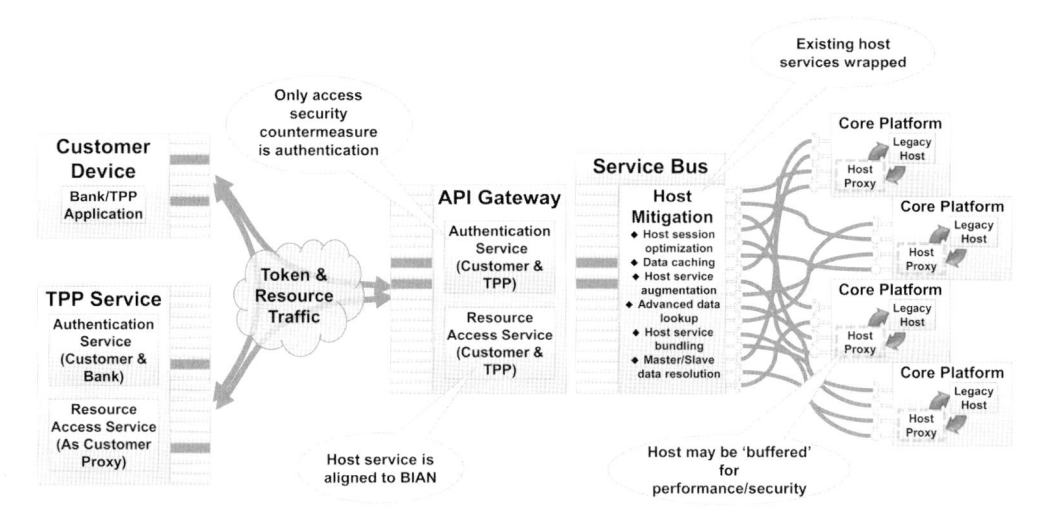

Figure 58: Level 2 layout

Key aspects of the approach
The main purpose of implementing a host-wrapping layer is to repurpose or extend the life of existing legacy systems and enable greater re-use of business functionality. In addition to addressing the listed shortfalls and improvements, API services are mapped/classified to BIAN and the ESB wrapper can be used to mask host-specific features thereby improving the standards alignment.

Wrapped host services can also support front-end (client side) application assembly approaches but this type of solution development is not shown in the diagram or considered here in any detail.

Advantages
- Core renewal – core/legacy systems can be repurposed to extend their production life, leveraging sunk investment and avoiding production disruption.
- Access management – the ESB can optimize host access, reducing systems loading and ensuring unintended patterns of host access are not permitted.
- Full standards alignment – the ESB can mask host-specific features allowing services to conform to open standards as far as they are available.
- Support for front-end application assembly – as noted.

Limitations

- Limited complex transaction support – the ESB may be able to support customer transactions that involve some level of cross contact session persistence and/or multiple system access.
- Limited front-end application support – the ESB environment itself is not typically intended as the platform for assembling elaborate front-end application capabilities – additional facilities are usually required.
- Authentication only access control – as with Level 1 solutions, the wrapped host architecture will use front-end access control mechanisms limited to authentication-based countermeasures.

5.12.3.3 Micro-service architecture

The most sophisticated level is where the host systems conform to a micro-services architecture with Service Domains (or groups of closely related Service Domains) acting as autonomous service 'containers' in a loose coupled service network. In this configuration a collection of Service Domains manages customer access, providing comprehensive services including access security, activity tracking and intelligent routing decisioning.

A micro-service platform that manages external access can link to different host configurations. Figure 59 shows how a customer access micro-service platform allows managed access to host systems conforming to different levels of API sophistication (direct to core, wrapped host and micro-service configurations).

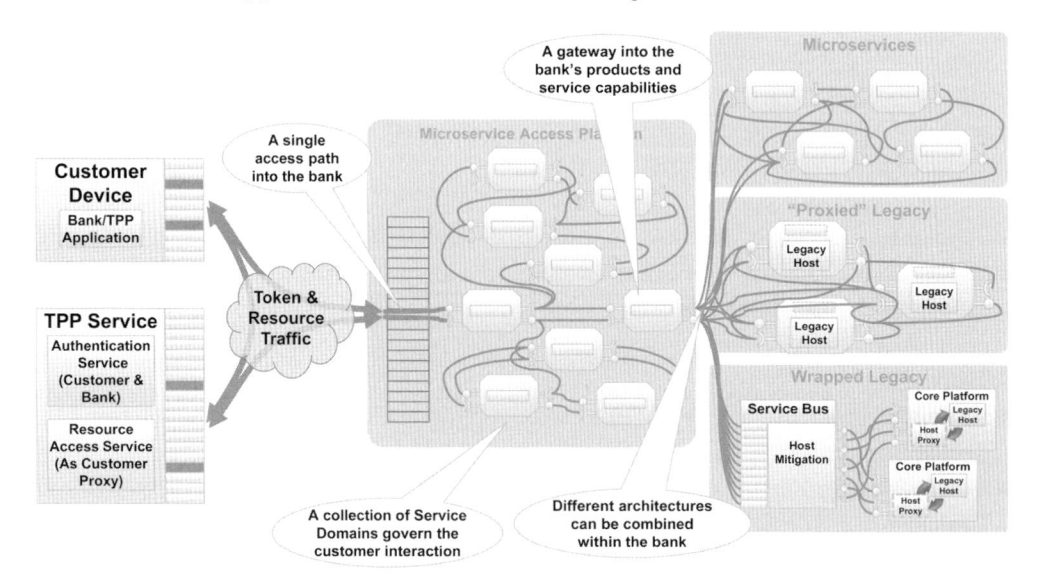

Figure 59: Level 3 Layout

Key aspects of the approach

The micro-service architecture approach needs to be considered in terms of two distinct aspects. The first as mentioned is a micro-service-based customer access platform that may include a range of facilities and utilities that support external customer access, again possibly through third party intermediaries. The second is the bank's product and service capabilities that may increasingly be supported using systems conforming to a micro-service architecture where this is appropriate.

A key advantage of aligning to the BIAN Service Domain and Service Operation standard for Level 1 and 2 solutions is that these interfaces can be subsequently integrated with a Level 3 front-end micro-service platform, requiring only manageable amounts of re-working.

Advantages

- Support for complex transactions – the micro-service customer access platform can include capabilities to orchestrate complex transactions that span contact capabilities and integrate multiple host capabilities over time.
- Comprehensive access security countermeasures – the micro-service access platform can integrate behavioral tracking capabilities and other security countermeasures in addition to authentication services.
- Support for flexible business models – a micro-service architecture better supports the integration of third party solution elements to provide enhanced and completely new business models.
- Enables background migration of core systems – a micro-service access platform can help manage the progressive evolution of legacy systems (through Level 1 to Level 3 changes).
- Supports integration of advanced solutions – a micro-service platform can better integrate components/containers that leverage advanced technologies for their own internal implementation.

Limitations

- Represents a significant investment – the development of a micro-service platform and micro-service solutions will require significant development costs and involves advanced techniques with elevated implementation risk that should be approached incrementally.
- Unproven in production/unpredictable business case – leveraging micro-service architectures to support new business models can result in unpredictable business results/practices.
- Evolving standards (BIAN/ISO/FIBO) – comprehensive development standards covering all aspects of micro-service design have not been defined and are emerging at varying pace. Early development risks non-conformity with later standards.

5.13 CASE STUDY

Aleksandar Milosevic, Chief Software Architect at banking software provider Asseco SEE explains the business benefits of working with BIAN to define standardized APIs:

"Using standard interfaces to consolidate and modernize portfolio
As a vendor that grew through acquisitions, we inherited a rich collection of applications that have their application-specific interfaces. Applications that had similar scope ended up having their specific interfaces for essentially the same responsibilities. One of our strategic goals was to cut integration time and cost and, over time, achieve plug-and-play interoperability between different applications in our portfolio.

Another goal was to hide any application or platform specifics behind the interfaces, so we can gradually modernize individual applications without disturbing the others.

Finally, our goal was to enable easier consumption of our interfaces from customers and partners. As we were already using BIAN as a map for application portfolio tracking and optimization we decided to go a step further with BIAN – to define standard A2A interfaces aligned with BIAN and retire legacy application-specific interfaces.

Asseco Reference REST APIs
We formed working groups made up of domain experts and gave them the charter to standardize REST APIs for Asseco SEE banking applications. One of the biggest challenges when defining a large set of consistent APIs is the alignment of their responsibilities and boundaries. Through our experience with BIAN we learned that we could utilize the landscape for functional decomposition of APIs in which each Service Domain becomes a
candidate boundary for an API definition. Having clear rules for establishing Service Domains reduced the risk of unclear boundaries and increased the productivity of our working groups.

Thirty APIs and counting
Since the beginning of 2016, our working groups were able to define 30 APIs and our many product teams implemented those APIs as both consumers and providers. Working on standard APIs had an integral impact on our development organization and helped broaden the perspectives outside organizational and application siloes. With three banks already using REST APIs and many more in the pipeline, APIs and their alignment with BIAN is a hot topic in almost any discussion that we have with banks today."

PART IV

6 Assembling a representative enterprise blueprint

The BIAN Service Landscape is a reference framework for classifying and organizing the complete collection of BIAN Service Domains. Each Service Domain is a general design of a discrete capability and the Service Domains collectively are intended to cover all aspects of the financial services industry. The BIAN Service Landscape is not a general model of a bank; it is more a structured 'library' index that contains one of each possible building blocks that might be needed to build any bank.

The existing BIAN Service Landscape has evolved in use over the years. Its structure and a general discussion of the way Business Areas and Business Domains are used to define a Service Landscape is described in Section 4.1. For the creation of the enterprise blueprint, a different layout of the Service Landscape has been developed. This layout better reflects some of the typical structure and flows/connections in a bank and, consequently, is a better format for assembling the blueprint. It does not change the nature or content of the Service Domains themselves, it is simply an arrangement of the Service Domains.

This alternative layout is called the 'value chain' view as it includes structures that align loosely to the value chain in service delivery.

The M^{4}Bank is a worked example where the BIAN designs have been used to define a representative organization 'blueprint'. The M^{4}Bank blueprint is assembled using BIAN Service Domains and represents a generic financial services value chain. It has four 'dimensions of complexity' (hence the name):
1. Multiple **products** - the enterprise supports a range of products and services.
2. Multiple **channels** - products and services are accessed through many channels and devices.
3. Multiple **lines of business** - the enterprise spans business segments/markets.
4. Multiple **levels of management** - the enterprise has global, regional and local management levels.

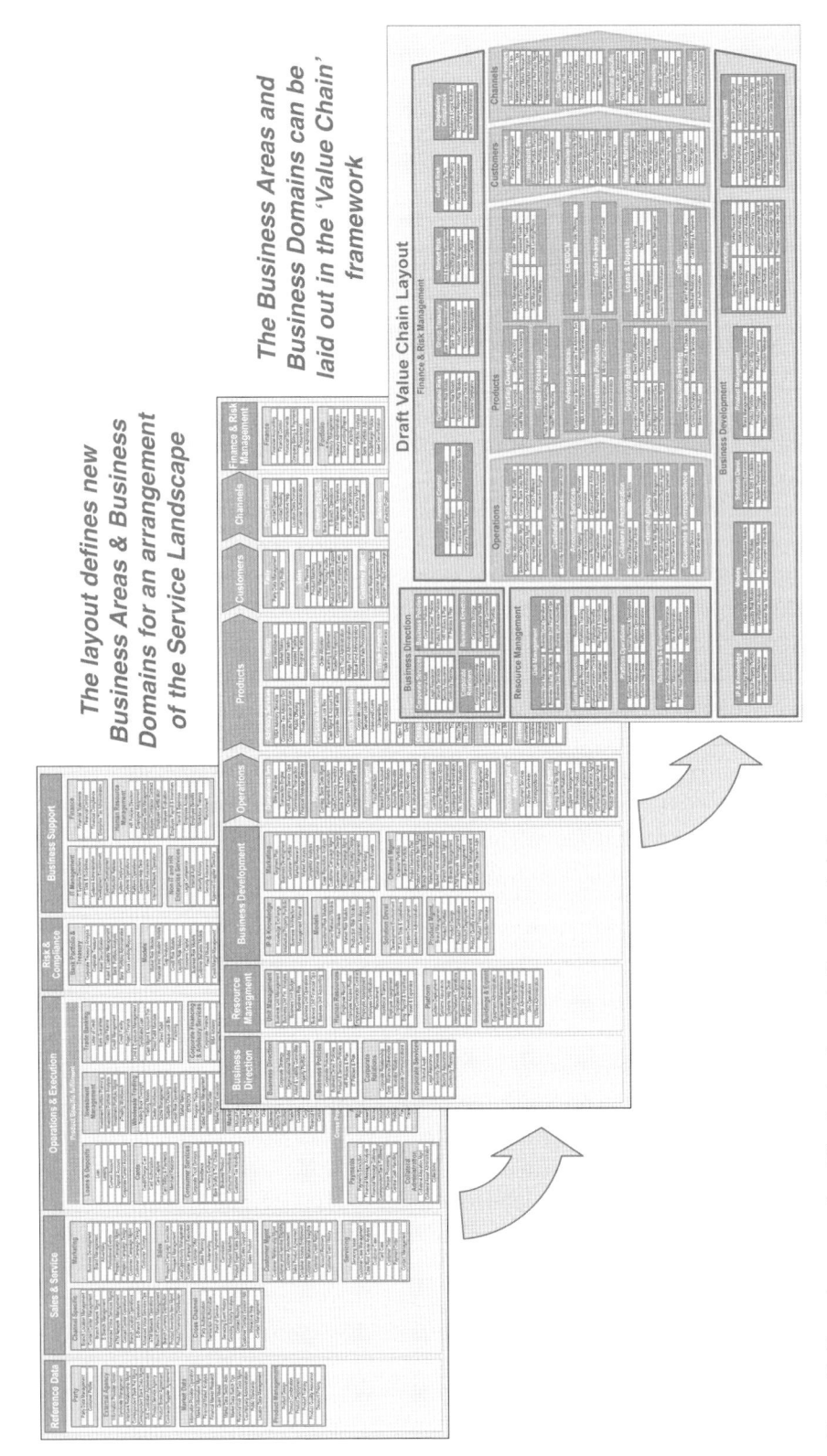

Figure 61: From the conventional Service Landscape to the value chain layout.

6 Assembling a representative enterprise blueprint

The Business Areas and Business Domains of the value chain layout are shown along with brief descriptions in Figure 60.

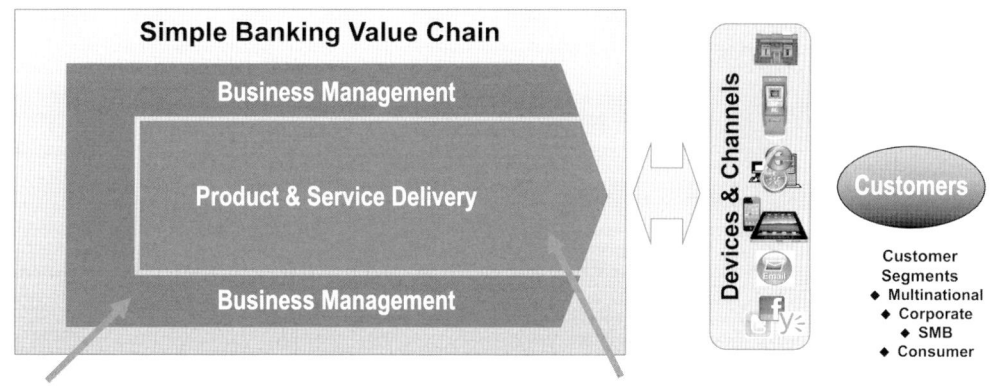

Simple Banking Value Chain

- Business Management
- Product & Service Delivery
- Business Management

Devices & Channels ↔ Customers

Customer Segments
- Multinational
- Corporate
- SMB
- Consumer

Business Management – defines the oversight, definition, development and support functions that surround and enable the core 'factory' that delivers products and services to customers

The Factory – contains the capabilities that are direclty involved in the delivery of services and products to customer

Figure 60: The scope of BIAN's M4 Bank model

To underscore the fact that the 'value chain' layout is simply a way to group and position the standard collection of Service Domains, figure 61 shows an intermediate layout where the Service Domains from the standard Service Landscape format are first reorganized into a second matrix format with the amended Business Areas and Business Domains that are used in the value chain layout. They are then repositioned into the framework of the value chain layout itself on the far right of the diagram.

■ 6.1　BUILDING THE ENTERPRISE BLUEPRINT FOR A BANK

This section describes the use of the BIAN Framework to develop an enterprise blueprint – the blueprint is often referred to as the 'bank on a page' view because it provides a concise representation of all the capabilities that make up the organization. The assembly of the enterprise blueprint for a particular financial institution involves three steps:
1. Select the Service Domains used by the enterprise;
2. Adapt the BIAN Service Domains as necessary;
3. Assemble the Service Domains in a structure matching the enterprise.

The three steps of the approach are summarized in figure 62. Each step is explained in more detail in the following sections.

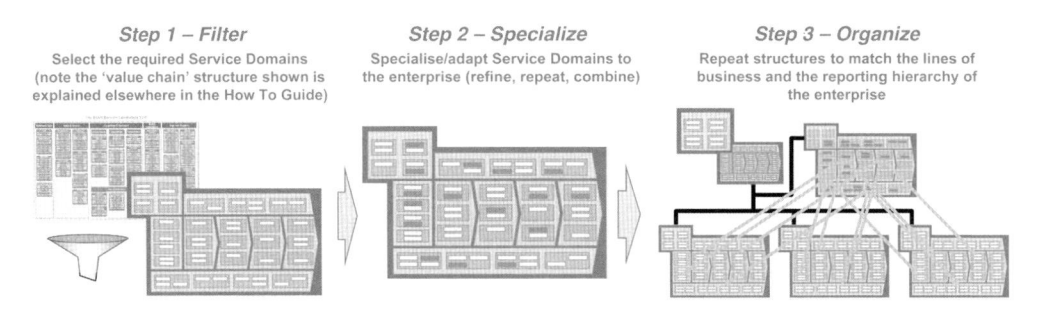

Figure 62: Three steps in developing an enterprise blueprint

Note: the approach is described as if the model is being defined to match the desired future state of the enterprise. Depending on the specific situation, the blueprint might be designed to reflect the current state and/or some intermediate states, particularly if a significant restructuring is anticipated.

6.1.1 Select Service Domains that match the enterprise activity

The first step is a simple filtering of the Service Domains of the Service Landscape to exclude any that support capabilities that are not required. As the BIAN landscape is intended to cover all possible activities that may be used in any bank, there may be product, channel and oversight activities that don't apply to a specific organization.

To streamline the process for members developing their own enterprise models, the BIAN Association intends to develop a collection of Service Landscape extracts suited to different types of bank and financial institutions. An initiative is currently under consideration with a leading Swiss academic body that will result in the development of a range of bank models based on established industry patterns using clusters of the BIAN Service Domains as the organizational building blocks.

An objective of this initiative is to define different operational partitions of a financial institution that can be viable stand-alone commercial entities (typically made up of several Service Domains). The anticipation is that the industry will continue to adapt and define optimized, specialized organizational structures that can be assembled more flexibly into different operating models.

In addition to this initiative, the BIAN Assocation will also develop standard example enterprise blueprints for different types of bank including:
- A local/regional bank (consumer and corporate customers);
- A national bank;
- A multi-national, full service bank;
- An investment bank;
- A hedge fund;
- A private bank;
- An Islamic bank.

Other types of banks and financial institutions may be added to the list. These examples will be developed in later editions of this book.

6.1.2 Adapt the general BIAN specifications as necessary

The BIAN Service Domains are intended to be canonical definitions of the 'elemental' capability building blocks, meaning that they define the mainstream features of a Service Domain in a way that can be consistently interpreted in different deployments. The techniques used to correctly scope and define the mainstream capabilities are described in Section 3.6.

BIAN Service Domains can be duplicated and specialized when the BIAN definition is too coarse-grained or combined when too fine grained. An example area of the landscape where this might be necessary is product fulfillment. BIAN defines generalized Service Domains for most main product types – an organization may well have many variants of these primary product types with their own P&L and delivery features that require their own appropriately renamed Service Domains.

The general BIAN Service Domain specifications may also need to be augmented with specialized features. These features may be applied to the Service Domains and their Service Operations. They may be needed for many reasons including to deal with local geo-political requirements, to support unique/differentiating business features and to address legacy systems behaviors.

The given names for BIAN Service Domains may also be changed to match the prevailing terminology in the target organization (if the business role is not changed). As the blueprint only contains the Service Domains as building blocks, any feature specializations within the Service Domains that may be required for the organization are not important at this level.

6.1.3 Assemble Service Domains in a structure matching the enterprise

The final step involves assembling the selected and amended Service Domains in a structure that corresponds to the organizational layout of the enterprise. This needs to consider the following main organizational considerations:

- **Discrete lines of business** – these can be based on geographic and/or market segment lines e.g. retail financial services in a country, global trading, etc.
- **Centralized operations** – this can be regional or global operations centers that support multiple lines of business e.g. a regional payments center, central training services.
- **Legal entity structure** – there can be head office, regional and local management units, each with their own legal entity structures and obligations e.g. a global holding company with regional and local subsidiaries.

When building the enterprise blueprint a value chain 'element' is completed for each line of business. The content of each value chain element only needs to include those Service Domains that represent functions performed within that line of business. This involves applying the same filtering as was done at the enterprise level in the first step for every line of business to create the collection of line of business value chain elements. Figure 63 shows an example of two different value chains.

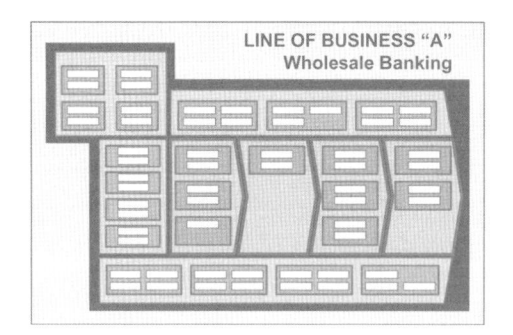

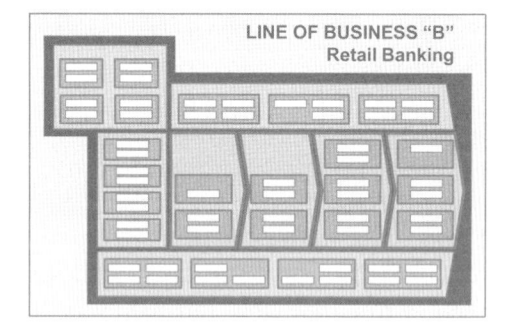

Figure 63: Two value chain elements representing different lines of business

One important advantage of the value chain layout is that it can be adapted to handle cross lines of business structures. These are needed in two specific instances in an enterprise:
- When activities that are performed at the local/line of business level in two or more locations need to be consolidated at a regional level – for example for the credit risk management of a multinational customer relationship.
- When a shared/centralized service is offered to two or more locations – for example, centralized payments services or trade clearing and settlement processing.

In these situations, an additional value chain 'element' is completed containing only those Service Domains that handle those common functions that need to be coordinated and any shared/centralized functions. The way that common and shared functions for two lines of business are linked to a cross line of business element is shown in figure 64.

The final aspect of the enterprise blueprint reflects the organization's legal entity structure. As the value chain model includes all the business capabilities that make up each individual operating unit, it can be used as a management dashboard to capture the reporting for all entities within that unit or 'element'. As the same value chain layout is used for a line of business or regional reporting center, the management region of the value chain can be used to support a reporting hierarchy from the individual lines of business through any regional units into the central head office management function.

6   Assembling a representative enterprise blueprint

Shared/Centralized Services – a connecting/proxy Service Domain links the local line of business to a shared facility

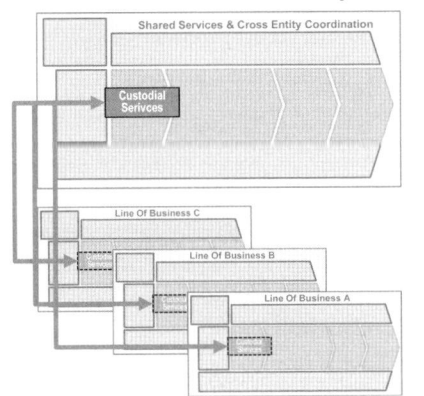

Coordinated Services – Consolidated Cross Entity views are coordinated through a central 'reporting' Service Domain instance

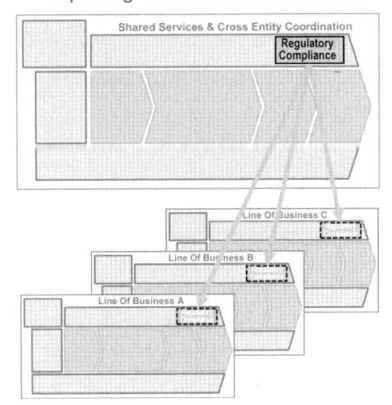

Figure 64: Two lines of business connected to a regional operation

This combined structure is shown in figure 65.

The Value Chain framework is used as a performance dashboard for the LOBs and Regional operations, reporting up to the Head Office

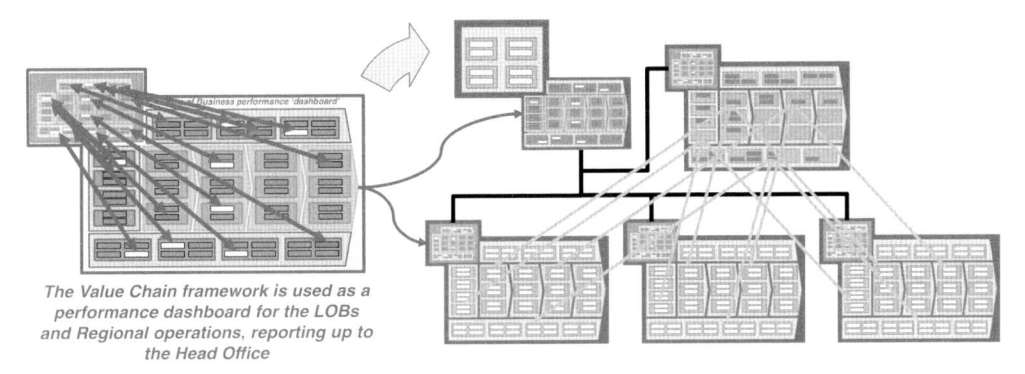

Figure 65: M4Bank with local units, regional and head office reporting

The line of business structure, make-up of any regional oversight or shared operations, and the legal entity reporting structure for the simple example above can clearly be adapted to represent the corresponding structure of any bank in order to produce their own specific enterprise blueprint.

6.1.4   Matching the enterprise segmentation approach

Different banks adopt different approaches to market segmentation, matching types of products and services to specific types of customer. An issue for banks interpreting the BIAN model is mapping their segmentation to the products and customer types reflected in the BIAN Service Landscape. To provide the greatest flexibility, BIAN seeks to define generic product types independent of the target customer type. These general products can then be aligned and, if necessary, specialized to support the target customer groups. In this way, a generic product Service Domain may be specialized to create multiple product fulfillment variants to match a specific bank's segmentation.

This concept is shown in figure 66 where generic product types are listed in the vertical dimension with generic customer categories across the top. Examples of specialized product variants can be seen in the matrix. This is an early stage concept for BIAN and it will be refined for later releases.

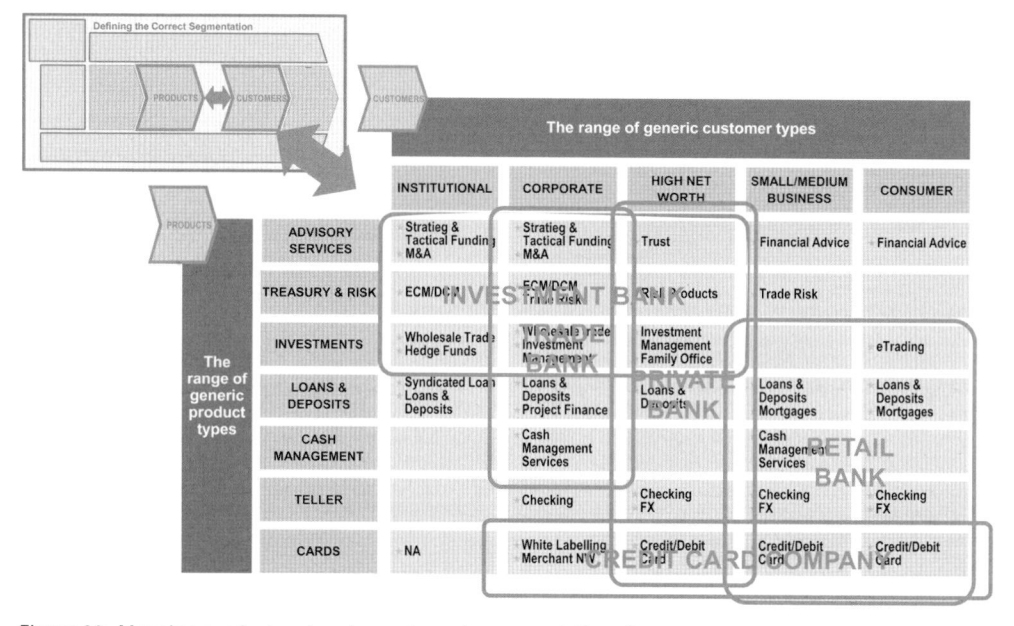

Figure 66: Mapping product and customer types to segmentation views

The same matrix layout has also been used to show the typical segmentation footprint of different types of bank. As this draft model is developed, additional detail in terms of product and customer dimensions and content can be added, as will different organization type profiles.

■ 6.2   CASE STUDY

Steven Van Wyk, Executive Vice President, Head of Technology and Operations, PNC Financial Services Group explains the benefits of aligning the bank's enterprise architecture to the BIAN model:

"The BIAN model fits perfectly in line with how we view enterprise architecture (EA) at PNC. One of the first steps we took as an organization was to bring a business perspective to enterprise architecture. To us, technology is not just a collection of servers and software, but rather a set of technical solutions that are aligned to specific business capabilities and functions.

Adding the business view
To begin, we looked at every application that existed in our portfolio and mapped it to the aligned BIAN Service Domains (specific business functions) in our EA management tool.

This gave us a clear view of systems that were providing similar or overlapping solutions, which could be optimized, while also creating a consistent and replicable way to evaluate proposed new solutions for our application portfolio.

Creating a bank on a page
This allowed us to create a business-driven 'bank on a page' heat map, using BIAN's M4 model, to show what areas were suffering from obsolescence and compliance issues. As we move forward, we can align our risk and project portfolio views to the same bank on a page overview.

Using BIAN's framework, we can move our core platforms into a componentized framework, which allows us to manage our transformation in logical steps that are aligned with the overall business strategy.

Positioning for disruptive industry change
Defining our technology into capabilities in this way also sets us up for future innovation. The proliferation of FinTech is setting new expectations with new business models that sometimes compete directly with banks. We are evolving our core banking capabilities into a componentized framework that will allow us to embrace evolving business expectations and customer demands. The search for innovation partnerships becomes easier when you are no longer tied to the past era's monolithic application approaches. We are exploring open banking APIs, for example, in a collaborative project with BIAN and Carnegie Mellon University.

By aligning with the BIAN framework we are assured that our enterprise architecture can continuously adapt to new market and technology demands."

7 An enterprise blueprint is a framework for analysis

An enterprise blueprint built using BIAN Service Domain partitions is a particularly good framework for management analysis and planning for several reasons:
- **Stable over time** - the roles of the discrete business capabilities represented by Service Domain partitions do not vary over time. The way they might execute and the patterns of collaboration that might be involved will change as new practices and solutions evolve but their specific purpose and hence their position in the blueprint is unlikely to change. As a result, a model built using these elements will itself be highly stable and enduring.
- **Concise, implementation-independent view** - beyond the broad-brush scope of business areas, the blueprint does not presume any specific organizational or technical approach. It can also be interpreted both by business and technical architects consistently, so bridging a design gap that often exists with other (incompatible) business and technology enterprise modeling approaches.
- **Suited for overlays/attribution** - the elements that make up the model can be associated with resources and current or target performance measures to support a wide range of business performance assessments.
- **High-level design** - the blueprint can also act as the top-level design of underlying organizational, procedural and information systems solutions, providing a planning framework for targeting investment and solution development.

The enterprise blueprint provides a framework that can support a wide range of planning and analysis functions. A list of projects that might make use of an enterprise blueprint are listed here, see also figure 67:
- **Application portfolio rationalization** - the target requirements and current application capabilities are overlain and shortfalls identified.
- **Mergers & acquisitions** - the combined application portfolios of the merged organizations can be mapped and, based on target capabilities, the optimum systems selected for the merged organizations.
- Etc....

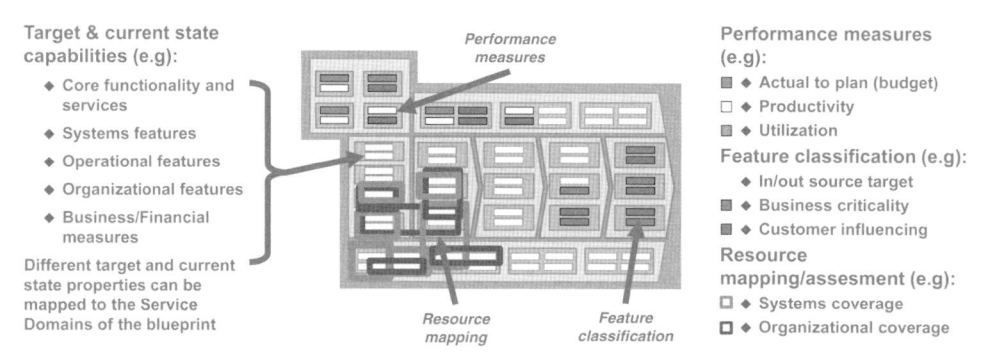

Figure 67: Enterprise analysis: a measurement framework

The model can be used to capture a wide range of current and target state capabilities, performance measures, operational features and resource mapping. The number and range of attributes that can be developed is unlimited. In addition, it is possible to combine and relate different measures with each other.

These projects and many other similar types of initiatives exploit the enterprise blueprint in a similar way: It can be used to associate required features and properties with parts of the business aligned to Service Domains. Note that the approaches described below may also be applied to coarser grained clusters of Service Domains within a Business Domain as appropriate.

Performance measurements can be set and tracked for these parts of the business and resources, such as staff and systems. These can be mapped across parts of the business to assess coverage, see figure 68. The following sections describe these types of use in more detail.

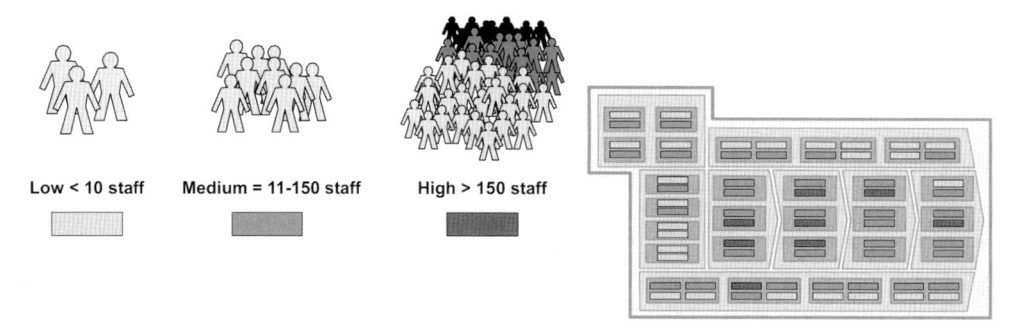

Figure 68: Enterprise analysis: a measurement framework for cost of staff

■ 7.1 THE BIAN SPECIFICATIONS CAN BE AUGMENTED

The BIAN Service Domain and Service Operations can be augmented to provide as much detail as may be required. We have alread discussedthe approach that can be taken to expand the features checklists in order to include the prevailing or target functionality for the Service Domain. There is also the opportunity for further specialization based on geopolitical scale and sophistication/maturity.

The Service Domains and Service Operations can also be matched to industry standards and proprietary specifications. The BIAN Association has completed a joint exercise with IFX to map a selection of Service Domain Service Operations to the established messaging standard. More examples of IFX message mapping will be developed in the future. Meanwhile, a white paper documenting the mapping exercise is available on both the BIAN and IFX websites. In addition, IBM (a BIAN Association member) is working on mapping its proprietary IFW model to the BIAN standard.

7.1.1 Feature attribution

In addition to adding functional detail to the model, a wide range of 'attributions' can be associated with a Service Domain. These features can relate to the supporting system properties or wider operational and business considerations. The features usually define target state requirements, adding additional insights to the target state functionality.

For some attributions the approach to assigning a value or rating is a simple direct assessment. For others, there can be a simple associated technique to determine which Service Domains make a specific contribution and to compare Service Domains against one another to obtain a comparative ranking. It is not the role of the BIAN Association to define these techniques, but by providing examples, it is intended that members and others applying the BIAN standard will develop their own approaches to leverage the standard.

As can be imagined, some attributions are simple rankings that can be applied across the blueprint quite easily, whilst others are a little more involved. Two examples are explained in a little more detail below.

In the specific case of *strategic intensity,* the Service Domains receive a relative rating at three levels:

1. **Commodity** - the performance of the Service Domain is commodity-based in nature – there are no optional features that provide differentiation – all participants needs to perform to the same basic level.
2. **Prevailing practices** - there is a range of operating capabilities and the organization needs to aspire to matching prevailing 'good' practices so that it is not compared negatively with its peer competitors.
3. **Differentiated** - there is some aspect of the operation that is unique or distinct from the competitors that provides a differentiating advantage in the market (faster/better/cheaper).

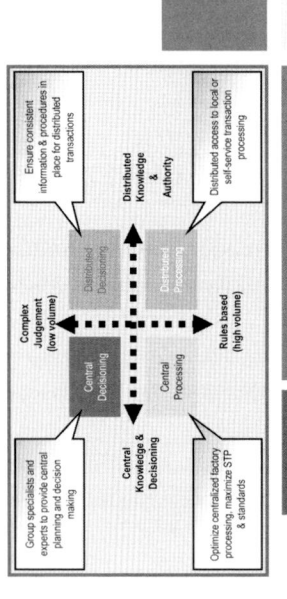

	Operational Rationalization Approaches	Organizational Rationalization Approaches	Systems Rationalization Approaches
CENTRAL DECISIONING Consolidate skills and expertise at the center. Ensure appropriate task scheduling/prioritization is in place and provide effective access from across the organization	▪ eliminate duplicate units ▪ consolidate operational resources ▪ define/leverage best practices ▪ establish shared service prioritization approach ▪ ensure access and adoption	▪ establish skills/expertise based centers of excellence ▪ define roles and responsibilities that leverage high value staff	▪ provide dedicated function specific support systems (likely to be function specialized) ▪ provide request capture and result distribution capabilities to link to the broader business community
CENTRAL PROCESSING Consolidate transaction processing in a shared/central facility. Minimize variations, maximize automation and ensure effective access from across the organization	▪ minimize processing variations ▪ streamline/optimize processes ▪ establish effective exception handling ▪ address potentially conflicting needs and priorities across service subscribers	▪ simplify tasks/leverage technology to reduce required skills/training levels ▪ implement effective exceptions and escalation handling arrangements ▪ establish optimal work scheduling locate to leverage staff demographics	▪ eliminate systems/application redundancy ▪ maximize automation, streamline processing (STP) ▪ enforce comprehensive technology standards
DISTRIBUTED PROCESSING Support automated rules based transactional decisions at distributed points across the organization (e.g. at branches) with structured procedures, standard information and decision criteria	▪ minimize processing variations ▪ streamline/optimize processes ▪ ensure standard information needs and decision criteria are established	▪ implement context specific training and support to ensure consistency ▪ implement access control to ensure qualified parties only participate ▪ leverage self service potential	▪ deploy standard rules based systems ▪ ensure integrated, standards based process design and data management is employed in systems ▪ leverage CBT and workflow systems capabilities
DISTRIBUTED DECISIONING Support local specialist decision making for high value and/or experienced based negotiation with effective procedures and information provisioning	▪ ensure authority is delegated to appropriate local units ▪ ensure required skills/qualifications and procedures are in place ▪ ensure activity reporting is supported to continually refine approaches	▪ establish clear business roles and responsibilities for local interpretation ▪ ensure staff give priority to high value activities ▪ consider incentive/appraisal tools ▪ ensure performance audit/assurance	▪ deploy standard decision support, analysis and information distribution systems ▪ integrate transaction capture and reporting systems to support audit/assurance reporting

Figure 70: Example approaches associated with an attribution

7 An enterprise blueprint is a framework for analysis

The assignment of competitive intensity to the Service Domains makes use of an analysis of the strategic intent of the enterprise. Given the strategic goals and objectives, it is necessary to identify which Service Domains contribute directly to the achievement of those goals and how they do so (Business Scenarios can be used to achieve this mapping if it is not obvious).

Two other attributions for *sourcing and centralization* use a quadrant ranking technique to classify a Service Domain. The quadrants for a centralization assessment are shown in figure 69.

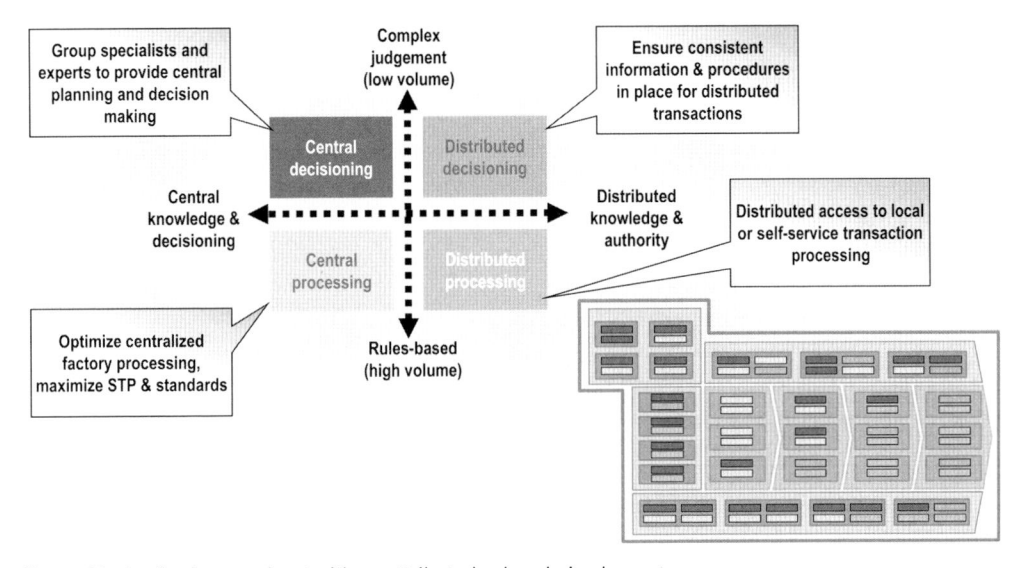

Figure 69: Attribution quadrant with an attributed value chain element

The Service Domains are assigned to a quadrant based on their business and operational characteristics. Using this classification, appropriate strategies and techniques can be associated with the organizational, operational and systems-related approaches for the Service Domain, see figure 70.

As noted, a wide range of attribution types and attribution techniques and guidelines can be developed and applied to the enterprise blueprint to help clarify the requirements/intent for the Service Domain-aligned business capabilities that make up the organization.

These attributions can be referenced in different combinations to inform investment decisions and help align subsequent investment projects.

7.2 TRACK BUSINESS AND TECHNICAL PERFORMANCE

The enterprise blueprint can also be used as a management dashboard. Because it represents a stable view of the capabilities that make up the organization, a wide range of performance measures can be associated with these individual 'units' and used to set targets and track performance against plan.

The measures can address systems performance or can target wider operational and organizational measures. As with attribution, the list of possible measurements is unlimited, some examples include the elements shown in figure 71.

Different systems and business cost and performance measures can be associated with the framework:

SYSTEMS RELATED COSTS
- Development & deployment
- Training, support & assurance
- Technology/platform operations
- Licensing/subscription/purchases

NON-SYSTEMS RELATED COSTS
- Workforce utilization
- Workforce training
- Location/equipment/utility/consumables
- Fixed capital allocation
- Fees/licensing
- Management overhead &support

Costs can be further analysed in terms including:
- Own Vs allocated
- Fixed/variable
- Book value/depreciating costs
- Repeating/ad hoc
- Volume discounts

SYSTEMS PERFORMANCE MEASURES
- Machine utilization
- Operating profile – schedule
- Security/resilience
- Performance profile
- User headcount, skill level & schedules
- Variability/configurability
- Advanced technology/practices

BUSINESS PERFORMANCE MEASURES
- Staff utilization/productivity
- Operating budgets
- User headcount/skills profile
- Working/commited capital
- Business criticality/contribution
- Reputational/customer exposure/risk profile

Figure 71: Systems and operational cost and performance measures

The enterprise blueprint itself can be used to format a management dashboard, with values/color coding related to the Service Domains to provide a succinct visual representation of the organization's operating state against the plan.

7.3 OVERLAY RESOURCES TO IDENTIFY SHORTFALLS

A final type of use of the enterprise blueprint is to overlay resources to identify shortfalls in the level of support. This approach was used in Section 5.11.5, where current systems and commercial offering were compared to the Service Domains for a point solution.

The same mapping approach, optionally using the finer grained feature lists for Service Domains, can be used across regions or the entire blueprint. Resources that can be mapped include systems/applications, personnel and utilities such as technology platforms, building and equipment facilities.

7   An enterprise blueprint is a framework for analysis

As described in Section 5.11.5, resource mappings can be used to highlight shortfalls such as gaps, duplication and misaligned resources, as summarized in figure 72.

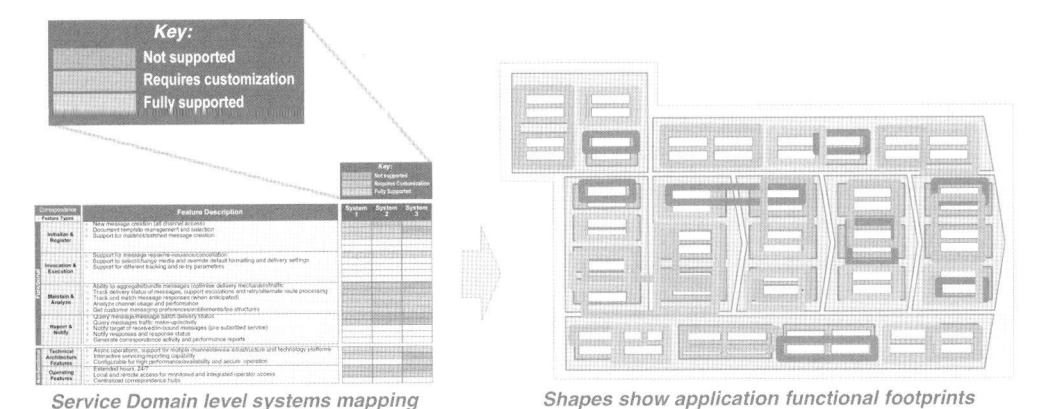

Figure 72: Overlay of systems on an enterprise blueprint revealing shortfalls

One final observation, having described the definition of the enterprise blueprint and the different types of analysis it can support. The elements of the blueprint aligning to Service Domains and those same Service Domains can be formally mapped to the supporting systems. As a result, the blueprint provides a representation of the business that can capture business needs and priorities and relate this to the underlying supporting systems as highlighted in figure 73.

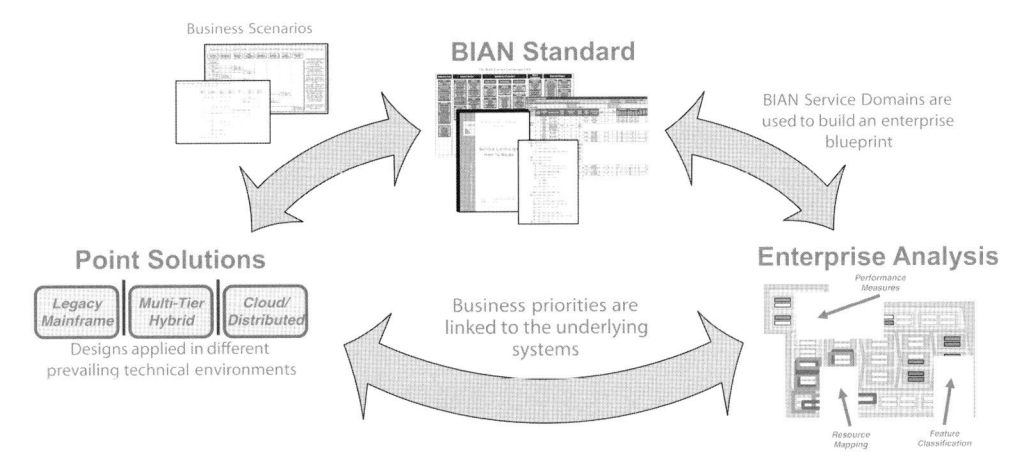

Figure 73: BIAN designs applied to point and enterprise solution

■ 7.4   ANALYSIS SUPPORTED BY THE ENTERPRISE BLUEPRINT

The BIAN Service Domains define discrete business capabilities at a high level. Once the Service Domains have been mapped onto an enterprise blueprint, the Service Domain-aligned elements of the blueprint can be augmented with additional specification details covering the target functional and non-functional requirements.

The BIAN Service Landscape can be used to support business and technical planning and analysis. Three broad categories can be considered:

1. **Capability overlays** - typically using more detailed functional specifications of the Service Domains; resources such as organizational units and, more commonly, production systems/business applications can be mapped to reveal gaps, duplications and misalignments.
2. **Performance measures** - target and current measurements can be defined and tracked for business and technology-related aspects. In this way the blueprint can act as a management dashboard.
3. **Feature or property** - different properties/characteristics can be associated with the Service Domain elements to guide planning decisions and analysis. For example these might include relative cost, business criticality and more complex characteristics such as centralized/decentralized, insourced/outsourced. The possible attributions are practically unlimited and can be selected and calibrated to match the types of insights/decisions they support.

The range of approaches, techniques and possible uses of the enterprise blueprint are extensive. Often the attributions will be applied to related groups of Service Domains clustered in Business Domains as the individual Service Domains can be too fine grained for the high-level analysis. A summary of the above description is captured in figure 74.

Target & Current State Capabilities (e.g):
- Core functionality and services
- Systems features
- Operational features
- Organizational features
- Business/Financial measures

Different target and current state properties can be mapped to the Service Domains of the blueprint

Performance Measures

Resource Mapping

Feature Classification

Performance Measures (e.g):
- Actual to plan (budget)
- Productivity
- Utilization

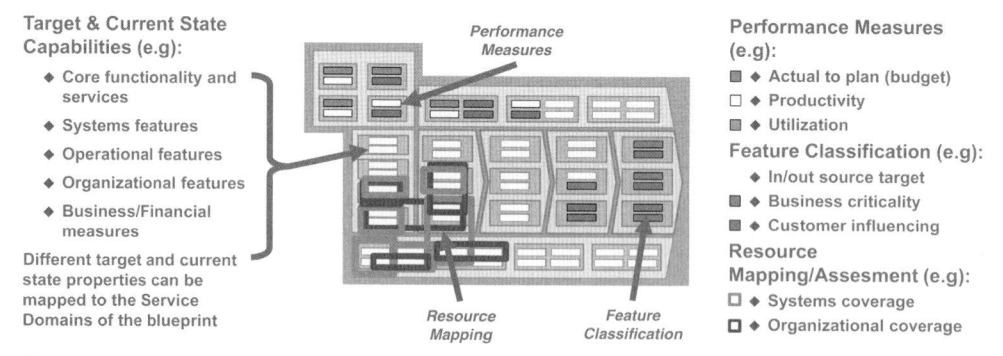

Feature Classification (e.g.):
- In/out source target
- Business criticality
- Customer influencing

Resource Mapping/Assesment (e.g):
- Systems coverage
- Organizational coverage

Figure 74: Using the enterprise blueprint for planning & analysis

■ 7.5 LINKING BETWEEN BUSINESS AND TECHNICAL ASSESSMENTS

The final observation in the previous section relating to the use of BIAN Service Domains to create an enterprise blueprint notes that the same elements in the blueprint map to those used to implement targeted solutions. Consequently, the link between the high-level planning and analysis performed using the blueprint and the underlying systems is greatly simplified. As a result of the common BIAN Service Domain partitions, investment decisions can be related directly to the underlying systems solutions.

PART V

Appendix 1: Service Domain descriptions (January 2018)

Service Domain Name	Description
Account Reconciliation	Match, reconcile and resolve identified discrepancies between accounts. Includes nostro/vostro arrangements.
Account Recovery	Handle recovery for a customer account where the standard recovery arrangements have been exhausted and a recovery plan is needed, which can include some degree of principal write-down and repayment restructuring.
Accounts Receivable	Manage the tracking, chasing and receipt of scheduled payments against issued invoices.
ACH Fulfillment	Operate the ACH access gateway.
Advanced Voice Services Management	Configure the PBX (telephony) channel for access, including embedded rules for self-service and routing, IVR capabilities if available. Note that aspects of the configuration can be dynamically optimized as necessary.
Advanced Voice Services Operations	Operate the telephone channel infrastructure, including the IVR and any other automated devices as appropriate. This includes default routing rules and intra-day/session adjustments to deal with peak load or other operational variations.
Advertising	Develop the plan for, and oversee, advertising campaign activity, including budget and resource management.
Approved Supplier Directory	Select and maintain a suitable collection of suppliers covering the range of requirements. Track performance and retain and deselect suppliers to maintain a competitive range of suppliers.
Archive Services	Provide long term archiving and retrieval services for documents and electronic media.
Asset and Liability Management	A central policy and direction capability that reviews consolidated bank P&L profile and performance, and defines and directs asset and liability policies. Also sanctions and/or influences large transactions.
Asset Securitization	Determine and select assets for securitization as needed to maintain and optimize the bank's portfolio. Administer the securitization process.
ATM Network Management	Configure the allocation of products and services across the ATM network and oversee ATM access registration and controls.

Service Domain Name	Description
ATM Network Operations	Operate the ATM network, including overseeing the physical movement of cash and documents, and the handling of device alerts and outages.
Bank Drafts and Travelers Checks	Administer the pricing, recording and generation of Bank Drafts and Travelers Checks.
Bank Guarantee	Orchestrate the pricing, issuance and subsequent fulfillment activities for Bank Guarantees as used in corporate/correspondent trade and project finance activity.
Bank Portfolio Administration	Consolidate, ratify, correct and present timely transaction information to support the analysis of the bank's consolidated 'book of business'.
Bank Portfolio Analysis	Define and maintain a broad collection of analytical views and ad-hoc analyses into the consolidated book of business for the enterprise. Develop and refine analyses in response to events and detected trends.
Branch Currency Distribution	Schedule and coordinate the secure distribution of cash inventory across the branch and ATM networks.
Branch Currency Management	Manage the secure movement of cash and currencies between branches/ATMs and central holdings.
Branch Location Management	Oversee/manage the day-to-day bank branch location activity, maintaining branch plans and budgets and reporting on branch activity.
Branch Location Operations	Administer the day-to-day activity within the branch - allocating tellers and customer relationship managers to positions and tracking availability/performance, ensuring cash floats and product consumables are on hand and that all facilities are in working order.
Branch Network Management	Configure the available services and products (ATM, office/table and teller assignments) for the branch locations across the overall branch portfolio. (Note an ATM is treated as a specific type of branch location in the BIAN model.)
Branch Portfolio	Evaluate coverage and relative performance of branches. Optimize product allocation and marketing activity across the available branch network.
Brand Management	Respond to events that potentially damage the brand or provide an opportunity to strengthen/leverage brand awareness.
Brokered Product	Administer any third party coordination with brokered products and service supplied through any bank channel.
Building Maintenance	Administer and execute site and utility maintenance and repair activities (building refit and decoration etc.).
Business Architecture	Develop and maintain a business architecture conforming to the corporate strategy and plan and operational configuration of the enterprise.
Business Development	Define, implement, track and assess the new business development plans for the enterprise or specific business divisions. This can cover business activities such as new market segment entry, product coverage and product specification development, brand development, new customer acquisition and existing customer cross-sell/up-sell and retention.

Service Domain Name	Description
Business Risk Models	Develop and maintain models that assess commercial/business exposures.
Business Unit Accounting	Maintain business unit accounting records.
Business Unit Direction	Define and orchestrate business unit activity against the unit business strategy and operating plan.
Business Unit Financial Analysis	Track and assess the financial performance of the business unit against projected performance and respond as appropriate.
Business Unit Financial Operations	Authorize and book payments and receipts against the unit's financial transaction account.
Business Unit Management	Track and report on business unit activity and financial performance.
Card Authorization	Execute the decision-based authorization and recording of proposed card transactions through the merchant network.
Card Billing and Payments	Process card customer statement issuance and billing and payments processing.
Card Capture	Capture the card payment transaction through the merchant network.
Card Case	Capture, track, resolve and report on card-related transactional disputes (includes card use and payment issues).
Card Clearing	Orchestrate: a) the capture and consolidation of card financial transactions originating from various sources, such as POS Network, E-Commerce Gateway, ATM Network or Card Case Management, and b) clearing of the transactions from the Acquirers to the Issuers through the Card Networks.
Card Collections	Administer the recovery of outstanding amounts from cancelled card accounts through internal or external collection agencies. This may involve negotiating payment terms or interest write-down.
Card eCommerce Operation	Orchestrate the processing of e-commerce transactions for authentication, authorization and capture of the financial transactions.
Card Financial Settlement	Orchestrate the settlement of the transactions between the Issuers and the Acquirers through the Card Networks.
Card Network Participant Facility	Orchestrate the activities related to the inclusion of new Acquirers and Issuers in the Card Network, their terms and conditions and their status.
Card Terminal Administration	Administer the POS Network including the inventory, terminal characteristics, deployment and status of the POS devices.
Card Terminal Operation	Handle POS operations including processing, capture and tracking of the transactions originating at the Point of Sale devices.
Card Transaction Switch	Orchestrate the switching and routing of Card Authorization and Financial transactions received through the Card POS Network, Card E-Commerce Gateway, or the ATM Network from the Acquirer to the Issuer through the Card Networks.
Case Root Cause Analysis	Analyze case resolution records for insights into product/service/operational weaknesses and to detect possible credit/fraud patterns.

Service Domain Name	Description
Cash Management and Account Services	Orchestrate the range of Cash Management services available for corporates (includes cash handling, account reconciliation, cash concentration, ACH, Positive and Reverse Positive Pay, Sweep and Wire services).
Central Cash Handling	Administer the central inventory of physical currencies and the allocation to/from branches/ATMs and with other banks and central banks to remain within desired levels of holdings across the branch network.
Channel Activity Analysis	Track and analyze channel activity to support relationship development, to detect unwanted behavior and constrain channel use as necessary.
Channel Activity History	Consolidated customer channel usage activity is captured to support activity analysis and is referenced for access authorization.
Channel Portfolio	Evaluate the coverage and relative performance of different channels with respect to the blend of service and product activity. Optimize channel use to minimize costs and enhance customer experience.
Cheque Lock Box	Consolidation of retail checks for a corporation (could be classified as another Cash Management service).
Cheque Processing	Process paper checks (MICR number handling) - creating payment transaction record stream.
Collateral Allocation Management	Administer the holding and allocation of collateral on behalf of a customer.
Collateral Asset Administration	Maintain the status of a collateral item, including scheduled and ad-hoc valuation and confirmation of the correct completion of scheduled maintenance tasks.
Collections	Administer the recovery and/or liquidation of collateral against problem accounts.
Commission Agreement	Maintain and administer the terms and transactions for employee and broker commissions.
Commissions	Capture and structure commissionable transactions that are subsequently processed against an existing commission agreement.
Company Billing and Payments	Handle the company billing and payments activity for company sales and purchases.
Competitor Analysis	Solicit, consolidate and analyze competitor-specific public domain data to develop competitor insights and comparisons.
Compliance Reporting	Report on applicable compliance checks that are applied to a transaction or facility fulfillment procedure.
Consumer Advisory Services	Provide consumer financial advice.
Consumer Investments	Handle the consumer front-end trading requests. These will typically be blocked/netted for market execution.
Consumer Loan	Fulfillment of a range of loan products for consumer clients.
Contact Center Management	Define and maintain the layout/ assignment of contact center resources to different contact traffic types (e.g. product/segment/ issue). This can include automated facilities as well as personnel.
Contact Center Operations	Administer the day-to-day activity in the contact center - allocate positions and track staff availability and performance.

Appendix 1: Service Domain descriptions (January 2018)

Service Domain Name	Description
Contact Dialogue	Handle/structure the customer narrative - consolidate and present data and guidelines, provide standard dialogue/scripting, provoke questions when appropriate, capture key data including relationship and sales triggers. Ensure the correct sequencing, content and derived actions are performed/initiated. Leverage the session as appropriate to provide customer notifications, status updates and undertake sales/marketing efforts.
Contact Handler	Handle the customer interactive contact, including the launching of one or more channel/device-specific sessions as necessary within the contact.
Contact Routing	Contact Routing tracks servicing resource availability, further qualifies and potentially verifies the contact and makes an optimal routing decision. This can include generating a screen pop if CTI is available and supporting multi-channel operations and onward routing of unfinished contacts.
Continuity Planning	Develop, maintain and test continuity plans and supporting facilities for an appropriate range of possible failure scenarios.
Contractor/Supplier Agreement	Maintain and administer master and project/task-specific contractor/supplier legal agreements. Confirm on-going compliance.
Contribution Analysis	Execute contribution analysis across customer/product activity to expose business development opportunities.
Contribution Models	Develop and refine contribution models to detect underdeveloped business relationships and other opportunities.
Corporate Alliance/Stakeholder	Manage key alliance and stakeholder relationship - define tasks needed to develop and maintain contact and ensure relevant information is shared as appropriate.
Corporate Communications	Develop and distribute key corporate messages as needed to support the strategy and maintain the enterprise reputation and brand.
Corporate Current Account	Orchestrate a corporate financial services account with the standard range of services and fees.
Corporate Deposits	Orchestrate the different flavors of corporate deposit accounting facilities (including term or demand) including the handling of associated services and fees.
Corporate Events	Administer the correct allocation of entitlements to a customer arising from corporate events (such as dividend and interest payments).
Corporate Finance	A fee or commission-based project providing specialized financing advice (tactical and strategic) to a corporation.
Corporate Lease	Fulfillment of a range of loan products for corporate clients for the purpose of leasing.
Corporate Loan	Fulfillment of a range of loan products for corporate clients.
Corporate Policies	Develop and communicate corporate policies that govern business execution.
Corporate Relationships	Manage corporate relationships with key parties such as major clients, political and industry groups, user associations etc.

Service Domain Name	Description
Corporate Strategy	Define and communicate the corporate strategy and plan. Direct business activity to meet, refine and improve the corporate goals and approaches.
Corporate Tax Advisory	A fee or commission-based project providing tax-specific advice, typically for corporate customers.
Corporate Treasury	Orchestrate the consolidation and presentation of summary transaction details in order to assemble a timely and accurate view of the overall treasury position of the bank at any one time.
Corporate Treasury Analysis	Track the consolidated treasury positions for the bank (includes liquidity and capital adequacy) and initiate interbank and market trades and hedging as needed to remain within desired boundaries.
Corporate Trust Services	Provide the range of fee-based trust services, typically offered to high net-worth customers.
Correspondence	Orchestrate the production of pre-formatted correspondence and batches of correspondence (e.g. mail shots). Optimize delivery bundling and channel selection. Route inbound correspondence.
Correspondent Bank	Fulfils a correspondent bank agreement between the bank and another bank, automated clearing house, etc. Handles the clearing and settlement of payments to/from the correspondent.
Correspondent Bank Data Management	Maintain correspondent bank details including the capture of transaction activity to track reciprocity.
Correspondent Bank Relationship Management	Handle the negotiation, development and tracking of reciprocal correspondent relationships.
Counterparty Administration	Maintain and provide access to the counterparty reference details to support trading/payment activity. This includes SWIFT addresses, standard settlement instructions that are published. The data is typically acquired using a market feed for the default values, but the facility can support the maintenance of specific details and instructions that apply to the counterparty relationship overriding the public default.
Counterparty Risk	Maintain and administer a counterparty risk rating.
Credit Facility	Maintain the availability and allocation of a negotiated credit line or facility for a corporate customer, including subsidiary allocations where appropriate.
Credit Management	A bank-wide function to qualify credit pricing for offered products and services to reflect the bank's appetite to write the business (overrides the standard product pricing procedure).
Credit Risk Models	Develop and maintain models for counterparty, issuer, and portfolio risk for all contracts, instruments and (sub-)portfolios respectively.
Credit Risk Operations	Provide an execution level check of credit exposure for market trading activity.
Credit/Charge Card	Orchestrate the scheduled maintenance and transactional activities associated with credit/debit card product fulfillment.
Credit/Margin Management	Determine and refine credit and margin directives and policies to reflect the overall risk/reward appetite of the organization and govern credit decisioning.

Appendix 1: Service Domain descriptions (January 2018)

Service Domain Name	Description
Currency Exchange	This is an over-the-counter service where currency is exchanged, and the transaction uses preferential rates and can include transaction fees. Note in some cases traveler's checks can be handled as a pseudo currency within this capability. Note also that Branch and teller currency inventory is administered by Branch Currency Management and Branch Currency Distribution Service Domains.
Current Account	Orchestrate a consumer checking/demand deposit account with typical range of services and fees.
Custody Administration	Administer the securities scrip (paper and electronic) for a custodial arrangement.
Customer Access Entitlement	Maintain the details of the products, services and channel access that the customer has in place. This profile is referenced in servicing and fulfillment activity. The view may also be compared to the full range of eligible products and services to identify business development opportunities.
Customer Agreement	Maintain a structured legal customer agreement. Note that a customer can be a complex corporate entity with multiple subsidiaries operating in different geopolitical areas. The customer agreement is linked to as many Sales Product Agreements as needed for all in-force products.
Customer Behavioral Insights	Apply behavioral analysis to customer event history to maintain ratings/scores (such as propensity to buy) and detect life events or trends.
Customer Behavior Models	Assess the coverage and impact of the portfolio of customer behavior models, and develop and refine the portfolio of available models.
Customer Behavioral Insights	Apply behavioral analysis to customer event history to maintain ratings/scores (such as propensity to buy) and detect life events or trends.
Customer Billing	Provide (central) services to compose, issue and track customer billing and invoices (see also accounts receivable).
Customer Campaign Design	Design and refine customer campaign specifications based on their impact.
Customer Campaign Execution	Execute a customer campaign (version) and track and respond to impact.
Customer Campaign Management	Assess the coverage and impact of internal/ customer campaigns and redirect campaign development and execution activity accordingly.
Customer Case	Initiate, track, resolve and report on customer cases (issues that typically require a corrective response to some financial transaction).
Customer Case Management	Track and assess case load and resolution activity - allocate resources as necessary to optimize case resolution performance.
Customer Credit Rating	Maintain and administer the credit scoring for customers based on consolidated internal data and optionally referencing external credit agency insights.

Service Domain Name	Description
Customer Event History	Capture, classify and store relationship, servicing and product-related customer events. In addition to transactional details, the log can capture life/relationship events.
Customer Offer	Orchestrate the processing of an offer for a new customer or an existing customer. The offer process is defined primarily by the nature of the product or service being considered, but can include actions such as document checks, collateral allocation, credit assessments, underwriting decisions, regulatory and procedural checks, eligibility checks, the use of internal and external specialist services (such as evaluations and legal advice).
Customer Order	Handle the processing of a customer order or request.
Customer Portfolio	Maintain a portfolio of view of the customer base with key customer data and consolidated activity details to support profitability and performance analysis across many possible customer dimensions.
Customer Position	Maintain a consolidated financial position of a customer.
Customer Precedents	Maintain/track the status of customer precedents.
Customer Product/Service Eligibility	Maintain a profile of the product and services for which the customer is eligible and any specific terms or other applicable considerations (supports relationship development and sales activity).
Customer Profile	Maintain a small amount of current customer status data to identify and influence any real-time operational interaction for sales, servicing and/or fulfillment (e.g. high value, eligible for campaign, account suspended, open case).
Customer Proposition	Support customer feature-specific product fulfillment.
Customer Reference Data Management	Maintain customer reference information.
Customer Relationship Management	Develop, maintain and execute a customer plan to maintain and build a customer relationship. Activities include maintaining customer contact, tracking internal and external events and activity of interest and relevance, product and service matching and sales, processing ad-hoc queries, trouble shooting and issue resolution including the initial phases of troubled account recovery.
Customer Surveys	Define, execute and analyze customer surveys.
Customer Tax Handling	Handle the consumer tax reporting obligations.
Customer Workbench	Provide a customer access portal to the bank's products and services through any suitable channel and device.
Dealer Workbench	Operate a dealer workbench, combining information feeds, deal capture, blotter, pricing tools and P&L analysis - this collection of capabilities is often referred to as the dealer position.
Delinquent Account Handling	Handle delinquent accounts (for active cards) for follow-up of payments due through periodic review and contacts. This process ends when the card account is cancelled and is transferred to Card Collections.
Deposit Account	Orchestrate the different flavors of a consumer deposit accounting facilities (including savings, term or demand) together with the handling of associated services and fees.

Appendix 1: Service Domain descriptions (January 2018)

Service Domain Name	Description
Development Environment	Select, maintain and operate the required combination of software development and operation tools, infrastructure and environments (includes version management).
Direct Debit	Fulfils a direct debit agreement. Handles the creditor side of direct debits.
Direct Debit Mandate	Manage the customer mandates associated with a direct debit processing facility for a corporate client.
Disbursement	Handle the disbursement of funds to newly established loans/facilities as necessary.
Discount Pricing	Maintain a current price list (with ranges and optional terms) by product/customer type for exceptional pricing conditions that override standard pricing as would be derived from the standard product specification.
Document Services	Record, index, classify, scan, store and retrieve any document in any media as appropriate. Includes electronic and physical distribution services.
Dunning	Handle the dunning cycle for a loan account that is behind payments.
E-Branch Management	Oversee and determine the optimum configuration for the product and service combinations available over the web.
E-Branch Operations	Operate the online electronic/web branch capabilities - control access and load balance across available communications and processing resources to optimize performance/availability.
ECM/DCM	Support the specification, pricing and issuance of ECM/DCM products for customer financing services.
Economic Capital	Develop, maintain and apply models that combine the overall risk over different risk types to determine the consolidated risk position for the bank.
Employee Access	Administer the systems and information access profile and authorities of an employee.
Employee Assignment	Orchestrate the assignment of individuals and groups to work tasks and positions, track current and projected utilization to inform resource planning and performance assessments.
Employee Benefits	Administer eligibility, subscription membership and access to employee benefits such as pensions, healthcare, holiday entitlement and services, personal finance advice, child care, counseling etc.
Employee Certification	Test, confirm and certify employees for recognized and qualitative skills, qualification and experience measures (e.g. education and industry qualifications, general skills, experience-based inferred skills).
Employee Data Management	Maintain a comprehensive record of employee-related details covering status and demographic attributes along with summary qualification, performance and appraisal data etc. to support workforce and individual management and administration activities.
Employee Evaluation	Periodically develop a fact-based assessment of employee performance, matched to agreed staff performance goals. Combine appraisal input from managers, peers, managed employees and external customers and evaluation agents as appropriate.

Service Domain Name	Description
Employee Payroll and Incentives	Administer the payment of salary, commission and incentives (includes stock/option grants) in compliance with the employment contract and discretionary awards.
Employee/Contractor Contract	Negotiate and maintain the employment contract for full, part time and contract workforce members.
Enterprise Tax Administration	Determine and optimize (though booking and allocation opportunities) the tax position of the enterprise and its subsidiaries.
Equipment Administration	Track the operational state and administer the assignment, maintenance and movements/inventory of available office equipment (printers, networks, faxes, shredders, buildings etc.).
Equipment Maintenance	Administer the regular and ad hoc maintenance and repair of office equipment (typically excludes IT).
eTrading Workbench	Operate the distributed consumer e-trading facility (local application and network connectivity to the bank). This environment hosts/supports a financial facility type product (Service Domain Consumer Investments) that customers use to trade securities on their own account through the bank. From the workbench environment using consumer investments a customer can initiate the execution of securities trades against their facility as well as applying service/facility fees and charges. The consumer investments capability accessed through the workbench integrates with the supporting customer accounting facilities which can include more complex margin accounts (and margin call initiation) as necessary.
Factoring	Factoring services allows for a bank to buy a customer's sell accounts receivable at discount to provide advanced income to improve short term liquidity.
Fiduciary Agreement	Fulfillment of a range of loan products on behalf of a fiduciary.
Financial Accounting	Financial booking of all business activity in a ledger/sub-ledger accounting structure/hierarchy according to the appropriate chart of accounts.
Financial Compliance	Track the resolution of detected non-compliance finance activities and instances.
Financial Control	Review and confirm the correct booking and financial conformance of financial activity to agreed budgets and procedures across the business units of the enterprise.
Financial Gateway	Operate automated message interfaces to secure networks such as SWIFT, TELEX, ACH and Exchange reporting services.
Financial Instrument Reference Data Management	Maintain a central reference directory of market traded asset/instrument details. The details are typically captured from one or more market feeds that publish market asset/instrument details but can include handling necessary internal processing in response to reported corporate events such as stock splits that impact the asset beyond simply updating the reference details.
Financial Instrument Valuation	Provide securities valuation services, including mark to market and other pricing mechanisms.
Financial Instrument Valuation Models	Develop and maintain a portfolio of valuation models considering currency, interest rate, instrument quotes, indices, commodity prices and other market, liquidity and credit risk factors. Support the use of these models in trading and pricing activity.

Appendix 1: Service Domain descriptions (January 2018)

Service Domain Name	Description
Financial Market Analysis	Analyze available sources of internal and external financial market information to develop insights and opinions on any aspect of financial market activity and pricing.
Financial Market Research	Consolidate financial market information from a variety of sources and optionally organize the consolidated information to align to different topics or categories for subsequent selection and analysis (see Financial Market Analysis).
Financial Message Analysis	Track and analyze financial message traffic to identify anomalies and potential fraudulent activity.
Financial Statements	Consolidate and present the enterprise financial statements: this includes the balance sheet, statement of cash flows, statement of retained earnings and the income statement.
Fixed Asset Register	Maintain a central register of fixed assets, tracking the status and applying appropriate depreciation to value representation.
Fraud Detection	Execute fraud behavior pattern scanners and threshold-based transaction triggering of possible fraudulent/AML activity.
Fraud Models	Develop and maintain a portfolio of fraud detection models and scanners. Support the use of these models in different production contexts and refine the models in response to new and changing exposures.
Fraud/AML Resolution	Review, diagnose and respond to detected production activity that has been identified as potential fraud/AML behavior.
Gap Analysis	Maintain and track projected consolidated cash flows to support evaluation and management of currency and interest rate risk positions, the bank's overall dispositive liquidity risk.
Guideline Compliance	Develop and apply a portfolio of guideline compliance tests to confirm adherence to agreed and regulatory imposed internal procedures (note one particular area of focus is investment management). Test on complete transaction data or a meaningful sample as appropriate to mitigate exposure to non-compliant behaviors.
Hedge Fund Administration	Administer hedge funds, allocate and rebalance the fund in response to market activity and funds sales and disbursements.
Human Resources Direction	Develop and enforce HR policies and the overall HR plan for the enterprise (in coordination with subsidiaries and divisions as necessary).
Information Provider Administration	Administer the information feed configuration and service agreement with the commercial information providers including subscription and service payment authorization activities.
Information Provider Operation	Operate the interface for importing data feeds from commercial information providers and internal broadcast pages.
Intellectual Property Portfolio	Administer the consolidated portfolio of intellectual property, ensuring entitlement and associated patent or copyright mechanisms are adopted and enforced. Leverage IP through licensing as appropriate.
Interactive Help	Provide employee or customer interactive context-sensitive guidance.

Service Domain Name	Description
Interbank Relationship Management	Manage the bank's relationship with other banks, covering any specific agreements that may be in place and overseeing operational issues.
Internal Audit	Maintain a portfolio of internal audit checks. Select and execute a meaningful sample of checks and identify and resolve non-compliance.
Internal Network Operation	Operate the internal data/communications network, including the administration of access rights to productivity packages/applications and production system and production data access.
Investment Portfolio Analysis	Assess and report on investment portfolio make-up, valuation and performance.
Investment Portfolio Management	Orchestrate the investment/rebalancing of an investment portfolio to optimize gains remaining within the terms of the portfolio 'charter' or agreement.
Investment Portfolio Planning	Agree the customer portfolio principles, guidelines and profile. Ensure disclosure and related obligations are made.
Investor Relations	Maintain investor relations, publish annual reports, interim statements and host investor meetings as necessary and appropriate.
Issued Device Administration	Administer the issuance of tokens such as cards, fobs etc. to customers. Includes tracking device operating system, version tracking and refresh.
Issued Device Tracking	Track and report on the status of devices such as cards, fobs, etc. issued to customers, including device cancellation.
IT Standards and Guidelines	Develop, maintain and enforce IT architectures, policies and standards as appropriate. Also, define the IT usage guidelines and policies governing systems use across the enterprise.
IT Systems Direction	Define, communicate and direct the execution of the IT strategy and plan in support of the broader enterprise business strategy, plan and policies.
Knowledge Exchange	Consolidate, classify and provide structured access to consolidated market intelligence, product and procedural knowledge gained from the workforce in the execution of business to inform business activity and support continual improvement.
Lead/Opportunity Management	Capture, classify and track a sales lead with an established client for additional products or services.
Leasing	Fulfillment of leasing products
Leasing Item Administration	Track the status of the assets underlying leasing agreements (for recovery).
Legal Compliance	Provide specialist legal advice, assess for legal compliance and resolve legal cases as they occur.
Letter of Credit	Orchestrate the pricing and issuance of Letters of Credit (typically associated with trade finance activity).
Limit and Exposure Management	Oversee corporate limits and exposures for the combined business activity.
Liquidity Risk Models	Develop and maintain models for dispositive and structural liquidity risk management, including Liquidity Gap Analysis, Liquidity at Risk (LaR) and Liquidity Value at Risk (LVaR).

Appendix 1: Service Domain descriptions (January 2018)

Service Domain Name	Description
Loan	Fulfillment of a range of loan products (including consumer and corporate loans).
Location Data Management	Maintain details of the use and state of locations of interest (e.g. shops).
M&A Advisory	A fee or commission-based project providing execution, pricing and deal coordination, and placement for M&A, IPO, LBO type transactions.
Management Manual	Develop, maintain and promulgate the management manual of required procedures and guidelines. Provide support in its reference and interpretation as appropriate.
Market Analysis	Analyze internal and external market information sources as necessary to develop specific market insights.
Market Data Switch Administration	Administer the internal information distribution 'switch' with internal and external market information feeds and associated employee access rights. Note this can include 'brokering' information access on a first come, first served basis for limited active user number feed services.
Market Data Switch Operation	Operate the day-to-day information distribution facility in compliance with administered access rights and the demand and availability of subscribed information feed services. Note, content is provided by the Market Feed Operation Service Domain for external feeds. Internal information can also be published over the channel from various content sources.
Market Information Management	Maintain/scrub/qualify/archive market information to provide structured/enhanced information views/history/logs.
Market Making	Orchestrate the market making of a security (matching buy to sell orders typically through coordination with a stock exchange).
Market Order	Orchestrate the completion of market orders from the customer perspective.
Market Order Execution	Orchestrate the completion of market orders from the trading perspective.
Market Research	Capture market research from multiple sources, classify and store information for retrieval.
Market Risk Models	Develop and maintain a portfolio of market risk models including currency, interest rates, instrument quotes, indices, commodity prices and other market and macro-economic risk factors. Support the use of these models in trading and pricing activity.
Merchandising Loan	Fulfillment of a range of loan products intended for the purchase of a larger merchandise item such as a car or boat. The item may be treated as collateral for the loan.
Merchant Acquiring Facility	Orchestrate the activities related to merchant fulfillment, merchant account maintenance, merchant transactional activities and settlement, including the billing of merchant fees and charges.
Merchant Relations	Administer the day-to-day interactions with merchants, for coordination of case resolution.
Mortgage	Fulfillment of a range of loan products for the purpose of property purchase.

Service Domain Name	Description
Mutual Fund Administration	Administer mutual funds, allocate and rebalance the fund in response to market activity and funds sales and disbursements.
Open Item Management	Handle the resolution of open items against a product or facility (such as overdue payments).
Operational Risk Models	Develop and refine operational risk models to detect possible exposures to operational failures.
Order Allocation	Apply appropriate rules to allocate a completed order across counterparties.
Organization Direction	Develop, maintain and implement the enterprise organization chart. Assign roles and responsibilities and track coverage.
Party Authentication	A cross channel capability that provides contact verification for a customer accessing the bank.
Party Data Management	Maintain a comprehensive set of party reference details, including legal entity structure, demographics, administrative, KYC-related properties, status and activity summaries.
Payment Execution	Orchestrate the execution of payments between accounts within the bank, or with other banks, selecting the appropriate payment mechanism.
Payment Order	Support customers in creating, changing, authorizing and tracking execution of payment orders.
Platform Operations	Operate the full suite of production platforms/infrastructure. Includes scheduled operations and back-up/recovery capacity assurance.
Point of Service	Administer all media connections (channel and application), inventory holdings (e.g. cash) provide support utilities and track activity at a servicing position - time spent, log activity, capture servicing events including commission and training-related activities.
Position Keeping	Administer the debit and credit entries against a financial position, keeping track of the balance.
Position Management	Maintain online and near-time cross account complex positions. Includes consolidated currency, instrument, sector and counterparty views as appropriate.
Private Placement	Project coordination and execution/ placement of a private offering of corporate equity or debt (avoids regulatory constraints of Public Placement).
Procurement	Coordinate the selection, pricing and execution of purchase agreements and ensure compliance with purchasing policies.
Product Broker Agreement	Maintain product broker contractual and service level agreements, and track and confirm compliance and volume goals.
Product Combination	Execute all combined product facilities which cannot be allocated to a single product in the product bundle. The fulfillment will mainly focus on (but is not limited to) the bundled pricing of the Product Combination resulting into fees, charges and equivalents such as bonus points.

Appendix 1: Service Domain descriptions (January 2018)

Service Domain Name	Description
Product Deployment	Plan and administer the deployment activities for new and enhanced products, includes training, inventory and solution deployment and coordination with operations, servicing, marketing and sales activities.
Product Design	Develop/refine product designs and supporting specification details
Product Directory	Keep information about the basic product building blocks, represented as Product Components with functions and features, as well as the completed product specification from SD Product Design.
Product Expert Sales Support	Administer the availability and allocation of product specialists to support sales activity (for both internal and external customer acquisition activity).
Product Inventory Distribution	Administer the ordering and distribution of product inventory across the branch network or direct to customers (e.g. mail).
Product Inventory Item Management	Maintain the available central product materials inventory in coordination with distribution activities and new product/materials ordering, receipt and warehousing.
Product Matching	Typically, an interactive capability used to match available product and product combinations to a customer type and situation. The mapping logic can be responsive to more dynamic factors such as prevailing business conditions.
Product Portfolio	Maintain and assess coverage and relative performance/ profitability of the full range of offered products and product combinations/ bundles. Direct product development/refinement is used to re-balance the portfolio.
Product Quality Assurance	Maintain and execute a portfolio of product quality assurance tests and, if appropriate, certifications. These tests can be applied to any specific aspects of product sales, servicing and fulfillment as might be appropriate.
Product Sales Support	Provide specialist support advice to customers for products and services on offer.
Product Service Agency	Maintain contractual and service agreements with transaction-related service providers (e.g. legal/tax advisors).
Product Training	Develop and provide product-specific training across the workforce. This includes all media and training mechanisms (online, self-taught, classroom etc.).
Production Release	Maintain and apply a comprehensive portfolio of functional and non-functional test evaluation criteria, and test utilities for pre-release and in-flight solution quality assurance of production IT systems.
Production Risk Models	Develop and refine production risk models to detect possible exposures to procedural failures.
Products and Services Direction	Develop and communicate product and service policies, and adapt in response to changing needs and to practical experience.
Program Trading	Automated trading of selected structured positions.
Project Finance	Provide project financing facilities and associated services.
Promotional Events	Develop and execute promotional events covering brand development and advertising. This can include participation in sporting/ entertainment events or more general promotional activity.

Service Domain Name	Description
Property Portfolio	Manage and evaluate the fit to needs and effective utilization of the site/property portfolio for owned and leased properties. Optimize the allocation of business functions/divisions to the building and track and project capacity requirements.
Prospect Campaign Design	Design and refine prospect campaign specifications based on their impact.
Prospect Campaign Execution	Execute a prospect campaign (version) and track and respond to impact.
Prospect Campaign Management	Assess the coverage and impact of prospect campaigns and redirect campaign development and execution activity accordingly.
Prospect Management	Capture, classify and track prospects to the point of initiating an offer for a suitably qualified prospect. Prospects can be sourced in several ways including the acquisition of prospect lists from third parties, general market research and solicited by brand and advertising activity. Prospect details are scrubbed and matched/checked against known customers to eliminate duplicates. Prospects can be tracked individually, by grouping criteria and by 'list'. Prospect Management handles the verification of the prospect, initiating the offer management process for suitably qualified prospects.
Public Offering	Project coordination and execution/ placement of a public offering of corporate equity or debt.
Public Reference Data Management	Maintain and provide structured access for standard 'global' reference data associated with market activity such as currency, country and segment identifiers. These values will typically be externally sourced as a market feed.
Quant Model	Develop and maintain a portfolio of quantitative analysis (quant) models that can be applied in different contexts across the business.
Quote Management	Provide buy/sell quotes for traded instruments
Recruitment	Administer candidate identification, selection, evaluation and on-boarding of new employees in coordination with internal management and external recruitment and advisory agencies as necessary (e.g. for background checks).
Regulatory and Legal Authority	Maintain effective relations with regulators, accounting and government agencies. Oversee interactions and reporting as necessary.
Regulatory Compliance	Interpret regulatory requirements and define a portfolio of regulatory compliance tests across all appropriate activities. Relate the regulatory checks to activities as necessary.
Regulatory Reporting	Administer and orchestrate the required regulatory reporting schedule of regulatory reports.
Remittances	Orchestrate national and international payment and remittance services. (Retain repeat transaction details where appropriate.)
Reward Points Account	Administer the booking and remittance of rewards points (basically a non-interest account with additional lifetime constrains on point validity).
Reward Points Awards and Redemption	Handle the allocation and redemption of rewards points for customer transaction activity.

Appendix 1: Service Domain descriptions (January 2018)

Service Domain Name	Description
Sales Planning	Plan and assess sales activity and re-direct resources and priorities as necessary.
Sales Product	A representation of a product as sold to a customer, covering the fulfillment requirements (as opposed to the legal terms handled by Sales Product Agreement).
Sales Product Agreement	Maintain a structured legal agreement defining the contractual terms and conditions for an in-force product.
Savings Account	Fulfill a savings account.
Securities Delivery and Receipt Management	Initiate settlement transactions and track to completion.
Securities Fails Processing	Capture, diagnose, resolve and report on securities-related issues and transaction failures.
Security Advisory	Provide specialist security advice and guidance for line management and projects as needed to ensure security arrangements across the organization.
Security Assurance	Maintain and apply a portfolio of security assurance checks, target selective assurance tests to ensure security countermeasures are in place and appropriate.
Segment Direction	Define market segments and develop and assess performance against the segment plan's performance goals.
Service Product	Represent the general facility at the core of the consumer and small business financial services activity. The fulfillment will focus on the pricing of the Service Product resulting in fees, charges and equivalents such as bonus points.
Servicing Activity Analysis	Analyze consumer servicing position activity, including teller, case/contact center traffic and potentially VoIP activity in more advanced situations. Analysis includes captured call/channel/device type, activity, onward routing and resolution decisions for operational and procedural insights and facility/process and training improvement (root cause analysis).
Servicing Event History	Capture, classify and store servicing activity and events to support root cause analysis.
Servicing Issue	Capture, track, resolve and report on customer servicing issues - note this excludes contacts that are resolved and cases that are raised. Issues are actions requiring some kind of follow-up by the contact service representative (CSR).
Settlement Obligation Management	Orchestrate the clearing and settlement of market transactions.
Site Administration	Oversee the configuration and assignment of committed space and facilities to business units to optimize facility leverage and meet business space requirements. Manage the assignment of access rights and security tags etc. to staff as necessary for access control.
Site Operations	Operate the day-to-day access and maintenance of work locations, including site access and environment security, assignable space and equipment allocation, facility/utility assurance and cleaning services coordination.
Special Pricing Conditions	Maintain a price list or single conditions (with ranges and optional terms) by various dimensions, e.g. customer segment (e.g. employee conditions), for exceptional product independent pricing conditions that override standard pricing derived from the pricing product.

Service Domain Name	Description
Stock Lending/Repos	Orchestrate stock lending and repurchase agreement (repo) transactions.
Sub-Custodian Agreement	Maintain sub-custodian agreement terms and track and report on sub-custodian activity.
Suitability Checking	Confirm that all involved counterparties are suitable for a proposed market trade.
Syndicate Management	Manage the membership and administration of syndicates in compliance with the agreed charter and operating agreement.
Syndicated Loan	Handle the processing of syndicated loans.
System Deployment	Plan and execute the production roll-out of new and enhanced systems solutions, including pre-planning, training, acceptance testing and production cutover and adoption support.
System Development	Manage and execute the multi-threaded development of application solutions spanning bespoke development and commercial package integration.
Systems Administration	Administer the licensing, maintenance commitments and assignment and usage status of IT assets.
Systems Assurance	Orchestrate scheduled maintenance, installation/upgrades and repairs/fixes on the IT infrastructure and production platforms.
Systems Help Desk	Operate the online/interactive production help desk and first level support activity. Capture, diagnose and resolve production systems issues and failures. Escalate issues to systems assurance as necessary.
Systems Operations	Operate the full suite of production applications. This includes scheduled operations and application data back-up/recovery procedures.
Trade Confirmation Matching	Match buyers to sellers in market trades.
Trade Finance	A collection of services associated with the support of international trade finance (including the coordination of correspondent banks, shipping, customs, lading, warehouse activity alongside financial management - LCs, guarantees etc.
Trade/Price Reporting	Operate a trade reporting facility as required by market regulation. Capture and transmit trades details to the exchange in line with an operating schedule.
Traded Position Management	Trade in the wholesale markets at the optimum price for both principle and advisory trading.
Trading Book Oversight	Define and track trading book activity against the established trading rules/entitlements and limits.
Trading Models	Manage the development and deployment of trading models to support automatic executions.
Transaction Authorization	A capability to provide a risk-based authorization for interactive customer transactions. This can combine the context (channel) transaction and customer details and recent activity analysis as appropriate. The authorization may require a specific level of party/customer authentication to get approval.
Transaction Engine	Orchestrate a schedule of payment transaction and reporting activities for the fulfillment of certain long-term instruments or structured facilities.

Service Domain Name	Description
Travel and Expenses	Administer the authorization, booking, payment, recompense and accounting for travel and expenses incurred in the execution of employment activity.
Trust Services	Provide trust services.
Underwriting	Manage the underwriting decision process and different levels of authorization required for proposed loans.
Unit Trust Administration	Administer unit trusts, allocate and rebalance the trust in response to market activity and funds sales and disbursements.
Utilities Administration	Administer the sourcing, service agreements and delivery of site utilities (heat, cooling, water, power etc.).
Workforce Training	Develop and execute a training syllabus covering all general and specific business skills/knowledge requirements and leveraging different training mechanisms and channels as appropriate (classroom, online/context based, self-taught, desk-side support etc.).

Appendix 2: BIAN and TOGAF's ADM phases

■ A2.1 RELATING BIAN TO THE PHASES OF THE ADM

This appendix describes where the availability and use of BIAN deliverables influences the way in which the TOGAF ADM phases are performed.

For each TOGAF ADM phase, only those BIAN deliverables are included that are a direct input for that ADM phase. Since the impact of those BIAN deliverables is fully integrated in the output of that ADM phase, the influence on later ADM phases is fully covered, see figure 75.

Applying the TOGAF ADM produces and enriches the BIAN Service Landscape and BIAN Business Scenarios specific to the organization. Furthermore, the results can be fed back to the BIAN community to extend and enrich the BIAN deliverables.

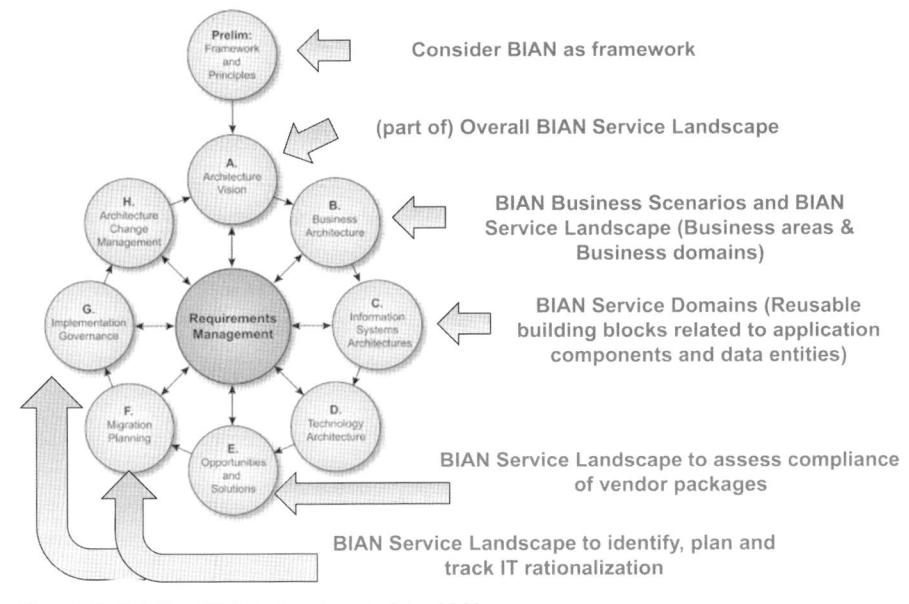

Figure 75: Relating BIAN to the phases of the ADM

A2.1.1 Preliminary phase
The Preliminary phase is about defining "where, what, why, who and how we do architecture" in the organization we are looking at.

This phase considers:
- That the existence of the BIAN network contributes to the awareness and acceptance of an architectural approach and, in that sense, can be used to create sponsorship and general commitment for the approach.
- That the use of the BIAN SOA Design Framework and related deliverables may be prescribed by the architecture.
- Whether or not to use BIAN input and principles during the architecture work.

A2.1.2 Architecture vision
Phase A is about validating the starting points, defining the scope and approach of the architecture development cycle, and recognizing key success factors:
- Relate the architecture development cycle to the use of BIAN deliverables. In the first instance, a decision must be made regarding the relevance and fitness-for-purpose of the BIAN deliverables for this architecture engagement.
- The parts of the BIAN Service Landscape and BIAN Business Scenarios that are relevant for the project can be used to identify possible stakeholders.
- The BIAN Service Landscape can also be used to identify other architecture developments in related areas of the organization.
- When using BIAN, certain re-use requirements may be applicable.

A2.1.3 Business architecture
The main objectives of Phase B are to describe the Baseline Business Architecture, to develop a Target Business Architecture, and to identify any gaps.

- The BIAN Business Scenarios can be used as a starting point, as an example, in describing the Baseline Business Architecture and defining the Target Business Architecture. The scope of a BIAN Business Scenario can be compared to that of a conventional high-level business process. The BIAN Business Scenarios are an example of how some BIAN Service Domains might collaborate in response to a business event. BIAN Business Scenarios can be matched to the internal (baseline and target) processes at a bank, whilst the BIAN Service Domains and their associated Service Operation boundaries can be used as an assessment framework. As noted previously, the BIAN Business Scenarios are indicative and, in matching them to a specific location, their sequencing and content may need to be changed to reflect the prevailing business rules and practices.
- The BIAN Service Landscape is structured according to a common reference hierarchy: a business breakdown in Business Areas and Business Domains. Although not a Target Business Architecture in itself, the BIAN Service Landscape can be used

as a starting point (or at least be used as a source of inspiration) next to the BIAN Business Scenarios for the set-up of the Target Business Architecture.
- As the BIAN Service Landscape is directly derived from the business breakdown, and validated via the BIAN Business Scenarios, it should be clear if and where the set-up of the Target Business Architecture deviates from this breakdown. This insight is needed to apply the BIAN Service Landscape in Phase C.

A2.1.4 Information systems architecture

The objective of Phase C is to develop Target Architectures for the data and/or the application systems domains and identify the gaps between the Baseline and the Target Architecture. Information Systems Architecture focuses on identifying and defining the applications and data considerations that support an enterprise's Business Architecture. It does so by defining views that relate to information, knowledge, application services, etc.

- BIAN provides the BIAN Service Landscape specific to the financial services industry, constructed of re-usable building blocks related to application components and data entities. As such, the BIAN Service Landscape can be used as a reference point for defining or assessing the Target Application Architecture of the organization. Its breakdown into Business Areas, Business Domains, and BIAN Service Domains can be applied in order to structure the application landscape. The principles applied in constructing the BIAN Service Landscape can be translated into application and data principles for the organization.
- A core activity is to relate the identified BIAN Service Operations at the target application level to the Target Business Architecture (developed in Phase B), to recognize the relationship between business processes and applications, and to analyze the relationship between business objects and data. The BIAN Business Scenarios in particular can support this mapping activity. In addition, the mapping of the main BIAN deliverables on the TOGAF Content Metamodel supports the execution of this activity.
- Equally, the BIAN initiative could benefit from this phase by updating the BIAN Service Landscape and BIAN Business Scenarios with the output of this analysis; e.g., the split-up or repositioning of a certain service, or the (updated) execution of a (new) business process.

A2.1.5 Technology architecture

The Technology Architecture phase seeks to map application components defined in the Information Systems Architecture phase onto a set of technology components.

Since the BIAN service definitions are implementation-independent, BIAN does not contribute to this phase directly. However, the result of Phase C will certainly contain specific technical requirements arising out of the BIAN service interfaces. (Note that BIAN Service Operations will be related to other standards such as ISO, IFX, etc., which may imply specific technology components.)

A2.1.6 Opportunities and solutions

Phase E generates an architecture roadmap, which delivers the target architecture. This typically includes deriving a series of Transition Architectures that deliver continuous business value (i.e., capability increments).

- The BIAN Service Landscape and other BIAN deliverables are created in co-operation with software vendors serving the financial services industry. Hence it is fair to assume that BIAN services leveraged in previous ADM phases will also be (in due time) physically available in the market as COTS software solutions or application components.
- The BIAN Service Landscape and BIAN Business Scenarios can also be used in requirements gathering and vendor and package selections, assessing the compliance of vendors and products with these BIAN deliverables. The compliance of products with the BIAN Service Landscape and BIAN Business Scenarios will increase the seamless integration of the software products in an existing (BIAN-compliant) target Business and Application Architecture and thus reduce integration costs.
- The BIAN Service Landscape and Business Scenarios can be used as enablers for designing COTS products in the financial industry space.

A2.1.7 Migration planning

The objectives of Phase F are to finalize the Architecture Roadmap and the detailed Implementation and Migration Plan.

There are no specific BIAN deliverables that act as direct input for this ADM phase. All relevant BIAN input is included in the output of previous ADM phases.

A2.1.8 Implementation governance

The goal of this phase is to govern and manage the implementation and deployment process.

There are no specific BIAN deliverables that are direct input for this ADM phase. All relevant BIAN input is included in the output of previous ADM phases.

A2.1.9 Architecture change management

The goal of Phase H is to establish an architecture change management process for the new enterprise architecture baseline.

There are no specific BIAN deliverables that are direct input for this ADM phase. All relevant BIAN input is included in the output of previous ADM phases. However, the tracking of BIAN changes and initiatives should be incorporated into the architecture change management.

A2.2 REQUIREMENTS MANAGEMENT

The goal of requirements management is to define a process whereby requirements for enterprise architecture are identified, stored, and fed into and out of the relevant ADM phases.

Leveraging BIAN deliverables in the ADM would guide and structure the capturing of requirements, along the BIAN Service Landscape (including its Business Areas and Business Domains) and BIAN Business Scenarios.

A2.3 RELATING BIAN TO TOGAF GUIDELINES AND TECHNIQUES

This section focuses on specific guidelines and techniques related to the ADM cycle that are relevant when using BIAN deliverables in an architectural engagement.

A2.3.1 Applying the ADM at different enterprise levels
The ADM is intended to be used as a model to support the definition and implementation of architecture at multiple levels within an enterprise.

In general, it is not possible to develop a single architecture that addresses all of the needs of all stakeholders. As can be seen from figure 76, an enterprise can be partitioned into different areas, according to 'Subject Matter', 'Time Period', and 'Level of Detail'.

The BIAN Service Landscape and BIAN Business Scenarios are especially useful in the following areas:
- The definition and/or assessment of the target architectures, especially business and information systems architectures (application and data) and the related definition of change from baseline to target.
- The assessment and selection of COTS solutions in the market, aimed at achieving compliance with BIAN deliverables and thus reducing integration costs.
- The BIAN Service Landscape is based on SOA principles. It uses a hierarchical decomposition of the business in terms of Business Areas and underlying Business Domains. BIAN Business Scenarios and the Business Domains from the BIAN Service Landscape might serve as a source of inspiration to define 'segments' and their relations (cooperation). For each Business Domain, the relevant BIAN Service Domains are recognized and described. This is more related to the 'capability architecture' level; however, BIAN does not provide the overall architectural insight at all levels of an organization (company, business unit, division, department, etc ...).

A2.3.2 Using TOGAF to define and govern SOAs
This chapter discusses the factors related to the adoption and deployment of SOA within the enterprise.

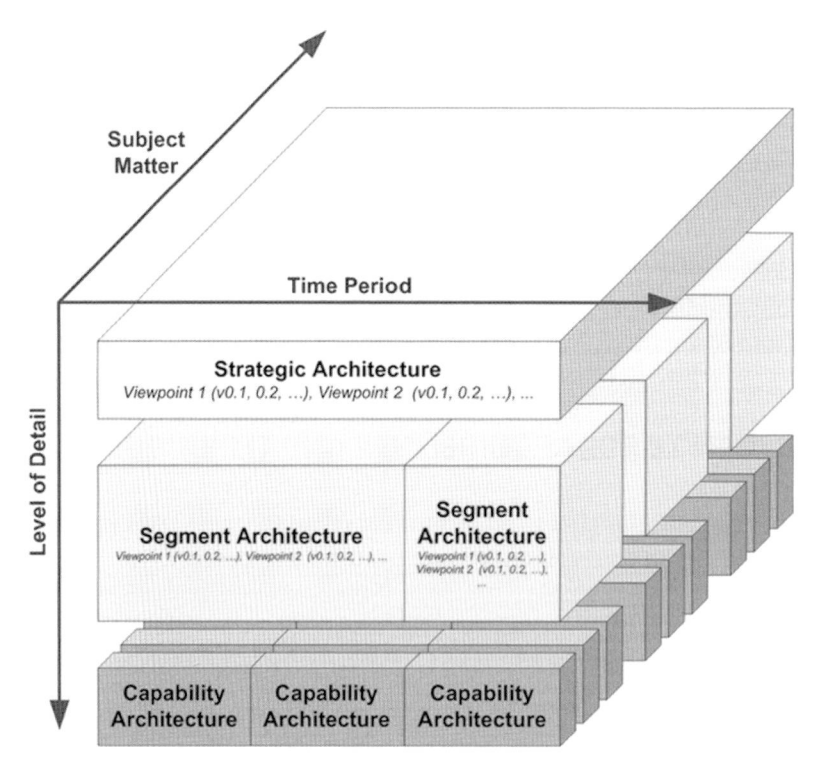

Figure 76: Different areas of an enterprise

- The BIAN Business Scenarios can be a useful vehicle to help introduce the BIAN service-oriented designs. They are initially used in a manner much like a conventional business process, representing the flow of activity associated with a familiar business event in a form that can easily be recognized and understood. The same BIAN Business Scenario representation can then be used to explain the concept of BIAN Service Domains by exposing the discrete role each plays in handling the selected business event.
- The BIAN Service Landscape is based on SOA principles. Hence, the architect should be aware of if and how SOA is leveraged within the organization. Where necessary, the architecture engagement should include activities required to apply SOA principles in the organization.
- To be effective, it is necessary to align TOGAF and BIAN terminology beforehand.

A2.3.3 Architecture principles
This chapter describes principles for use in the development of an enterprise architecture.

The definition of a principle is: "a qualitative statement of intent that should be met by the architecture". This applies to principles that:
- Govern the architecture process;
- Affect the development, maintenance, and use of the enterprise architecture;
- Govern the implementation of the architecture.

BIAN has developed various design rationales and supporting design techniques, mainly to define a BIAN Service Domain. Examples include:
- BIAN Service Domain Operational properties: clearly bounded and with a unique business purpose, a focus object record with full lifecycle handling of its focus object, exclusively service-based, loose coupled and location independent.
- BIAN Service Domain Design techniques: right-sizing the BIAN Service Domain's focus objects, assigning a single functional pattern and confirming its role through BIAN Business Scenarios.
- Not all BIAN design principles are canonical and fully and explicitly described in the BIAN Metamodel. As the construction of the BIAN Service Landscape is based on these specific design principles, it is important to make them as explicit as possible during the execution of the different ADM phases.

A2.3.4 Architecture patterns
In TOGAF a 'pattern' is defined as: "an idea that has been useful in one practical context and will probably be useful in others".

Patterns describe how, when and why building blocks can be applied, and which trade-offs must be made in doing so. In that sense, BIAN can be used as an additional source for best practices. The BIAN Business Scenarios describe typical patterns of service usage and service interaction. Additionally, BIAN provides patterns for service design.

A2.3.5 Interoperability requirements
Defining the degree to which the information and services are to be shared.

This is a very useful architectural requirement, especially in a complex organization and/or extended enterprise and key in BIAN's focus. BIAN provides guidelines (in terms of structure with the business landscape or BIAN Service Domain design principles) and content (the BIAN Business Scenarios) that should be met with respect to interoperability.

■ A2.4 BIAN AND THE TOGAF ARCHITECTURE CONTENT FRAMEWORK

The TOGAF Architecture Content Framework consists of the relevant artifacts produced in the ADM cycle. As shown earlier in Section A2.1, the use of BIAN is relevant to several phases of the ADM. These dependencies make it straightforward to map the BIAN deliverables onto the TOGAF Content Metamodel.

It should be noted that the only BIAN deliverables that are mapped are those that provide a direct input in an ADM phase. This means that not all parts of the TOGAF Metamodel are related to specific BIAN deliverables.

A2.4.1 Deliverables, artifacts and building blocks

Figure 77 shows the relations between the different concepts (deliverables, artifacts and building blocks) in TOGAF. Building blocks refer to descriptions of specific parts of an architecture. They are devised in terms of architecture building blocks and solution building blocks.

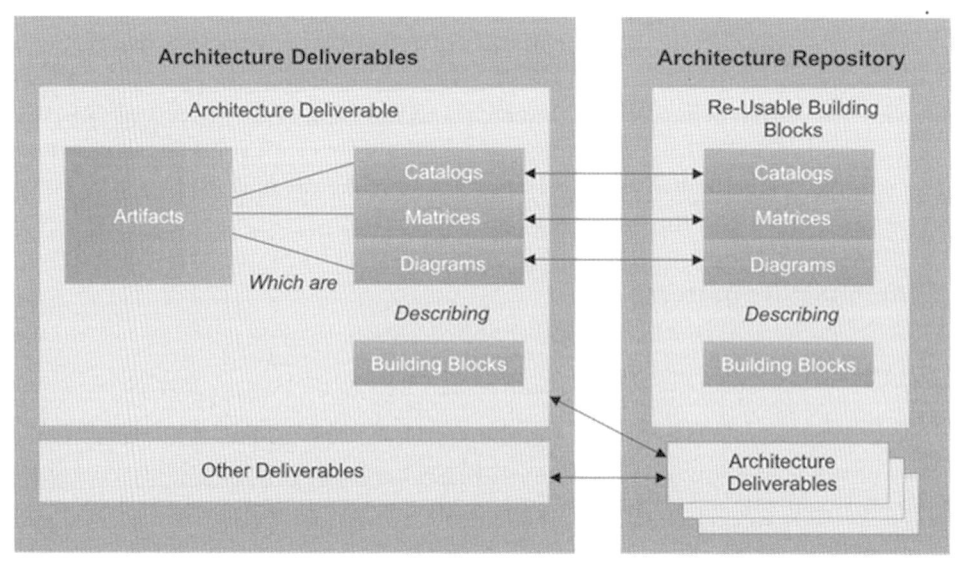

Figure 77: Deliverables, artifacts and building blocks

BIAN focuses on those IT services relevant to the financial services industry. The structure is based on a common understanding of the business and systems in use. The BIAN Business Scenarios are used to validate the completeness of the Service Landscape. In TOGAF terminology, the BIAN Service Landscape is a structured description of the various architecture building blocks needed to provide the required capabilities in the financial services industry.

A2.4.2 Mapping the BIAN deliverables to the TOGAF Content Metamodel

The BIAN deliverables listed below can be mapped onto the TOGAF Content Metamodel; BIAN Service Domain principles ensure consistency within a Business Domain:

- The BIAN Business Scenarios used to validate the BIAN Service Landscape and to ensure completeness can be used as best practice process templates.
- BIAN focuses on application-to-application integration relevant for the various logical application components.
- BIAN service definitions are canonical, implementation-independent descriptions of logical components; hence, physical and technical layers are out of scope.
- BIAN Services are clustered around focus objects and manage their full lifecycle.
- Focus objects are relevant to logical Data Architecture.

Appendix 2: BIAN and TOGAF's ADM phases

Using BIAN deliverables in an architecture engagement may require a TOGAF Content Metamodel extension with respect to the BIAN Service Landscape and BIAN Business Scenarios. The services extension is intended to allow more sophisticated modeling of the service portfolio by creating a concept of IT services in addition to the core concept of business services.

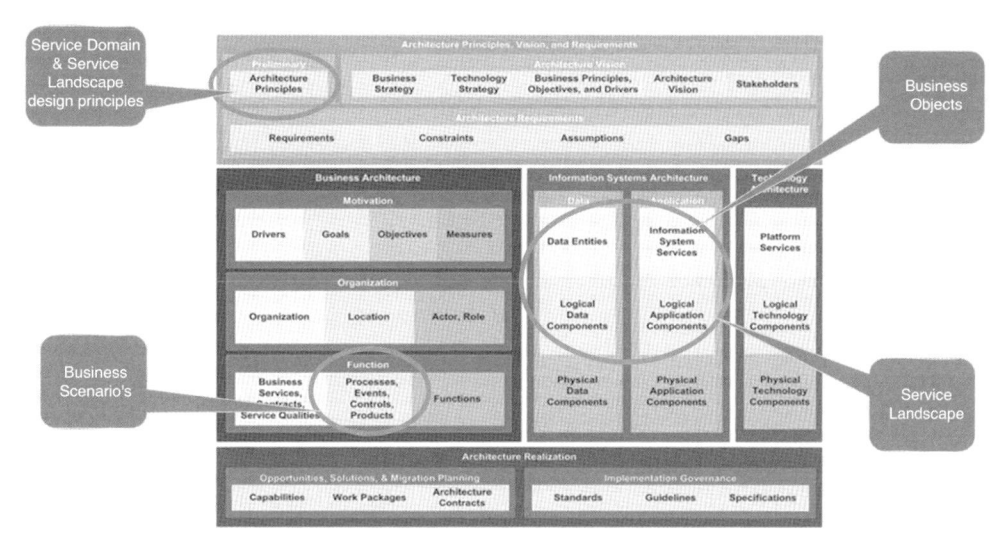

Figure 78: Mapping BIAN deliverables onto the TOGAF Content Metamodel

Appendix 3: The BIAN organization

This appendix provides an overview of the BIAN structure and bodies.

The BIAN structure is influenced by two major thoughts:
- BIAN is a not-for profit association and thus it has the bodies required by this type of organization, including a General Assembly and a Board of Directors.
- BIAN is dedicated to gathering and defining content, which occurs in Working Groups with a central Governance structure and Architecture Committee.

Figure 79 shows the major bodies and entities of BIAN as of 2018.

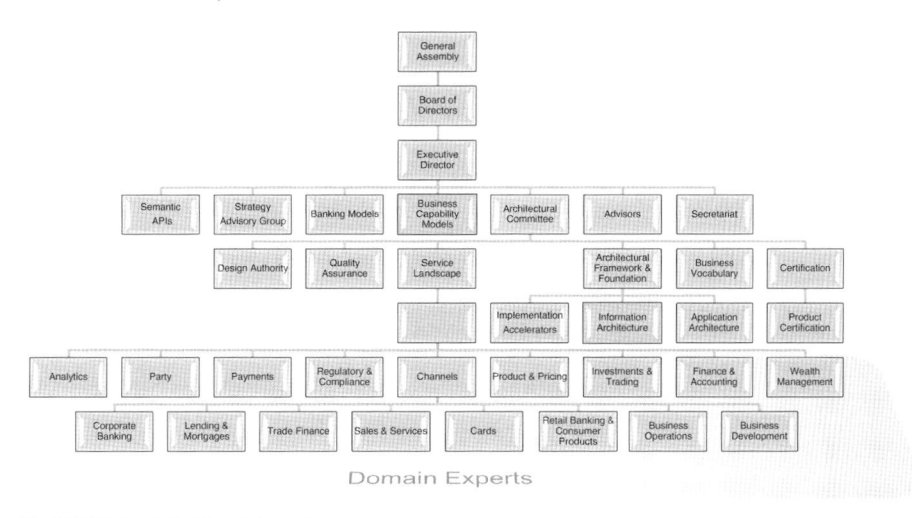

Figure 79: BIAN's organizational overview

■ A3.1 GENERAL ASSEMBLY

The **General Assembly** meets regularly (typically once a year). Each member has one vote (all members are equally represented). The General Assembly elects the Board of Directors and the Board reports back to it on a yearly basis. A General Assembly can be initiated by members, for example if it needs to approve changes to the statutes. Additionally, the General Assembly approves the strategy and budgets regarding BIAN content work.

■ A3.2 BOARD OF DIRECTORS

The Board of Directors defines and executes the strategy of BIAN and consists of at least three directors (up to a maximum of 20). The Board officially represents BIAN, whilst the day-to-day operations are delegated to the Secretariat.

■ A3.3 SECRETARIAT

The **Secretariat** runs BIAN on a day-to-day basis, including all organizational aspects, such as member administration, finance administration, project support and setup, event management, managing the public and internal website and the like.

The Secretariat consists of the Executive Director, support staff and advisors. A Program Manager has specific responsibility within the Secretariat to ensure the propagation of the content work and control the progress of one or more Working Groups.

■ A3.4 WORKING GROUPS

The **Working Groups** are the main entities responsible for the content and definition work which is undertaken by experts from the BIAN members. In particular, the IPR-Policy is managed using the construct of Working Groups.

Members formally join one or more Working Groups. A Working Group elects a Chair and a Vice Chair and provides a charter, which must be approved. Deliverables are defined and decomposed into tasks which focus on iterative development and fast delivery. Experience shows that the key to successful work outcomes is an actively maintained documentation of results, which is constantly monitored.

The three major content topics of BIAN are:
- Service Landscape/Service Definition;
- Architecture;
- Building Blocks.

The first two of these are interdependent activities, whereas Building Blocks are self-contained and independent from the other two. In addition, Building Blocks take account of results coming out of Architecture to avoid any overlap with work that has already been done.

The programs are explained in more detail in the following sections.

A3.5 BIAN SPECIAL PROJECTS

Where there is a specific requirement the BIAN Board can establish a project. These projects will be topic driven, such as APIs, and will be supervised directly by the BIAN Board.

A3.6 COMMUNICATION BETWEEN A MEMBER AND BIAN

A major factor in the success of BIAN is the effective communication between each member and the BIAN organization.

BIAN's executive body is the **Secretariat**. It is responsible for leading all the projects, organizing all the events and driving the definition work.

The main contact on the BIAN Secretariat for the experts and possible Working Groups and module lead is the Program Lead, who is responsible for managing the individual programs and their deliverables.

A3.7 OFFICIAL ROLES OF MEMBERS

BIAN as an organization has multiple facets and aspects - as the overall structure outlines. Thus, a member can take up various positions and act in different roles. The major roles of members are:

- **Delegate**: the representative is a senior manager of the member company, who can speak for the corporation and place votes accordingly. The Delegate will join the General Assembly.
- **Director**: the members elect directors, who form the Board of Directors. Directors should be senior and well known, industry-recognized personalities. Their responsibility is to formally represent BIAN to the outside world and to be responsible for BIAN operations.
- **Representative:** every member should nominate a Representative. This person should be familiar with the requirements of the member and advise on content questions from a member's viewpoint, as well as being able to place the appropriate resources into BIAN Working Groups. The Representative acts primarily at the content level and participates in the official BIAN events (Chapter Meetings).

- **Expert:** each member can send multiple Experts into different Working Groups. The Experts contribute expertise and know how. Any active Expert can join the official events. Typically, Experts are involved in the definition and delivery of content and join module workshops and sessions. The role of an Expert has multiple facets or areas of interest. Experts receive the big picture of BIAN in the Chapter meetings.

A3.8 BIAN EVENTS AND CHAPTER MEETINGS

A3.8.1 Scope and content

The overall target of the Chapter Meetings is to provide the **big picture** of all the activities currently being undertaken in BIAN. The attendees of the meeting will benefit from receiving details of all the results achieved in BIAN via presentations by members and from the market. Chapter Meetings also contribute to the skills enhancement of all attendees.

And last but not least the Chapter Meetings should support the creation of trust, strong networking and relationship building, a shared view and dedication to the vision to bring high value to the financial services industry by making IT more flexible.

Chapter Meeting agendas typically include:
- Obtaining feedback through members presenting the strategic roadmap decided by the Board of Directors.
- Discussing new ideas for the strategic roadmap that have been put forward by members.
- Discussing the presented results of the definition work undertaken by the Services programs, Architecture and Building Blocks.
- Assessing and refining the mode of working and the work schedule.
- Providing a forum for presentations from members about their Architectural experiences and for presentations from outside the BIAN community which provide a broader view of the topics of interest.

A3.8.2 Where should members participate?

Looking at the member roles, namely Delegate, Director, Member of the Strategy Advisory Board, Representative and Expert, it is clear that the Chapter Meetings are dedicated to encouraging knowledge exchange and to get participants involved in the content definition work.

This means that the events are designed for all member organization's experts.

A3.8.3 Location and frequency

The Chapter Meetings are held regionally with the composition of the BIAN community defining the location of these events. Currently, the events take place in Europe, North America and Asia-Pacific.

In terms of frequency, it is planned to have two events in each continent per year in order to continuously provide the big picture for each participant.